Getting Naked and Mark Grayson

"Mark Grayson is a thought leader among a generation of men advocating for a new healthy masculine culture of connection. He invites men to follow our joy and our curiosity, to self-reflect on the vast capacities and interests we can all choose to hold. His work as a c-suite leader, a father, a writer, and as an advocate for men's wellness shows how, over the course of time, an ongoing self-reflection about men and masculinity invites us into spiritual frames of understanding. Mark's writing documents his striving for what is possible for all men, a model of masculinity which is a combination of deep contemplative thought merged with action and doing. His work as founder of the Trinity Spiritual Center is an expression of exactly this."

—**Mark Greene, founder,** *Remaking Manhood* **podcast,**
author of *The Little #metoo Book for Men*

"In his timely book, Mark Grayson makes the urgent point that men like all humans have a soft or what has been deemed "feminine" side to themselves that includes their capacity to be emotionally sensitive and expressive, empathic, and connected to themselves and others. These qualities are essential to their health and wellbeing, and are also the driver of their relational intelligence or their capacity to be curious about others which is essential for human connection. The book is beautifully written and filled with practical advice that will be helpful most assuredly not only for men but to all who read it regardless of one's identities."

—**Niobe Way, professor of developmental psychology at NYU,**
the author of *Deep Secrets: Boy's Friendships and the Crisis of Connection*

"Mark Grayson has an uncanny way of capturing the emotional climate of this moment on a micro and macro scale. His writing spans the entire range, connecting the deeply vulnerable and personal to the political and cultural zeitgeist. His curiosity takes him places where readers do not usually find themselves—for that and many other reasons, I love him and his writings."

—Sunny Bates, author, entrepreneur, advisor

"Mark Grayson has written poignant, often self-reflective, and compelling essays about experiences and situations, personal and professional, that would be insightful and helpful to the vast array of readers who deserve to read and learn from him. He's also a splendid person with an impressive career, so he has much to share to inspire and help guide the rest of us."

—Tamera Luzzatto, Senior Vice President, Pew Charitable Trusts, former chief of staff to Senators Hillary Clinton and Jay Rockefeller

"If you're looking for a roadmap on how to live as a man for the 21st century and beyond, look no further. Mark Grayson's writing is chock full of guidance for all males but particularly younger men who might feel as though there are no clear guideposts on redefining and expressing what it means to be male. Through Mark's personal and professional experience, both his successes and failures, he recognizes that life is most meaningful when it's expressed through connection and love. Grounded in his lived experience as a man of the world who is deeply spiritual, and integrating ancient wisdom as well as contemporary insights, he offers a path out of the current cultural conventions that constrain men and harm women. He is a practical, steady guide–a bold, funny, irreverent, wise leader–for these times."

—Sadhvi Bhagawati Saraswati, Ph.D., world-renowned spiritual advisor

"What immediately impressed me when I first met Mark Grayson was his creative energy, his overwhelming and communicative enthusiasm. I realized later in our discussions how open he was to new ideas, how he was able to always overcome his own prejudices to discover new ideas, and how he was able to promote these new ideas. It is truly exceptional that such an accomplished man, with the highest university education, who is also a family man, who has worked at the highest level in marketing, in communication, in the film industry, has been able to maintain such freshness, such enthusiasm, such social and spiritual commitment."

—Raphaël Liogier, author of *The Heart of Maleness* and the forthcoming *The Anguish of the Void*

"I recall the first time Mark Grayson spoke up in my class. Whatever it was he said, it was so brilliant that a few people actually laughed. That's the way students acknowledge something that they dimly perceive as blazingly insightful, but that they don't quite comprehend. Through his suggestions—his provocations—Mark profoundly changed the direction of my scholarship, and my career."

—Morris Holbrook, William T. Dillard Professor Emeritus of Business, Columbia Business School

"The beautiful thing about Mark—and specifically his work and writing about men—is his unquenchable curiosity. He doesn't operate from a realm of ideology and instead allows himself to be fully present to life and his subject matter. Mark has the ability to turn vast amounts of knowledge and experience into clear articulate prose that lands directly in the heart of the reader. Curiosity and humility is what is required in these strange times, allowing people to discover what is true for themselves. Mark has this unique skill of leading people toward their own authenticity."

—Michael Hebb, founder of Death Over Dinner, writer/social activist/restaurateur

"I've known Mark Grayson for over 20 years. I've always been surprised by his fresh ideas, boundless energy, and his ability to decipher the kernel of wisdom from within utter chaos! As a public policy advocate for over 30 years, I have worked with him closely and witnessed his ability to identify patterns, connect dots, draw expertise from an impressive array of high powered—and oftentimes famous—mentors, creating truly amazing outcomes in the end! Mark is a mesmerizing spokesperson who can communicate others' complex ideas while remaining true to himself as the thoughtful and kind person that he is."

—Jocelyn Hong, President, the National Institute for Lobbying and Ethics and Chair of the H Street Group

"Mark Grayson is a man who, as Dorothy Day put it, loves truth enough to live it. From childhood he refused to buy into beliefs about who he was as a male that he sensed even at a very early age were not only false but damaging. Over time his struggle and resistance against the pressures of conformity forged in him a calling. Now, in *Getting Naked: A Field Guide for Men*, that calling has become wisdom. The power and authority of Mark's story arise from his candor and searing honesty about what it has taken to win his spiritual liberation as a man. I can think of no better guide than one who has lived the truth like Mark has, to guide others towards a similar discovery of who they were born to be."

—Courtney Cowart, Executive Director of the Society for the Increase in the Ministry, and former Associate Dean and Director of the Beecken Center at the Sewanee School of Theology

GETTING NAKED

A FIELD GUIDE FOR MEN

MARK GRAYSON

Cover design by Kostis Pavlou.
Copyediting by Stephen Foster.
Typesetting by Susan Gerber.

For media inquiries, questions about bulk purchases, permission to use any of the content of this book, or speaking availability, please visit www.nakedmancollective.com.

Library of Congress CIP is on file.
ISBNs:
979-8-9901355-0-5 (hardcover)
979-8-9901355-1-2 (paperback)
979-8-9901355-2-9 (ebook)

 NAKED MAN COLLECTIVE

For Parker and Philip,
the best sons a guy could ever have,
and Sarah,
who has the courage to love us so deeply

CONTENTS

AUTHOR'S NOTE

I am an extremely lucky guy who has moved up in the world from some fairly humble roots, having been born into a family of farmers, small business owners, and educators living in rural Ohio before we moved to Central Texas. My life trajectory from there accelerated quickly upwards as I was a good student. I eventually attended educational institutions that some would consider elite and built a life rubbing shoulders with a broad, diverse group of highly successful men and women of all races and socioeconomic backgrounds.

I make these statements so that you understand that my worldview is broad, and I have lifelong friends across the full spectrum. That said, I am sensitive to the fact that as a cis white straight male my experience is not universal, and I am aware of its limitations. I have done my best to engage all points of view in writing this book, comparing the research to the actual lived experience of men in my networks.

I am particularly concerned that because I have been lucky in life, this book might not be perceived as representative or relevant to the men whose roots I share and are so deeply encoded in my DNA that my great joy to this day is returning home to the places where I can be a small-town boy. (Our sons have inherited my genetic predisposition as well.) I may not have joined the military or taken up a trade, but that does not mean that I do not feel an affiliation to these men. I suspect that I have more in common with them than the guys with whom I have interacted professionally over the past forty years.

The amazing thing that I have learned in my quest to develop an authentic expression of my own masculinity by studying the men around me is that under the swagger of nearly every male beats the heart of a really sweet man looking for companionship on life's journey. I am utterly convinced of the inherent goodness of men. It's only our cultural conditioning and our flaws in being human that get us into trouble.

To the women who are reading this book I would like to say upfront that I know that many of the observations that I make about men apply to women as well. Rather than call that fact out repeatedly, I have chosen to assume that you will recall this statement periodically throughout the book and indulge and support me in my focus on building a new narrative for men.

INTRODUCTION

This book is an attempt to provide a roadmap for men who are seeking greater personal satisfaction and more fulfillment in their lives.

In August 2018, I attended a men's retreat in Ojai entitled "Women Teach Men" with a buddy who was turning 40. The #MeToo Movement had exploded on the scene during the previous fall, and 100 guys, mainly ages 30–45, came together to explore how we might respond to the complex challenges that engulfed us. The retreat was organized with the intention of reversing the traditional power paradigm—all the speakers were high-powered, accomplished women. Between sessions we attendees gathered in squads of six to eight led by a male facilitator to talk about how men might take on the challenge of working with our brothers to effect a shift in men's behavior.

In our breakout group was a brilliant twenty-five-year-old tech exec who had been excoriated for some statements he had posted online in college about the interactions of men and women prior to the #MeToo moment. He was reserved and gun-shy about speaking up, but clearly had a ton on his mind. Feeling his pain, my friend and I chatted with him about our own sense of frustration and alarm that the movement was tearing men and women apart, even as it uncovered serious issues that needed our attention and deep wounds that we needed somehow to heal. We discovered that we had a lot in common, even at ages 25, 40, and 60. Our new friend inquired whether I had done some thinking on this topic. I admitted that I had in fact done quite a lot of thinking and writing privately about all this. He asked to read some of my stuff. I sent a piece to him to read that night, which he did.

Later we attended a men-only session with psychotherapist Esther Perel. From the outset we agreed to create a safe space where we could share our dark secrets in confidence and speak of our swirling emotions and insecurities without shame or embarrassment. I heard things that I never thought a man would admit even to himself, much less to others. There was an overwhelming outpouring of pain and confusion. These revelations were not just related to the mixed set of feelings that men were experiencing about the #MeToo Movement—which ranged from extreme outrage at bad actors, feelings of complicity, and anger at being condemned for merely being male—but the challenges of being a man, in general. There was talk of the dark underside of men's sexual drive—the thrill of aggression, our need to consume, possess, or conquer. The prevalence and persistence of premature ejaculation, well into our 30s for some, and the general embarrassment of not being able to maintain more control over our impulses. The agony of wanting to form deep connections with women without having the emotional capacities or communications skills to do so. The frustration of being punished for the sins of our brothers, along with the acknowledgment that on some level we were, all of us, guilty of exploiting women. It was 1:30 AM before Dr. Perel closed a session whose dialogue showed no sign of ever ending.

The next day the retreat was buzzing with men connecting in ways that we typically do not. There wasn't any posturing, just a fierce desire to continue the conversation of the night before.

At the end of the retreat, I found myself standing in a sacred circle with the legendary Rev. Jo from Agape Church in Los Angeles. Her towering presence could inspire fear in men, as you knew that without lifting a finger, she could invoke the wrath of God. One by one we stood before her and made a solemn vow to act on some insight of the retreat. Shaking like a leaf, I heard myself swear from out of nowhere that I would begin to publish my writing.

That was a big, scary departure for me as I had long ago decided that I could not openly discuss my several-decade exploration of modern masculinity in public. It would have been too high risk for me professionally, as I was a non-profit exec and a producer of children's programming. I could not expect to remain employed if I were to share my thoughts about unexpected hard-ons, the range of sexual impulses that men feel, relationship challenges, and feelings of inadequacy and failure.

However, as I stood before the group and reflected upon the collective pain that I had witnessed that weekend, I realized that men who have been trying to reframe and expand traditional notions of masculinity need to step up during these contentious times, overcome our reluctance, and put ourselves at risk of retaliation for speaking out. In that pivotal moment, I decided that the positive impacts that I might generate in joining the men who were committing to making a shift, no matter how small, far outweighed the personal consequences of doing so.

Nevertheless, it took me a couple of months to screw up the courage to begin posting my thoughts online. I, too, had some prior history here. The previous January, just a few months after the allegations against Harvey Weinstein were made, I had submitted an essay to the *Los Angeles Review of Books* proposing an action step that men could take to reframe their understanding of the issues. To say that my proposal was unconventional is an understatement. It was so out of bounds that you could think of it as a piece of Swiftian satire—"An Immodest Proposal"— as the essay suggested that men pose nude for a female photographer to better understand the impact of the male gaze. To my great surprise and amazement, the essay was accepted and published by BLARB, LA Review of Books's online platform. This caused a mini firestorm in my family, as everyone thought I was a fool to pull this stunt and jeopardize my career. My piece wasn't remotely G-rated.

So, I hesitated to cause them more pain and risk triggering negative professional ripple effects from which I might never recover. But, remembering my promise that I would share my thoughts with the men in our tribe that are in crisis . . . on a cold Sunday afternoon in October, I sat by the fire and reworked the BLARB piece, using my "chest" voice (as I would telling a story to guys at the bar) instead of the heady, intellectual voice of the original. Continuing watching TV, I sent it off to Lisa Hickey, the publisher of The Good Men Project, thinking I might hear back in a few weeks. Two hours later, I received a positive response, with an inquiry as to whether there were other topics that I might want to write about. I dashed off twelve ideas without giving it much thought and got a second quick response. Fifty essays and five years later, I am still writing.

        ▨ ▨ ▨

This guide is for men who are eager to reframe the behavioral patterns that are deeply engrained inside us about what it means to be a "real man," despite these patterns being at odds with the new set of expectations that confront today's men. These patterns have been categorized by social commentators as the "Man Box" because they are so deeply encoded into our society and our individual behaviors that many men find it difficult to challenge its "rules." Men have created these definitions of masculinity over time as a way to distribute and control power. Although the "Man Box" is a prison for many (some would argue all) men, there is a payoff for men in maintaining the status quo as we benefit from this system of oppression. For a host of reasons that we'll discuss in the book, it's long past time for us to take responsibility for making a cultural shift that better supports the needs of all individuals, including our own. *Getting Naked* attempts to answer the question of how we might evolve from being emotionally detached providers, warriors, and protectors into becoming compassionate nurturers, companions, and seekers as well. It suggests ways in which aspects of our personalities that are conditioned out of us can be reclaimed and turned into strengths. It reflects forty years of experience trying to expand the narrow, rigid definitions of manhood that our society forces upon men, along with the latest academic research and the stories of other men who have been fellow travelers on this journey.

I hope that these pages provide insights that will advance the current conversation about what it means to be a 21st-century man. My deepest wish is that this book inspires generations of men to develop their innate capacities to engage with their wives, partners, children, colleagues, and friends in an open-hearted way that will enable them to experience the grace, power, and joy of being alive, connected, and unabashedly male.

CHAPTER I

THE INCOMPLETE MAN

When our older son was five, he took a series of developmental assessments to determine his readiness for elementary school, including a Gesell "Incomplete Man" Test.

Afterwards, his kindergarten evaluator informed us that our son had meticulously filled out the left side of the figure in great detail, but running out of time, he had left the right side blank. This "error," along with the fact that he had given his Incomplete Man a penis, was interpreted as evidence that our wonderful boy was developmentally delayed. It was unlikely that he would ever catch up and thrive at the school's kindergarten that she was interviewing him for. She advised us to seek admission elsewhere. (He graduated from Harvard seventeen years later.)

At the time I didn't understand how much my son's assessment mirrored my own lifelong journey (and that of generations of men) as we attempt to frame new forms of masculinity that more authentically respond to today's requirements. Much as we have tried, most of us are still struggling to develop a complete picture of what it means to be a good man in a world where the concept of masculinity and the dynamics between men and women are rapidly changing. Although we know we need to make a shift, we are unable to frame and step into our new role.

We remain frozen in part because the old models of masculinity are strictly enforced, and the potential social and financial consequences of exhibiting our full humanity as men, in defiance of their edicts, holds us back from moving forward. Our inertia is also due to the fact that the way in which we are raised to fulfill the expectations of these traditional models often forces us to hide or erase the very capacities we need in order to make a shift. As a result, we remain "Incomplete Men," stick figures missing critical pieces of our male identities. *Getting Naked: A Field Guide for Men* offers a framework, a set of key insights inherent in our evolving understandings of masculinity that might help you move forward.

This is not the first time that men have tried to reframe the way we roll. In the early 1980s and 1990s, the mythopoetic men's movement aspired to deepen our understanding of the male psyche and clarify how it might differ from the new identities women had assumed as a result of the feminist movement. The ideas expressed by Robert Bly (*Iron John*, 1990), Sam Keen (*Fire in the Belly*, 1991), Joseph Campbell (*The Power of Myth*, 1988), Robert Moore and Douglas Gillette (*King, Warrior, Magician, Lover*, 1990), John Eldredge (*Wild at Heart*, 2001), and Richard Rohr (*From Wild Man to Wise Man*, 2005) continue to be touchstones for today's men who are committed to preserving and protecting "the best parts" of traditional models of masculinity. Although much effort has been poured into a "new masculinity" movement which builds on these models, men's retreats can often become trauma centers where guys can safely reveal their pain, without forfeiting their standing as a "real man," but are still not given the tools to effectively shift behavior. We grieve, we attempt to improve our interactions and relationships with loved ones, but much of our behavior remains unchanged. A further problem is that these gatherings can often become ways in which we reify and reintegrate some of the negative norms of the male code and can even reinforce social structures that contemporary society is evolving away from. Today's men's retreats are an important step in the journey, but they don't offer a complete roadmap of possibilities for moving forward.

The great risks and destructive impacts that are inherent in maintaining the status quo have become vividly clear over the past few years. Richard Reeves's excellent analysis *Of Boys and Men: Why the Modern Male Is Struggling, Why It Matters, and What to Do About It* sounds an alarm that we must take seriously.[1] His findings confirm that millions of boys and young men are struggling in school, at work, and in the family at a level that exceeds our prior estimations. In his view, in addition to the work that needs to be done at the individual level, men's struggle is a structural problem that requires meaningful policy solutions. This book will focus on the former—the work that we can do now as individuals while other experts address structural issues. It's clear that something must be done to reduce the current pain points experienced by men and women.

MAN BOX CULTURE

We are going to organize our search for solutions at the individual level using a framework that shines a light on the set of behaviors that have trapped men for years. The consequences of men performing these traditionally masculine behaviors were first codified by Paul Kivel and Tony Porter as the "Man Box." They have been dramatically articulated by Mark Greene, former senior editor of The Good Men Project, and a good friend, in his excellent précis, *The Little #MeToo Book for Men*.[2]

His brief, incisive prose distills Kivel and Porter's construct into an actionable set of understandings of how men are caught in a web of expectations of what it means to be male from which it is difficult to escape. It's a must read for every man eager to throw off the yoke of its oppression.

Here's a quick summary of Mark's brief. The Man Box is a narrowly defined set of traditional rules for being a man that are enforced through shaming and bullying, in order to enforce conformity to our current culture of masculinity, and to perpetuate the domination, even exploitation of people who are perceived to be "other" or of lesser stature when compared to straight men—most often, women and the LGBTQIA2S+ community. In this model of masculinity, a man is expected to be:

- Strong and stoic
- Unemotional, expressing no feelings except anger and lust
- Providers (never caregivers)
- Heterosexual, hyper-masculine, sexually dominant
- Able-bodied, a person who never asks for help
- Someone who plays or watches sports
- Domineering in every exchange

Each deviation, no matter how small, is policed. It is important to note that many aspects of this culture of masculinity cut across race and the socio-economic spectrum, providing a point of common experience and set of expectations for all men around the globe. It is a universally shared understanding among men, for better or worse.

The objective of this dominance-based culture of masculinity is to eradicate and target difference in male norms, granting permission for aggression—large or small—so that power can accrue to the guys on top. It is a narrow and repressive form of manhood that is defined by violence, sex, status, and assault, a cultural construct where strength, power, and status are everything, and showing emotions, being open, or engaging in relational empathy are signs of weakness. A social system where sex and aggression are the yardsticks by which men are measured. One of its main strengths is that it insists on acquiescence and silent acceptance. That means that most guys don't challenge the paradigm or the misdeeds of other men for fear of retaliation.

The culture of masculinity is very hierarchical. One of the key tenets of the "Man Box" is that in order to sit at the top of the hierarchy of men, we must reject the personal qualities that our Western society identifies as "feminine." The world of emotions and social cognition—being empathetic, networked, connected, open, and transparent—is devalued as unmanly. Instead, this macho code of behavior reveres a male that is silent, tough, independent, hyper-competitive, and it bears repeating, hyper-sexual. Greene and others contend that this hierarchical system for establishing a man's relative status and power is responsible for the current epidemic of loneliness, depression, substance abuse, and suicide among men, because of the way that the Man Box forces boys to detach from their emotions and adhere to a rigid set of expectations that inflict significant damage. We will talk more about that in Chapter 4.

A veritable platoon of sociologists and psychologists—William Pollack (*Real Boys*, 1998), Michael Gurian (*The Wonder of Boys*, 1996), Dan Kindlon and Michael Thompson (*Raising Cain*, 1999), and later Michael Reichert (*How to Raise a Boy*, 2019)—have documented the destructive emotional training that our society imposes upon boys. The irony here is that the way we men are raised prevents us from having the very tools we now most need in order to initiate a paradigm shift. We have neither the emotional conditioning nor the communication skills to navigate a "highly polarized system between women and men."[3]

Two decades have passed since some of these popular bestsellers armed a generation of parents, myself included, with an understanding of the importance of nurturing the emotional intelligence of young boys. You might have thought that by now a new generation of men would exhibit less of the derogatory, dismissive behavior that prior generations have shown towards women. Instead, as we have recently learned from Peggy Orenstein in her book, *Boys and Sex: Young Men on Hookups, Love, Porn, Consent, and the New Masculinity*,[4] if anything "the definition of masculinity seems to be contracting,"[5] and the exploitation of women continues. Much as we would like to believe that the new generation of men is behaving better than their fathers, the evidence is not encouraging.

Indeed, men and women seem to be locked in a battle to determine what the prevailing model of masculinity and its corresponding attitudes towards women going forward will be. Many pundits observed that the 2020 presidential election asked voters "to consider what masculinity means," forcing us to choose between a version of masculinity that stresses macho, plain-spoken toughness, and another model that emphasizes family empathy, caring for and protecting others. As feminist author Susan Faludi, and journalists Claire Cain Miller and Alisha Haridasani Gupta brilliantly observed in their pieces for the *New York Times* just before the election, the stakes just keep getting higher and higher.[6] The challenge is that this debate is all too often framed as males having to make a choice between being either traditional or progressive, when the invitation that is being offered men in this moment is the choice to be both.

Further complicating men's ability to make a shift is the dark underbelly of our tough, self-confident male egos. We struggle with deep-seated shame about our bodies and sexual impulses. In diametric opposition to its adoration of the breast and vulva, our culture treats the penis as an object of ridicule and scorn. At a very early age our initial delight in our unusual piece of anatomy is replaced by a sense of embarrassment instilled by our elders, which is later amplified by the non-stop messaging by men, women, and the media that the penis is a sexual assault weapon. Making matters worse is the fact that the penis seems to have a mind of its own. Increasingly research confirms that we all occupy a spot on the spectrum of desire that is a mix of hetero- and homosexual impulses, as Kinsey first reported in 1948. It further suggests that men's sexual impulses are likely not singular and fixed. Indeed, the research indicates that our "orientation" may be a pattern of preference (sometimes the result of a committed partnership) that at any time could change. That is, our sexual orientation is not a neurochemical phenomenon that is static and stabile (though our preferences may be for a host of reasons). Uncomfortable with our bodies, and unable to process the underlying fluidity inherent in our sexuality, men do not permit themselves to acknowledge and express the full range of their impulses, except within the narrow band of behaviors that society validates. This is, of course, extremely challenging due to the insistent biological imperatives that will not be denied and every man experiences throughout his adult life. We are, both men and women, by nature, extremely physical, sensual, sexual beings.

A final force holding men back is the fact that our secular society does not encourage men to be spiritual. Although the Pew Research Center reports that significant demographic segments are moving away from religion while continuing to believe in a higher power, most men are groomed to devalue their spiritual leanings in favor of exhibiting an orientation towards material achievement that is required to be considered a successful adult male. Our inexperience cultivating the life of the Spirit removes a key instrument for change in a guy's toolbox, one that it is my contention is absolutely essential. Why? Every wisdom text from around the world has recorded that all fundamental, long-lasting, transformational change comes from within.

All these challenges have been brought to a tipping point recently by the onset of COVID-19. The fundamental assumption underlying traditional constructs of masculinity—a man's personal agency to achieve a desired outcome in a system where he has some control—was removed, at least for that moment. The question is: In which direction will men make a shift after this disruptive period? Will we return back to the old models that are well-rehearsed, understood, and safe, but do not serve us well, or will we leap into a new, emerging paradigm? Do we even have a choice? Is this powerful disease forcing men to learn lessons that we have long resisted, demanding that we adopt new behaviors? Is the virus virulent enough to create permanent and lasting change in the way that we live? What will the new norms for being perceived as a 21st Century Male look like in this modern era? Will these norms be adopted by a broad spectrum of men, not just the current pioneers? And what is the critical path for getting there?

I believe that men are ready for a fresh look at how we might construct our own authentic form of masculinities, with new norms of what it means to be a man. I also believe that this effort must literally strip men down (as all male initiation rites since the beginning of time have done)—physically, emotionally, mentally—so that we can build our new identities from the ground up, inside out. We will never experience the change we seek unless men recover and re-energize the innate capacities within us. We must learn how to be bold and at the same time fiercely loving and kind. Everything else will follow.

A ROADMAP FOR MAKING A SHIFT

Recognizing that broad platitudes will get us nowhere, I have identified seven areas of exploration that men can focus on in order to move forward, based on studies by sociologists and other academics observing male behavior, conversations with several psychotherapists whose client lists skew towards men, and my own personal experience. I will describe each of these seven areas in the succeeding chapters, offering research findings, illustrative stories from my own life and from the lives of others, along with some practical suggestions and exercises that you might find useful.

I am proposing these seven areas for personal exploration in order to create a significant transformation in your life, from the inside out.

Each territory for investigation enables men to disable a key tenet of the Man Box's influence over our behavior, so that we might create our own new, more authentic way of being male.

A Seven-Part Journey Towards Becoming a 21st Century Male

1—Get naked

Men are trained to reject any behavior that seems weak in order to become competitive, aggressive warriors as adults. To counteract and balance this training, men also need to learn the power of being open, vulnerable, and transparent. *Getting Naked* proposes that every man who is ready to make a shift literally and metaphorically should strip down physically and mentally at home—as a rite of passage indicating that he is open to the change that he seeks. With this new mindset, men will also begin to develop a much healthier relationship with their own bodies and stop buying into the shame that we are taught. We can learn to see grace and beauty in every male form, at every age.

2—Get in touch with your "feminine" side

Because the Man Box rejects the "feminine" as "other," men need to reclaim the feminine wisdom within them in order to become whole. We need to learn the value of being networked, creative, intuitive, body-conscious (in a healthy way), grounded in ordinary life, and nurturers/caretakers that are emotionally connected. We know that teamwork and collaboration produce better results than a strictly competitive approach, and that diversity, emotional/relational intelligence, and social cognition are the doors to success.

3—Learn how to engage and express the heart

From a very early age, boys are touched less, and they are conditioned to detach from their emotions in order to become tough, successful adults. Man Box culture trains men to be "calm, cool, collected," instead of showing their feelings. "It isn't manly." Men are therefore complicated creatures emotionally, and because we are not taught how to handle or communicate our feelings, we tend to explode in anger or lust. We need a system upgrade that enables us to open our hearts, one that provides us with a broad range of tools—verbal and nonverbal—to respond in more appropriate ways to people and events around us.

4—Acknowledge the full range of your own male sexuality

The Man Box asserts that "real men" are both hyper-sexual and hetero-sexual, despite the latest research on male sexuality indicating that men experience a broader spectrum of sexual and romantic impulses than we are willing to admit. We therefore need to reframe what it means to be a "Real Man." Men need to get in touch with their actual sexual identities and the range of appropriate ways in which they can express and enjoy them.

5—Develop a daily contemplative practice

Since the early eighteenth century, the ideal man has been perceived to be rational and detached, an individual who is in control of his thoughts and impulses so that he can seize every advantage while retaining his "killer" instinct. We need to develop the skills that empty and still the mind, so that the authentic man within, not some social construct heavily shaped by the expectations of culture of masculinity, can emerge. We need to create an inner space where fundamental change can occur, as grace appears only when we pause in life, surrender, take off our armor, still the body, open the heart, and quiet the mind, so that the transcendent which is our birthright can expand our being.

6—Make time to withdraw completely from the world for a period of rest and retreat

A core proposition of the Man Box is that the primary role of men is as providers in a winner-take-all world. Western society's extreme emphasis on "doing" or "accomplishing" things is a heavy burden for men, who are taught from an early age that they must aggressively compete for money, power, recognition, and status in order to be successful and happy. We men need to give ourselves permission to take a break from the 24/7 pace so that we might regroup and redesign our lives both individually and collectively.

7—Reframe definitions of success

New definitions of success are essential in order to weaken the Man Box's grip on our souls—both the drive to be successful and the fear of failure if we do not abide by our culture of masculinity's expectations are significantly limiting to men's fulfillment. A framework for Designing Your Life developed at Stanford offers a good starting place for this final step.

WHY AM I YOUR GUIDE?

You may now be asking why I'm the person to guide you on this journey. Here's my answer.

Forty years ago, in an act of self-preservation, I rejected the tribal narratives of what it meant to be male that I had learned growing up in the remote corners of rural Ohio and Central Texas. I knew that I had to choose either to adhere to the macho male code or leave it all behind.

I never really did fit the traditional masculine mold. Yeah, I was athletic, and as a youth participated in all kinds of neighborhood sports, but in high school instead of football, I played soccer and ran track. Instead of summer jobs involving heavy manual labor, I taught summer school and worked as a lifeguard at the pool. Instead of driving a pickup truck, I drove an MGB convertible. Instead of hunting and chasing cattle or deer for fun on the weekends, I went hiking. Instead of drinking beer with the guys, I enjoyed partying with women and men. After finishing college, I finally realized that the "Texas Plan"—leaving the state for college and then returning home—also expected me to settle down, put on a pair of boots, get married and start a family, so I left. I wanted all that, but on my own terms, and I was tired of being labeled as "gay" for not trying harder to be one of the guys.

It all came to a head when the only job I could find in Austin after graduating from Harvard was calling on bad debt for the largest John Deere dealership west of the Mississippi. (Although that propelled me out of Austin, in search of work and an identity that was more aligned to my soul, the job actually turned out to be a terrific experience.)

My trek into a new masculinity frontier wasn't what I expected. Instead of being rejected, I was embraced first by the last generation of Mad Men in advertising, then by a bunch of Hollywood bosses, and finally by the pioneers of impact investing, including Charles R. Schwab.

If there was a theme across all these male friendships and professional working relationships, it was "Breaking Free." As we were creating new products and services, and new forms of organization, we were also recreating ourselves as men who aspired to more meaning and purpose than earning a paycheck. We introduced fashion watches at a reasonable price point, wine coolers, Captain Morgan Spiced Rum, Bill Nye the Science Guy, Rabbit Ears Radio (Hollywood celebs and world-class musicians telling classic children's stories), Schools Attuned (for teachers, parents, and students struggling with differences in learning)—each in its own way dedicated to making the world a better, more exciting place for ourselves and our families. (And yes, despite all the temptation to behave otherwise in New York, Hollywood, Paris, London, Rome, San Francisco, and DC, we were all family men, just like I would have been back in Texas. I did not succumb to the behavior that the #MeToo Movement has so vividly condemned.)

Because I traveled a lot for business, I missed being present daily during our sons' elementary school years, ironically, as I led an education start-up to national prominence. But, despite being on the road, I did figure out how to attend all their poetry recitations, most of their important games, and concerts. I made it a priority even when many of the other dads who were only commuting to NYC did not. Then my career hit a brick wall for a completely unexpected reason, leading to an unplanned transition and loss of income. This sudden shift shook the very foundation of my masculinity: *being the provider.*

Seizing the opportunity to make a fundamental change in the way I rolled, I launched a small business and reorganized my life so that I could be more present at home. Fifteen years ago I learned to juggle the demands of being an entrepreneur, father, and spouse, while working remotely, much as today's men are learning now.

When forces that I eventually understood were beyond my control took charge of my life, I decided to go with the flow and demonstrate my willingness to be open, transparent, and vulnerable in direct defiance of the traditional male code. That took a level of courage that I still don't quite comprehend, and the full support of my loving wife as I struggled to find my footing.

After this act of surrender, a series of extraordinary experiences began to unfold. Self-help books flew off the shelves to get me started—the ones I needed at the moment, but didn't even know existed, would actually drop into my hands in the store. Then a series of spiritual advisors showed up. A pre-cognitive psychotherapist, who taught Transcendental Meditation trainers. A demanding but loving female guide (who is also a world-class triathlete). A former Ogilvy exec who is expert in research on the mind-body-heart connection. An inter-spiritual mystic traveling the world, who was a close friend of Ram Dass. An Episcopal monk. All welcomed me into a deepening exploration.

It became clear that I was now on a spiritual adventure, taking me to new territory—both internal and external—consolidating what I had been learning all these years about the essence of my male psyche. Three major projects came out of nowhere and took off seemingly of their own accord, gathering a momentum that has propelled them into the national limelight.

Conventional notions of manhood are shifting now for many reasons. Scrutiny of male entitlement and hypersexuality exposed by the #MeToo Movement, changing roles (long in the making) now amplified by COVID-19 requirements to shelter in place, male push-back against those advocating for making a shift in male roles and attitudes, and other social forces have brought men to a place where we need to decide how we are going to move forward.

How should we respond? Should we return to our old routines? Or should we reorder our priorities and reorganize our daily lives? I think the latter.

My life and writing have provided me with insights that men might find useful on this journey of collective redefinition of masculinity that we have begun. It has also provided me with access to researchers and thought leaders in the new masculinity/male spirituality space, and legions of men who are willing to share the stories of their struggles to make a shift.

I fervently believe that together we can create the change we all seek, preserving the best parts of our old male code, and inventing the new. So, let's begin our journey.

CHAPTER 2

STRIP DOWN

I travel a lot for business and make a point of working out at local gyms whenever possible to observe the behaviors of men of all ages and backgrounds, listening to their banter in the locker room. It's an informal field study that I have conducted now for forty years.

During that time, I have witnessed the emergence of a peculiar convention among young men: dressing and undressing under a towel, and the introduction of the shower stall.

Wanting to better understand the mindset that is behind this trend, which is so counter to the communal showers that I grew up with, I recently consulted my friend George, a twenty-five-year-old, hale and hearty male.

"What's up with that?" I inquired, baffled.

"Well, you know, from age five on boys are taught that your privates are private. You never show your penis."

"Not even in front of other men?" I asked. "I mean, we all basically have the same equipment. It's not exactly a mystery what's down there."

"No," he mused, thinking for a second, then went on. "I played soccer in school. It was a big shock when I got to college and had to undress and shower in front of the other guys."

"Why? What was so hard about it? What did you feel?"

"Embarrassment, insecurity, shame."

I told George about my own experience confronting my negative feelings about my body when I posed for a female photographer to better understand the impact of the male gaze. She confirmed that every man that she had worked with on her nude male project, "CFNM (clothed female/naked male)," had expressed an enormous amount of shame, even the actors and models who were used to putting their bodies on display.

George responded, "Yeah, we need to learn the difference between modesty and shame."

"Exactly. Of course, men shouldn't run around flashing their junk, but why should we be made to feel ashamed about having a penis?"

He paused and said, "Well, I don't know how it is for you, but guys my age don't hear many positive messages about being male."

I nodded, reflecting on the string of negative statements that I had heard over the decades from men and women that viewed the male body and men's sexuality as bad, scary, or dangerous. A beast to be controlled. I shifted gears. "The funny thing is that there is enormous power in a man's ability to stand in his own naked truth."

"Yeah," George agreed. "It's the opposite of what we are taught. It makes you a better man."

There are many entry points into the journey to become a more "complete" male, filling out our frames with key components of our masculine identities that have been conditioned out of us. Once you commit to undertaking this adventure, you will quickly discover that there is no prescribed sequence of tasks to accomplish other than the ones that call for you as they appear before your eyes. The path forward reveals itself when you are ready to take another step. This book is therefore not a "how-to" manual but a guide to the issues that you may encounter.

That said, when guys ask me "Where do I begin? How do I take my first step forward out of the Man Box?" I always tell them that the best place to start is the hardest and most unlikely.

"You need to get naked. Physically, emotionally, psychologically, and spiritually, you need to get naked."

WHY?

Getting naked is a reliable, proven step in identity transformation. Since time immemorial public nudity has been used in all sorts of rituals designed to induce altered psychic states in tandem with the cycles of nature and milestone moments in our adult journeys. In his ethnographic paper "Naked, Mute and Well-Hung: A Brief Ethnographic Comparison of Kengpa and Related Ritual Performers in the Eastern Himalayas and Beyond," Prof. Antoni Huber of the Institute for Asian and African studies at Humboldt University in Berlin traces naked dances still practiced today back to the Stone and Bronze Ages. A common feature of rites of passage conducted by a vast array of cultures around the globe—Hindu, indigenous African, Native American, South American, Aboriginal, Buddhist, Okina Noh—includes the removal of one's clothes in exchange for new garments more in keeping with the identities individuals will adopt in the next chapters in their lives.[7] Lest we think that public nudity is a parlor trick among ancient or less advanced civilizations that is not relevant to contemporary life, it might be worth noting that Mormon "Initiatories" (washing rites for initiates) were conducted fully nude into the 20th century, and were only banned in 2005, when modern sensibilities forbid them.[8] And military organizations around the world strip recruits down in cohorts, taking away civilian clothing, standardizing appearance, and conducting physicals prior to beginning the process of building the identities of soldiers during boot camp.[9] All these traditions recognize the value of physically removing the childhood identities of adolescent men and women, and investing them with new names and the tools they will need to fully participate in the life of the community as mature adults. These rituals have a profound psychological impact, enabling individuals to reframe the narratives that they have accumulated. They offer the possibility for a fresh start.

It has been my experience that even without community context in which these rites of passage are performed, a similar, powerful transformation can be triggered in men when we are forced to stand in our own naked truth and allow ourselves to be seen. (This is not the many, naked, weekend warrior workshops that the men's movement has organized for several decades, though that can be a good place to begin. What I'm talking about is deeper, more personal, ongoing, as rebuilding male identities is a process that occurs over time. More on that in a moment.)

A second reason why I recommend getting naked (and/or adopting a "naked" mindset) as a good first step is that the act of allowing yourself to be seen in your natural state in public requires "balls," a bit of brazenness. It is a demonstration of a level of commitment to change irrespective of the consequences that men must summon during these challenging times. This type of personal bravery is essential to the journey of becoming a new man, as you will most likely encounter some pushback from colleagues and friends (men and women) who are uncomfortable with the shift that you will make because it may be at odds with some of the conventions of our day. Given that Man Box culture is so persistent and invasive, bold, strong action and a fierce, focused mind are required to eradicate its impact. There is no better way to remove the physical, mental, and emotional armor that you have worn for most of your life. Getting naked puts you in a new frame of mind and telegraphs to the world that you are willing to buck conventional expectations in order to rebuild your identity "from the studs up," revealing the man that you truly are, not some caricature of manliness that our culture promotes. (Note: Later in the book, we will discuss the difference between Man Box culture and traditional forms of masculinity, some of whose features often do serve us well.)

There is a third reason for getting naked, and it's the most important. In addition to the benefit of putting yourself in the mindset of being committed to change, getting naked (both physically and symbolically) puts you in the best possible position to make the most dramatic gains from the explorations that you will undertake on your journey. You will discover that stripping yourself down and revealing yourself to others in your natural state will help you release the narratives that you have wrapped around your psyche about what it means to be a man. It's a bit like jumping off a cliff into a pool of water below. Once you conquer your fear and take the plunge, ripple effects occur afterwards. Many opportunities for personal growth will arise before your eyes, drawing you forward on your journey, and your concerns about stepping out of the Man Box will diminish. Unfettered, you will be more able to recover pieces of your identity that have been conditioned out of you, expanding your vision of what it means to be fierce, bold, loving, kind, and unabashedly male.

If you have any doubts about the value of a naked mindset, you might be interested to know that there was branch of psychotherapy in the '60s and '70s in which nude therapy was practiced. No less than the eminent Abraham Maslow (best known for the "Hierarchy of Needs"), then president of the American Psychological Association, endorsed this therapy organized around encounter groups that were so prevalent at the time. Columbia- and Duke-trained psychologist Paul Bindrim pioneered this form of group psychotherapy based on Maslow's work. "Maslow had become disillusioned with psychoanalysis, behaviorism and the focus on psychopathology. He called for a focus on personal growth, authenticity and transcendence, and he viewed nudism as a viable path to those things." Bindrim organized nude therapy encounter groups around the idea of the naked body as a metaphor for the "psychological soul." "It was believed that uninhibited exhibition of the nude body revealed that which was most fundamental, truthful, and real." In group sessions, participants' bodies were studied with scientific discipline in an attempt to free the self from its socially imposed constraints and related narratives. By the late 1970s and early 1980s, nude therapy fell out of favor, as societal attitudes started becoming more conservative, and some of the therapeutic practice was downright weird (pressure to disclose intimate secrets to a group of strangers, "crotch eyeballing," intense sleep deprivation).[10] Even though this form of therapy has since been discontinued, the psychological benefits of getting naked remain relevant, due to the personal transformation that it can put in motion.

Getting naked has other benefits. You may rediscover components of your personality that society judges as "girly" as we delve into the wisdom of the sacred feminine and its relevance to men. With the vulnerability and accessibility that getting naked psychologically creates, you may regain a long-lost ability to open up your heart and express your emotions in ways that build your most important relationships at home and at work. You may find that the increased transparency equips you with a new ability to communicate your thoughts and feelings, as well as listen to those of others (in defiance of cultural edicts that "real men" must be strong, silent types). You may learn that being better connected to (and in command of) your own body will help you develop a fluency in the language of non-sexual, consensual touch that is so important to our physical and emotional well-being as humans (instead of acting as if touch is some form of sexual foreplay). You will most certainly need to get naked to be able to empty out all the crap in your soul so that your true calling in life can emerge (rather than running the playbook that the Man Box dictates). It will also provide you with a blank slate upon which to write the new definitions of success that are required to end the "How Big Is Your Bank Account/Paycheck/House/Car/Wife's Boobs/Dick" narratives by which most men operate.

There is another intrinsic benefit, however, that makes getting naked a good idea in and of itself for men: so that we undo the harm caused by the negative perceptions we secretly harbor about our own male bodies. These perceptions weave themselves into so many aspects of our behavior and experience that a close examination of their impact is an essential step in our self-discovery process.

Our culture's conflicting attitudes regarding the male body can fundamentally shape our identities as adult men, equipping us with an extremely complicated relationship to our embodied presence. In some settings, we worship the male form; in others, we demonize it. For cisgender men, the mixed messages begin early. Although our culture celebrates ways that the male body can be used as an instrument for good, men are also taught to feel shame about their bodies, specifically their genitals, from preschool on. As we mature, our dominance-based culture of masculinity repeatedly sorts men into cohorts organized by our physical appearance and strength. During early childhood, performance in sport and other body-centric activities begins to define us. When puberty kicks in, we are sorted again by looks, height, and build—which adds to our general insecurity about our rapidly changing bodies, no matter what relative position we occupy in the emerging hierarchy of men surrounding us. During this period other people's assessment of our bodies and their comparison to various ideals deepen our negative self-assessments and the shame that we have learned to attach to our physical being. Many women go through a similar damaging reassessment of their bodies at this time, and the increase in the incidence of eating disorders and body dysphoria among both genders in this age group begins to rise. This is also a period when women and men begin to perseverate about breast and penis size. Compensating for any bodily deficiencies that we perceive we may possess as we move into our adult years and become sexually active, we men once again use our bodies to measure our manliness once more, utilizing how much sex we engage in (or claim to) as another identity marker. This sizing each other up in the

locker room of life is deeply ingrained—physically, mentally, sexually—
and never stops. To begin to re-humanize and de-weaponize the male
form, we need to reduce the stigma that we attach to men's bodies. And
getting naked is a good way to begin.

POWERING DOWN TO POWER UP

My journey to make such a shift in my perceptions regarding my own
body got started in a pretty unusual way. Initially, my objectives were
very much a product of Man Box culture. Around the time I turned 50, I
went through an unexpected career crisis—one so dramatic that I knew
I would need a total system reboot before I took my next swing. Since
getting fit was something that I could do while I was waiting, and something that I could control, I poured myself into what I hoped would be a
life-altering exercise regime for several months. I also decided to create
a written record of the mental shift that I was making as a man no longer
defined by his job, and a photographic record of the physical changes
that my body was undergoing as I entered my golden years, hoping both
would confirm that a robust man still firing on all cylinders was coming
out of this very trying period.

In order to capture the full impact of this transitional period in my
life visually, I decided to pose semi-nude in my briefs for a professional
photographer. I admit the thought of doing so made me a bit uneasy,
since there was no way that my middle-age frame would compare well
with the younger models, actors, and athletes that we see in underwear
advertising campaigns on bus stops all over the country. I also have neither the good looks nor the charisma that older celebrities possess that
would transform my imperfections—love-handles and padded midriff—
into their star-studded status. I just wanted a photo confirming that I
was making a big shift, since the camera doesn't lie. For weeks I struggled to determine who I could ask to undertake such a strange request.

My wife was adamantly opposed to my tomfoolery. The only guy that I knew would be a safe co-conspirator was a thousand miles away. Then I stumbled upon a photographer whose exhibition of nude portraits of regular guys was causing an uproar in SOHO. Fascinated that the artist's innocent portrayal of everyday men's bodies had triggered both strongly positive and negative reactions, I set up a meeting to learn more, and to determine whether a private portrait for my own purposes was possible.

My heart stopped when I discovered that the photographer who had convinced guys to pose in such a relaxed and natural state was a younger woman, Bek Andersen. Could I ever get comfortable in my skivvies in front of her? It seemed unlikely. Reassessing my request when we met, I heard her express many of the ideas that I had been writing about since my early twenties as our conversation flowed back and forth effortlessly, but from a distinctly feminine and feminist perspective. One of the aims of her work was to help disarm the male gaze, turning the tables on men, so that we experience the way in which we anatomize and objectify women, triggering all kinds of responses about which we are not always consciously aware beyond our ever-pressing desire to get laid. Later in our discussion, she began using language that seemed to directly quote my own writing, as well as the words of a female coach that I was working with. Sensing a direct command from the Universe, I threw caution to the wind and heard myself inquire whether she would do a private portrait of me fully nude. She agreed, but only if I would pose for her project as well, surrendering my entire masculine frame to the unblinking eye of her lens. When I asked her how the private commission would differ from her project, she replied that I would have to give up my manly, "I'm-in-charge" attack on life for an afternoon, following her every direction, no matter how uncomfortable I felt. As I later discovered, this was a critical step in my journey. For reasons that I will never be able to fully explain, I agreed.

When the day arrived that Bek Andersen came to photograph me, my heart was racing wildly. I was terrified by the thought that I was allowing my body to be seen by a stranger, as a prelude to it eventually being seen by the world. Would the photographs confirm what an utter fool I am? What if I got a hard-on in front of this beautiful young woman that I had only met just once, and had grown to respect and admire? Wasn't it inappropriate for me to flash my junk in front of her?

Bek tested my mettle from the beginning, wanting to confirm that I was prepared to keep my promise that she could photograph every inch of me in whatever state I happened to be, as she directed the shoot. For my first pose she insisted that I stand buck naked in the front door to our house. Because the residents of our bucolic, gentrified community regularly walk past our house for exercise, I prayed that she would finish our first set of pictures without my arrest (or her embarrassment) due to my body's rapidly rising response to all the adrenaline pumping through me.

Having introduced my full anatomy to her camera lens and the outside world in such a bold, out-of-the-box fashion, the remainder of our session turned out to be an exhilarating study of the many unique ways my body presents as male—goofy, loose, dancing through life. I was amazed at how quickly things shifted once I took my clothes off. I discovered that my innate modesty was a useless hindrance in this setting, so I discarded the red robe we first thought I might wear between shots and stalked around the house like a leopard uncaged. As Bek distilled the essence of my manhood in the gorgeous, pale, yellow light of a New England fall afternoon, I found myself relaxing, dropping my guard, releasing my subconscious worries, and enjoying the moment, finally comfortable in my body and able to respond to her direction, including her request at one point that I regain my edge and "rearrange" my flaccid junk to offer the camera a livelier presentation of my version of masculinity as a cis male.

To fill the time as Bek shot hundreds of images, I began to ask her for more details about the experience of photographing other guys, and her extraordinary ability to capture men in their natural state. I knew from our prior conversation that she had worked with a wide range of males, some of them her friends, some volunteers off craigslist that she knew not at all. Ever a paternalistic figure, I asked whether she was ever concerned about her personal safety in these settings. (For our shoot, she did not bring her male assistant. I guess she assessed that I was "safe.") Was there a common thread among us all? Were we—indeed, were *all* men—just basically peacocks showing off our feathers?

I wasn't prepared for her answer. Without hesitation she responded, "Shame. Every man I've worked with has expressed an enormous amount of shame about his body. It is so toxic that it usually takes me two days to recover."

After our shoot, I was astonished by the images that Bek had made of me. I barely recognized the man that she had recorded. Despite my status as a man exiting his prime, staring me in the face was a spectacularly strong, virile male presence, exuding a confidence that radiated energy off the page. Untethered by the personal and tribal narratives of what it meant to be male, and finally able to be open and receptive, I felt released, unleashed, finally free to project the real, crazy dude within.

My experience was a total revelation (in more ways than what appeared on camera). It was only when I allowed myself to be vulnerable that I was able to see the grace, beauty, and unbelievable strength and charisma of my own, unadorned body. Was it the equal of any poster boy that Hollywood or professional sports might serve up? No, but the image had captured a man in full possession of his powers. I also learned how much harm the male gaze—our brain's insistence that we anatomize the women we lust after, the men we size up in the locker room, and our own bodies—does to all, ourselves included. In addition, I was forced to acknowledge that the very image that I found so stunning might someday be viewed by others, not just women, but also men. Yikes. The hunter had become the prey, trapped by the male gaze. It was equally uncomfortable and thrilling.

Several years later, after I was stripped of all the markers that I considered key indicators of success as well, my life began to unfold in a strange and wonderful way. Just like any rite of passage that I might have encountered in another tribal community across the world, posing nude for a female photographer turned out to be the trigger point for a series of extraordinary events. This breakthrough ultimately unleashed a complete rebuild of my identity across several dimensions of my being—personal, professional, civic, and spiritual. Getting naked forced me to confront the enormous amount of shame and insecurity that I experience regarding my own body and started the process of jettisoning a ton of other emotional baggage that I carry.

But all that occurred much later.

SHAME

The shame that we men possess and the compensatory strategies that it triggers are a root cause of some of our bad behaviors. While not all our discomfort and insecurity can be attributed to negative perceptions about our physical presence, it is foundational, and often inter-mixed with other feelings of inadequacy or embarrassment we might hold in our bodies. So, getting naked is a good place to begin to tease out and reveal the various ways that we experience shame, in order to eradicate or mitigate their impact. Below is a short list describing the layers that have surfaced in my own reflections and in discussions with other men. They may offer a useful starting point for your own investigations.

As noted earlier, some of our shame is physical, and it begins early. Sometime during pre-school, Western society teaches boys that the great delight that we take in our unusual piece of anatomy is a forbidden pleasure that must be kept under wraps and only shared in socially approved ways. (Yeah, right. Good luck with that.) That physical shame sticks with us as we mature into adolescence and become adults. Under this shadow, sex takes on all kinds of dark characteristics, instead of being an expression of our joy with life and our delight in each other.

A second source of shame involves the feelings that surface as we use our bodies to engage in a wide range of sexual activities, some of which may not conform to our culture of masculinity's "rules." Having been told that enjoying your penis is a forbidden pleasure that must be undertaken in private, we are also fed a host of lies as to what great sex is, drawing lessons from older, equally clueless peers, and pornography. Exercising our libidos becomes an activity conducted with furtiveness, aggression, possessiveness, and exploitation, with an extreme focus on intercourse at the expense of other forms of sexual activity that might be part of our repertoire (if we're lucky) for the remainder of our lives. Paul Nelson, a NYC-based therapist who specializes in men's sexual issues and founded FrankTalk.org in 2008, the first non-commercial website for men with ED, made the following observation about men's view of sex in a conversation we had on the topic of male sexuality for this book: "For most men sex is a clearly defined, highly repetitive ritual that reproduces a porn scene. Men think perfect sex is making out followed by oral sex leading to intercourse that ends in simultaneous orgasms. The goal of having sex for most men is validation and approval from their partner, so much so that many of us ask afterwards 'How was it for you?' hoping for a higher score than our last performance. We need to expand our horizons." All too often, our sex lives are needlessly riddled with frustration or embarrassment, simply because our culture forces men to focus on "scoring" as the benchmark of having successful sex. As a result, we boast about our exploits in a practice that many times we know little about.

A third source of shame is religious, at least in the West. Although most faith traditions assert that the body is a temple that should be maintained so that it can be of service to others and give praise to the divine, far too often a second, double-edged message is imparted:

namely, that our bodies are the source of our carnal desires, and that enjoyment of our physical presence for our own pleasure is an evil to be avoided. Christianity is a prime example of these conflicting views. A central core idea of the Christian faith, as revealed by Jesus of Nazareth, is that heaven is both here and now and yet to come, and that the human body is the material embodiment of the divine which we should use to perform good works. Unlike some faith traditions, Christians are taught not to transcend or reject their physical bodies for spiritual concerns, but to utilize the body's material gifts so that they have a positive impact, concerning ourselves not only with others' spiritual states, but their physical well-being also. (It is important to note here that deploying the body in service to and for the pleasure/benefit of others is, of course, a key ingredient of healthy masculine identities.) Nonetheless, as Richard Rohr observed in a recent lecture at Chautauqua on "the evils of the flesh" as misconstrued by Christians, "religion after religion has localized the heart of evil in sex."[11] This misperception is especially acute regarding the male body as an instrument of the profane that is unfortunately sometimes accurate, as far too often men are flawed creatures who carry the burden of utilizing their bodies for their own personal enjoyment in ways that are harmful to others. For these physical and moral errors in our behavior, we bear another measure of shame. However, the demonization of the body by religion adds another level of negative perceptions about one of our most exquisite gifts: the human form.

A fourth source of shame is the prevailing social customs of our day. While going shirtless is acceptable for men in mixed company almost everywhere around the world, full male nudity is not. Celebrities, models, or athletes who possess physiques essential to their discipline may sometimes appear naked professionally or for commercial purposes (and on exotic beaches where local authorities permit), but even in these moments, full-frontal male nudity never goes without public comment. Meanwhile, a double standard prevails, as women appearing naked or topless seldom sparks as much public outcry, as in a male dominated world women's bodies have been displayed and adored for eons. This inherent double standard and negative bias against the male body, and the harmful promotion of ideal body types that we encounter on social media and in advertising, exacerbate men's body consciousness and feelings of inadequacy and shame.

It is interesting to note that this double standard was very much on display even in the tony, sophisticated art world of Vienna a couple decades ago. While museumgoers have enjoyed looking at female and male nudes for centuries, there was never a blockbuster exhibition solely devoted to male nudes until 2012, when the Leopold Museum organized "Nude Men—from 1800 to the present day." Initially, the museum's outdoor advertising campaign featured an image (from the exhibition) of three soccer players standing side by side each other on the field before a full stadium of fans in nothing but their socks and cleats. The general public's outcry was so strong that the museum was forced to add a red stripe covering their genitals. (Somehow the giant outdoor poster of a recumbent naked stud that was hung horizontally in front of the museum survived censorship, perhaps because of its breathtaking brazenness and its proximity to the actual exhibition.)[12]

A fifth source of shame is psychological, derivative of our discomfort with the realities of our bodies and its unpredictable, biochemical responses in men. As we will learn in Chapter 5, the narrow articulation of heterosexuality that so dominates Man Box culture is a total myth that is decidedly at odds with the emerging research about men. It turns out that many men have a mix of impulses, even if one identifies as straight. Though the methodology of his studies have been questioned at times, Kinsey identified early on the phenomenon of heterosexual men having sex with (or having sexual impulses about) other men. In an article published by Kinsey, Pomeroy, and Martin, it was reported that "a considerable portion of the population, perhaps the major portion of the male population has at least some homosexual experience between adolescence and old age. In addition, 60% of pre-adolescent boys engage in homosexual activities . . . In these terms (of physical contact to the point of orgasm) the data in the present study indicate that at least 37% of the male population has some homosexual experience . . . Among the males who remain unmarried until the age of 35, almost exactly 50 per cent have homosexual experience. . . ."[13]

Though underreporting of actual sexual behavior is endemic among men, more recent studies by Ritch Savin-Williams, Jane Ward, and Zhana Vrangalova (among others) confirm and elaborate on Kinsey's early findings. It appears that scholars are gathering ever-increasing evidence of a much higher incidence of men who identify as heterosexual that are (or have been) sexually active with men. This gap between the expectations that are set forth by society and what actually occurs in life is another source of shame and embarrassment for many men, especially since many men rarely discuss the realities of their sex lives. Gay and trans men go through an even harder oscillation of defining/denying their sexual identities and exercising their libidos in defiance of the traditional, hetero male constructs. The shame that gay men who do not identify as heterosexuals experience has been well documented in such books as *The Velvet Rage* by Alan Downs[14] and *Straight Jacket* by Matthew Todd.[15] We have yet to learn the full scope of the trauma and shame that trans men experience, though books like *Becoming a Visible Man* are beginning to paint that picture.[16] As our understanding deepens, we may discover that straight men have much to learn from their gay and trans brothers and sons about how to rebuild our identities so that they more accurately reflect who we are.

A sixth source of shame that has arisen more recently is societal. This is perhaps the most alarming of all. The wrath that has been recently leveled against men who have sexually assaulted women as revealed by the #MeToo Movement has engendered a negative view and distrust of men in general, no matter what our track record may be. Harvard evolutionary biologist Carole Hooven openly lamented this phenomenon in an interview with Andrew Sullivan,[17] breaking down in tears about the impact that the very negative views of men may be having on the emotional and psychological development of an entire generation of young men, including her own adolescent son. Post #MeToo, all of us, whether consciously or unconsciously, rightly carry a layer of collective shame regarding the actions of our brothers and forefathers. As this may serve as a deterrent for some men inclined to misbehave, this lower level of shame might be a good thing. But it is also having disastrous consequences on a generation of men who are having less sex than their forebearers at a time of life when their libidos are on overdrive.[18]

A NEW RESPONSE

How do most men respond to the deep sense of shame that we carry, and the insecurities that we possess about our manly frames? Simple. We develop macho narratives that deny our brokenness, presenting as strong, hyper-sexual creatures to hide our weaknesses. (This is true for all men regardless of their sexual orientation.) We throw ourselves into the gym where we muscle up and sweat out our anxieties in a culture that prizes athletic prowess as a proxy for competitiveness, assertiveness, aggression, and conquest, indicators of male success in life.

The warrior male has been a presence among us since the beginning of time, and athletic competitions for demonstrating our physical prowess have been a beloved feature of every society through the ages. There is nothing new in our obsession with strength and power on the playing field and at work, except, however, the ways in which men document and share their manifestation for public view in the 21st century. Some of our training and exertion of strength is healthy conditioning; some is a form of showing off that is normal and benign. Recently, however, the pressure to demonstrate prowess has become narcissistic and self-serving, taking on more harmful consequences.

It's hard to pinpoint when this trend started. Our current preoccupation with sports in the West as an indicator of future success in life seems to have taken root during the heyday of the British Empire in the mid-nineteenth century when the muscular Christianity movement arose in public schools (the equivalent of our private schools) to build the body in pursuit of health and character—physical vigor, courage, strength—making the body subject to the soul. This movement differentiated its aims from pure athletics, tying its training regimens to a higher purpose, in contrast to the self-serving body-building activities of men:

"A man's body is given him to be trained and brought into subjection, and then used for the protection of the weak, the advancement of all righteous causes, and the subduing of the earth which God has given to the children of men . . . For mere power, whether of body or intellect, he has . . . no reverence whatever."[19]

Disseminated to English-speaking countries around the world, the movement morphed into the cult of athleticism, with an emphasis on amateur sports and health(ism) that has had such an enormous impact on our secular culture that we assign virtue to celebrity athletes. We worship these warrior-heroes, many of whose main motivation is securing the financial and sexual rewards that professional sports afford. We want to be like these fierce competitors and share in their spoils.[20]

It wasn't always like this. Americans have always been fascinated by the athletes and movie stars who animate our imaginations, but until recently few men aspired to attain the bodies for which today's stars are so handsomely paid. In fact, the extreme body self-consciousness that most men experience today really wasn't as common among mid-20th-century guys. In the forties and fifties, *Life* magazine routinely published photographs of young men naked while off-duty during World War II and in the locker room after a game. None of these "regular joes," nor the magazine's readers, thought twice about the nudity. Then in the '60s and '70s, an entire generation of youth promoted some very casual attitudes towards nudity and sex. Feminists, asserting that what was fair game for men was also appropriate for women, created *Playgirl* in 1973 (after Helen Gurley Brown published the first male centerfold in *Cosmopolitan*[21]), and in short order full-frontal, male centerfolds were the norm.[22] These early photoshoots seem wholesome within the context of the rampant pornography today. Indeed, the scenarios depicted are innocent, as if the photographer captured each man in a private moment where he just happened to be nude, not unlike Bek Andersen's work. The question is how and when did we become so body conscious and the penis become so demonized?

In decades prior to the '80s, hitting the gym really wasn't a thing guys did, with the exception of body builders and gay men who were more body conscious than most straight males. Men tended to run, play tennis or golf, and generally let our bodies go to shit, once we got married. The fitness revolution of the '50s, '60s and '70s was mainly a girl thing (*The Jack LaLanne Show,* Weight Watchers).

Then, a seminal, watershed event occurred, triggered by an image of a nearly naked male that *American Photographer* has identified as one of "10 Pictures That Changed America."[23] In 1982 Bruce Weber photographed Tom Hintnaus, the "Boycott Olympics" pole-vaulter, in Calvin Klein underwear and plastered his perfect frame on a towering billboard over Times Square. Living in New York City at the time, I recall this cultural moment vividly. An enormous outdoor ad visible for blocks down Broadway (and Hintnaus's unretouched shaft) became the talk of the town. Clearly, the ladies were thrilled by the stunt, and like many other guys eager to get laid, I bought my Calvins, alongside the idea that I needed to try to be Olympic-level fit in order to be sexually attractive, an idea that survives to this day. (It also taught me another lesson, a harbinger of things to come: never doubt the power of a photograph to change your world.)

As it became increasingly apparent that fortunes could be made by simply achieving the "god-like" body that well-built men in Hollywood, male modeling, and sports have monetized, we have now arrived at a place where a key marker for manliness is rocking a six-pack, bulging biceps, and other well-endowed body parts. For most men the gap between this iconic ideal and our physical reality is significant and ever-present in our mind, thanks to social media and mainstream advertising. Feelings of inadequacy and shame abound, no matter what our station in life. Men at the top of Man Box hierarchy attest that they are on a hamster wheel of round after round of fitness regimens in order to prepare for their next contest. A former trainer for a Division I baseball team comments:

> "Even elite male college athletes have major insecurities about their bodies. Many struggle with eating disorders. There is a lot of injury due to 'over lifting,' even among the guys that knew they were being drafted. They all know that they are good-looking, physical specimens, but the 'not enough'/'bigger-faster-stronger' mentality is deeply ingrained in sports from an early age."

He went on to indicate that guys worry endlessly whether they are better looking than their teammates and are more likely to hook up with the most beautiful women in the school. The "gods" that we idolize have bought Madison Avenue's message encouraging us to oversexualize our bodies. Figuratively for all men, the competition on the field continues in bed.

Of course, some of today's body consciousness is probably a good thing, as compared to the way in which prior generations of men paid little attention to their fitness. A Harvard-educated MD who has been an internist for 50 years and whose practice is two-thirds male, many pretty healthy in their 20s, 30s and 40s, says that how you navigate through the early decades is absolutely critical to a long life. "You need to not stress eat, not drink too much, and make time to exercise, even as you are juggling so many balls in the air—the kids, your wife, the high-pressure demands of your job." His bottom line is simple, "Don't gain weight after you get married, so you don't get diabetes and coronary disease and die when you are 65." For those of us who are older he notes that "you have to learn how to go hungry and exercise more to maintain a lean body as you age." In his view, some basic body awareness is essential to maintaining health, but he agrees that today's craze is only exacerbating the epidemic of insecurity and anxiety that he is seeing in all men, especially among millennial males. "It's an alarming trend, and it takes a huge toll. There's a general feeling of inadequacy derived from career and marriage in your middle years that spills over into how men's bodies perform, and their libidos. I remember feeling overwhelmed by the pressure of it all at age 38, but our generation experienced a general optimism about our futures. It's not the same today. As a result, I'm constantly having to remind younger guys that you don't have to have intercourse in order to connect and feel sensual, and you need to schedule a date night with your partner."

What's the alternative to this mad obsession with maintaining ideal physiques? How can we develop a healthier perspective of the male form? While the tenets of the body positivity movement must play a role in shifting our self-perceptions, I think it's unlikely to provide the whole solution to our negative views of the male body. Guys tend to be creatures who like to imagine that they have some personal agency in creating their own reality. What is required are better definitions of health, wellness, and fitness for men. Our goals need to be less about body shape and strength, and more about a life-long experience of all forms of health (physical, mental, spiritual), flow, and output. Indeed, if our goal is to get laid, research among women seems to indicate that we need to tone it down in the gym, as they actually prefer bodies that are less bulked up than we do.[24]

As for optimizing health and wellness, there is a ton of new scholarship that suggests we should expand our focus on strength training and cardio fitness to include more holistic practices. Shane O'Mara lays out a compelling description of the basic neuroscientific understandings of the able body-mind connection and their impact on wellness in his book *In Praise of Walking*. (Spoiler alert: He argues that if we do nothing else but walk 10,000+ steps daily, we can expect to experience better health outcomes across the board for the remainder of our days.)[25] A second resource that deepens our understanding of the mind-body connection and health is Van der Kolk's *The Body Keeps the Score* which examines the primary stress responses that create functional and chemical changes in the brain. His clinical research, and studies by other academics, offer a strong argument that yoga can restore homeostasis of the automatic nervous system when we experience trauma.[26] The net take-away from these studies is that what matters most is not a bulging physique. What's important to success in life is highly balanced and integrated neurocognitive and biochemical systems. Health. Flow. Output.

There are many forms of ancient body-mind practices besides yoga whose restorative capacities can help to establish a positive body-mind-soul relationship, many of which are being documented by researchers; these include Tai Chi, Qigong, Reiki, and Systema. As I discovered in the yoga studio just prior to Bek Andersen capturing it all on film, in order to experience the full benefits of these practices, it is essential for men to enter into these spaces without the mental baggage of pursuing fitness and stress reduction as their goal. Leave your manly output and optimal performance mantras at the door, and let the discipline do its work unimpeded by your goals and expectations. (This is another reason to strip down and leave it all behind, as guys do in hot yoga. Are you sensing a trend here?)

GET NAKED

My advice as to how to combat the negative perceptions that we carry about our bodies as men is therefore relatively straightforward and simple. Get naked. Try to reject or reduce the shame that you carry. Stop hiding your version of being male. Instead of using your manly frame to perform a narrow cultural construct of masculinity that may not fit who you are, stand in your own naked truth. Let go of all the lies that you have told yourself about the rules that you must follow and ways in which you must behave in order to be a "real man." Stop hiding your version of being male. Your spouse or partner(s) will thank you. Your children and family will benefit. Your colleagues will appreciate the transparency, openness, and ability to connect that will begin to govern your life.

What you will begin to discover as you strip down and open up is that our inability to express intimacy, our unwillingness to show our emotions and connect in a transparent way is really our refusal to get in touch with our true self and share that as a gift with others. My good friend Harry Schmitz, who has been a clinical psychologist and consultant to Fortune 500 companies on mental health issues for over 50 years, observes:

> "There is no difference between the CEO's and the linemen of the world. The issues are always the same. Our pain as men is profound. Bullshit reigns supreme because it's too scary to express our true self. Our demons won't let the true self out."

We throw up blocks to cover the full shape and dimension of our beings because we are afraid to be who we are. Remove these blocks. Rediscover your innate capacity to be a connected, authentic male. If you take this step, you will begin to discover not only who you truly are, but your purpose and meaning in life.

So, get naked—body, mind, and soul—however much that you can in this moment in time. Force yourself to confront the shame and insecurity about your body that you carry. Reveal the lies that you have told yourself about what it means to be a man. Acknowledge it, and let it go.

The old narratives that you have embedded into your soul to conform to the rules of the Man Box will begin to vanish. A new you will emerge, one that is based on the strong, virile presence that you actually possess.

GETTING STARTED

So how do you begin to get naked?

Set aside an afternoon and ask your spouse or partner to photograph you nude. If that's uncomfortable, hire a professional. Set a firm date so there is no backing out. As a warm-up for your portrait, spend some time attending to your daily chores around the house with no clothes on. Find an outdoor space in the privacy of your own backyard or a remote wilderness setting where it is legally okay for you to take your clothes off and accept the possibility that you might be seen. If you are lucky, you will be, by an acquaintance who won't think that you're a nut job.

Stop changing under a towel at the gym. Indeed, if possible, force yourself to take communal showers with other men so that you can get comfortable with allowing your unique physical presence to be on display. Swim and sunbathe wherever legally possible nude.

I understand that for many taking this step may seem like a nonstarter. It requires a leap of faith to jump from a great height into the waters below. For a host of reasons, personal, situational, even practical, it may be too much (though I would challenge you to make sure you aren't making excuses). Nonetheless, accept this invitation to nakedness and disclosure in whatever lower risk way is comfortable for you with the expectation that any small success will get you started and encourage you on to greater heights. This is a process that will continue to unfold and reward you with many benefits over time if you stick with it, and you will need to. What we are striving for is a new mindset that allows for a level of openness and vulnerability that men are taught never to show.

You will most likely experience the greatest transformation if you choose a like-minded buddy to go on this journey with you. Someone you can trust with whom it's safe to share your most intimate and private thoughts. Start there. I would also say that it is helpful if you both have a belief in a higher power (not necessarily God) to ground you. Where do you draw your strength? Your spouse/partner, family, an ideal? What is driving you? Share that as well and pray that it will be revealed in your physical body as the superpower that you totally own. You'll be amazed by what your body will tell you when you get in better touch with it.

SEEK THE SACRED FEMININE WITHIN

Tom and I share a mutual friend, Fred, whose TV room is our communal man cave. Fred's wife, Jo-Ann, loves to entertain, so our Sunday afternoons and evenings are often spent at their house. I have never been a big sports junkie, but I enjoy the wisecracks that flow between us as we watch football, hockey, baseball, or golf.

You would think after fifteen years of spending so much time together I would know a lot about Tom, but I really didn't until recently. I knew that he had played hockey professionally for a few years, was on the town council for a dozen, became a state representative, then returned to his life as a building contractor and self-storage unit operator.

Tom is probably the most macho man I know. Strong, fit, handsome, rugged, he lifts weights. Still plays hockey. Nice guy. A man of few words, at least socially. Tom, Fred, and I each have a son the same age who are also best friends, so it's been interesting to watch our own behavior patterns play out in the next generation.

A couple years ago we all decided to attend Fred's son Collin's senior recital at Oklahoma City University, the legendary launching pad for many musical theater careers, including Kristin Chenoweth and Kelli O'Hara. Tom and I decided to sit towards the rear of the auditorium, so that Fred and his family could be together during this milestone moment.

It was not all that different from most Sunday afternoons. We were once again in the dark, glued to the performance in front of us.

Towards the end of the recital, Collin sat at the edge of the stage and sang "It's Hard to Speak My Heart/All the Wasted Time" directly to his parents in such a profoundly moving way that, suddenly, Tom started crying. I wept, too. Afterwards, Tom spoke eloquently about how deeply moved he was by what we witnessed. I echoed his thoughts. It was impossible not to respond to the love that Collin was expressing to his parents, but it was the last thing that I had expected to share with my most macho of male friends. Tom had never so openly conveyed his thoughts or feelings in front of me before.

Somehow, because Collin had shown us how to unleash the depths within, and Tom and I had done the same, we now have a lot to talk about when we get together on the weekends. The fierce love that poured out of Tom's and my souls for our best friend's son, and our ability to show it, articulate it, were to me the perfect embodiment of the sacred feminine, a secret capacity that we now share.

One of the key tenets of the Man Box is that "real men" do not behave like women. As a result, men must root out even the smallest gesture, the tiniest nervous tick that does not fit the traditional masculine profile, or risk being teased by our male peers as "Girly" or (God forbid) "Gay." "Other," "Not Manly," "Not Masculine," "Not Male."

This is, of course, absurd. We live in a world where we long ago realized that men and women possess a mix of personality traits to varying degrees which our gender-oriented culture construes as masculine or feminine. (Note: I will not wade into the nature-versus-nurture culture wars as to how gender is constructed here, as at the end of the day I believe it is more important to focus on the way in which we experience gender as it exists now and consider whether and how we need to expand our current concepts of what it means to be a man or a woman.)

Over the past few decades our American way of life and our values have permeated societies around the world—democracies and totalitarian alike—including our dominance-based culture of masculinity. It appears that this may be having disastrous consequences for both men and women far beyond our own shores, which if it continues, will cause extraordinary harm. Why? The evidence is mounting that Man Box culture may be driving a tsunami of health issues—physical, emotional, mental, spiritual, as well as political. The statistics in America are alarming.

For over thirty years NYU Professor of Developmental Psychology Niobe Way, founder of the Project for the Advancement of our Common Humanity, has been studying the social and emotional development of adolescent males and females, and the cultural ideologies that influence developmental trajectories. She lays out the growing evidence that a crisis in connection is now wreaking havoc on our lives:

Growing levels of distrust
- Only 19 percent of millennials in the US think that "most people can be trusted," as compared to 31 percent of Gen X and 40 percent of baby boomers.

Decline in empathy
- 40 percent decline in empathy since 1979

Increase in depression and loneliness
- 3 in 5 Americans (61%) report feeling lonely—Cigna (2019)

■ Depression is a leading cause of ill health and inability to work worldwide—WHO (2020)

Increase in anxiety

■ All Americans under 65 recommended for anxiety screening by National Health Council (2022)

The violent consequences of the crisis

■ Suicide rates among youth ages 10 to 24 increased by 57% between 2007 and 2018

■ Hate crimes in the U.S. rose to the highest level in more than a decade. FBI (2020)

■ Those under 25 are now called the mass shooter generation[27]

In addition to the above, there has been a 23% increase in alcohol abuse, a 16% increase in substance abuse[28], and a 30% increase in drug overdoses during COVID[29], amplifying the underlying trends that were already in place before the pandemic arose, with males accounting for 62 to 63 percent of the gender distribution of patients.[30]

In the 1990s and 2000s, Carol Gilligan, Judy Chu, and Niobe Way challenged many assumptions about the nature of boys.[31,32,33] In particular, their research documented that young boys start off life—in pre-school and early adolescence—defying conventional perceptions that men are emotionally inert and non-communicative. The researchers assert that it isn't until later adolescence that young men begin to emotionally detach in order to conform to our society's thin culture concept of what masculinity is.[34] They perceive this process as ultimately leading to the current crisis in connection and what is now a global pandemic accelerated by social media and COVID. In their more recent work, this "triumfeminate" has made a compelling argument that the root problem here is that we are conditioned as young boys *and* girls to reflexively devalue and dismiss the characteristics that our culture considers feminine. Most importantly, we are taught to value being strong, silent, and independent, in direct opposition to the very quality that defines us as the human species—our ability to form deep, powerful social connections—because this quality is considered "feminine" in our male-dominated world.

To add further irony to our present situation in these gender fluid times, millennials and Gen Z are now choosing their personal pronouns. In doing so, according to Way, they are reifying the status quo using the same preconceptions of what it means to be masculine and feminine as have been in place since the 1950s as gender identity markers. According to Niobe Way[35] and Peggy Orenstein,[36] the younger generations use adjectives to describe masculinity and womanhood in much the same way that the Silent Generation did. In her presentation at Trinity Spiritual Center on November 20, 2022, Niobe Way remarked,

> "When I asked my students last week what stereotypes they associate with masculinity, they said 'tough,' 'academically competent,' 'strong,' 'dominant,' 'aggressive.' Many positives. When I asked about femininity, they used words such as 'delicate,' 'pretty,' 'emotional,' 'weak.' Not nearly as positive. The stereotypes that were coming out their mouths weren't even from my generation. They were from my mom's generation. We're going backwards."[37]

So much for changing stereotypes among younger generations . . .

Under these circumstances the question is: If our dominant culture of masculinity is literally killing us, should we not try to figure out how to restore the pieces of our humanity that we have been taught reflexively to reject? Should we not come together as men and women to reintroduce the sacred feminine wisdom that has been driven from our lives?

I can already hear the saber rattling of men who want nothing to do with this discussion, having heard for too long that they need to adopt a "softer" approach to some of the problems that they have confronted. These suggestions, however well intended, are often dismissed, because they challenge a male "identity" that has been carefully, painfully constructed and that most men will protect at all cost, for fear of being seen as unmanly. As a guy who has struggled with such advice for over forty years, I can understand your hesitation. I can also hear the protests of men who will be damned if they will be turned into a "soy boy" or "metrosexual."

Let me assure you upfront that I am not suggesting that the positive characteristics we share as men should be diminished in any way. Believe me, I know that it is essential to be strong, assertive, competitive in many situations in life. I know what it's like to go toe-to-toe with masters of the universe.[38] Chuck Schwab once muttered under his breath at a tense Board meeting which he chaired and I staffed, "Jesus, Mark, you're one of the toughest execs I've met." I'm just saying that we don't have to roll that way all the time. There are settings where we do have other options, and we should use all the tools we have in our toolbox. Not every problem is a nail that requires a hammer.

So, the goal of this chapter then is not to change you, transform you, or turn you into what you are not. My purpose in exploring the sacred feminine is to help you recover the pieces of your early masculine personality that may have been groomed or conditioned out of you as a child, pieces that are just as inherently male as they are feminine, pieces that our society labels (and devalues) as womanly. Our goal is to help you reclaim your entire identity as a man, so that you might more fully participate in life as you were originally intended to do.

Our guide on this journey will be Mirabai Starr, a friend and award-winning author of creative non-fiction and contemporary translations of sacred literature. Mirabai taught Philosophy and World Religions at the University of New Mexico-Taos for 20 years and now teaches and speaks internationally on contemplative practice and inter-spiritual dialog. Her latest book, *WILD MERCY: Living the Fierce & Tender Wisdom of the Women Mystics,* was named one of the "Best Books of 2019."[39] She lives with her extended family in the mountains of northern New Mexico.

WILD MERCY is an excellent field guide through this terrain that is foreign to most men. It is a summary of what we can learn from female wisdom figures through the ages—the perspectives, energies, and insights that male-dominated societies around the world have rejected as alien to our dominant global culture of masculinity.

We will focus on six areas in which the sacred feminine offers important insights that run counter to key understandings that we integrate into our identities as we grow up within the Man Box culture: the joy inherent in ordinary life, the transformative power of creativity and clarity of expression, our roles as nurturers and caretakers, new perspectives on the body, the gifts of intuition, and the power of community and connection. (We will explore a seventh dimension—emotional and relational intelligence—in the next chapter.)

Let's begin.

JOY IN ORDINARY LIFE

It's hard to ascertain when exactly men's love affair with superheroes begins. We seem to be born with an innate attraction to larger-than-life individuals—first our parents, siblings, and grandparents, perhaps a pet. We then become fascinated by the fairy tale/television/feature film/book characters that animate our imaginations and our fantasy lives.

Our adoration of the out-of-the-ordinary never ends, as we transfer our attention from the gods and goddesses of our childhood to a new set of heroes in sports, music, media, politics, and business. We begin to compete first on the playing fields, then at work and in the community, many of us hoping that we will rise to participate in the pantheon of the men and women whom generations down the road may remember.

There is certainly nothing wrong with pursuing our need for recognition and to be seen for who we truly are. There is also nothing wrong for some men to seek to achieve the extraordinary, the exemplary, or the unusual, which now seems even more within reach in this modern era due to social media's ability to make one an instant celebrity. But I suspect that Teresa of Avila, if she were alive today, would have none of this. As Mirabai Starr reminds us, the Spanish mystic famously asserted that "God lives among the pots and pans."

Teresa of Avila's insistence that divinity can be found in the mundane is more than a celebration of the intimate details of hearth and home that so many of today's lifestyle mavens post about on Instagram, and tastemakers in every generation make serious claim to. It is more than a spiritual practice for creating environments where connection and creativity thrive in balance within the grace, ease, peace and serenity of the space offered. These are worthy undertakings whose values I certainly don't mean to diminish. But Teresa of Avila was talking about something more.

Mirabai Starr's account of Teresa of Avila's thinking indicates she was convinced that God was present in the dirt and grime of housekeeping, the annoyance of attending to our daily chores, the mess that's involved in cooking, cleaning, organizing, and caring for the physical needs of others. Starr's portrait of this beloved sixteenth century Carmelite nun, mystic and religious reformer is that of a prototypical rebel. A feisty figure—dramatic, a bit of a wild child as a teenager who did something scandalous, enough to land her in a convent. Not interested in getting married and having children, she decided to remain. A very practical woman, she founded seventeen monasteries and convents. She loved to cook. Yet on the inside her life of prayer was filled with great longing for connection, a fire of desire that would fill her with visions and locutions that she subjected to great scrutiny. Her autobiography, her record of these investigations and her life of prayer, and her literary work *The Interior Castle*[40] describe a journey of faith. They remain widely read classics that inspire millions to this day.

St. Teresa's (and Starr's) attention to this feminine wisdom of knowing that enlightenment—rebuilding one's identity from the inside out so one's life can be transformed—is found in the "pots and pans of life" is notable in our extraordinarily overscheduled and busy lives. This spiritual practice in no way impeded her astonishing record of reforming a monastic organization that has survived on to this day, evading the Inquisition that threatened her very existence, and authoring several treatises that still shape our thinking about the meaning of life. Her life is proof positive that attending to the sacred mundane can have an energizing, liberating impact.

So what does this mean for men seeking to incorporate the positive impact of this insight into their lives? Well, for one, it's more than men doing "their half" of the household chores, as is now increasingly the custom in more homes thanks to COVID. It's finding the pleasure and joy in completing these tasks, and experiencing their ability to anchor, root, and ground those of us who are otherwise way up in our heads, much like Teresa was, and most men are.

The list of chores that can open our appreciation of the ordinary is endless. It's really a matter of attitude and attention. Two of my favorite examples of guys who embody this joy and appreciation for the mundane are my own dad and stepdad. Both had extraordinary careers throughout which they were skilled practitioners of "Householder Yoga"[41] long before their own peers and later generations ever had a clue, indeed before today's young dads were even born. It's important to understand that this is more than a lifestyle choice for both my dad and stepdad. It is a values statement, a discipline, a practice of staying humble and connected to the ordinary, which they observe to this day.

CREATIVITY AND CLARITY OF EXPRESSION

Another rule of the Man Box is that "real men" are not overly expressive. They choose their words carefully, and communicate most effectively with as few as possible, showing little emotion, and sharing their innermost thoughts with no one. We make this behavioral choice because we believe that we live in a dog-eat-dog world where few can be trusted. It is therefore best not to make oneself vulnerable by sharing too much. In a culture that prizes individuality, self-reliance, and independence this makes logical sense.

Our strong preference as men to observe this socially approved restriction appears to gather force in adolescence. As noted earlier, both Judy Chu and Niobe Way have provided significant documentation of the fact that younger boys demonstrate extraordinary emotional sensitivity and a keen ability to express themselves with precision and nuance prior to the pressures that puberty and the need to perform as "mature" men set in. Unfortunately, as boys grow older, if they are too expressive or intimate in their behavior, they are often tormented by their classmates—male and female—as being gay, an anathema in a culture that is still deeply homophobic, despite the gains made by the LGBTQIA2S+ community recently. (One need look no further than the constant refrain of "No homo" among men ages 12–30 for evidence.)

While social media has liberated millennial and Gen Z men from the staid, stolid, non-expressive norms of prior generations, the carefully crafted identities or brands that young men are creating online still predominantly conform to the Man Box code, with its emphasis on promoting one's sexual attractiveness. The lengths to which men will go to attract partners on social media remind me of the Satin Bowerbird, a vain, violet-blue-eyed avian in Eastern Australia with shimmering blue feathers. This ingenious bird decorates its lair with blue, yellow, and bright shiny objects—ribbons, straw, flowers, berries, shells, even ballpoint pens—in order to lure females into his bower. I suppose that there is a universal understanding that inventiveness and distinctive calls are acceptable, even desirable for men to use in expressing their lust, one of the two emotions that it is "okay" for men to express. (The other is anger.)

Because men are taught that a gift for creative flair and clarity of expression makes them vulnerable to accusations of being girly or gay, many straight men are wary of sharing whatever imaginative endeavors they might secretly pursue in their personal life. If we do reveal our gifts for activities that society perceives as unmanly, we do so without demonstrating too much effort or flair—cooking (grilling, esoteric ethnic, farm to table, not spending days to perfect a haute cuisine dish), gardening (tending to vegetables and the lawn, not flowers), writing (non-fiction, not fiction, unless you're a Southern gentleman), music (rock, rap, or jazz, not classical). Heaven help the man who puts too much passion into these pursuits.

Celebrities in the arts get a pass, but their sexuality is always under suspicion. For some reason, we are willing to believe that their creative bent predisposes them to bat for the other team occasionally, despite their impressive public sexual records otherwise. Ordinary men, real men, who are active in the arts are not given the benefit of the doubt.

Sacred feminine wisdom offers a decidedly different point of view on the arts. As Mirabai Starr details in her book *WILD MERCY,* a host of goddesses across all wisdom traditions have shown us the benefits of creativity and self-expression as a way of problem-solving and making meaning of our experience. For example, in the Hindu understanding of the world, Shakti is the primal energy of the Universe. She embodies the force that animates creation. All forms are manifestations of Shakti. In addition to representing the movement of the One into many, she also dissolves the boundaries of the separate self, restoring essential unity with the Supreme Being.[42] In short, she is a big deal, standing equal with Shiva, the god of destruction and transformation. Shakti has her own power of destruction, an ability to disintegrate whatever stands in our way of becoming fully alive, real.

Another goddess of creativity, again of Hindu origin, is Saraswati. Mirabai paints a vivid picture of this Hindu deity, detailing the many gifts that she embodies and bestows upon mankind. Saraswati is a goddess who uses words to transform consciousness, meditation to deepen concentration, creativity to refine wisdom, and music to awaken the heart.[43]

She reminds us that creativity and artistic expression help us clarify our thinking, give voice to our deepest understandings, and surface answers to our questions. This feminine wisdom is therefore an absolute essential component of the male psyche whose presence we must revive.

I am, of course, biased here, having used writing and singing and dancing my entire life in order to animate my being. Speaking from experience, I am constantly amazed that when I begin to feel "dead" in my professional work, it sometimes only takes a couple hours of self-expression to restore my energy level. Indeed, sometimes just a walk can put me in the zone where the creative process kicks in, solving whatever program I am working on at work. (Neuroscience supports my impression of how this happens.)[44] It has also been a joy to watch the few men that I see attending spiritual workshops discover the benefits of turning off the brain and relaxing into a mindset that is less time-sensitive and outcomes-oriented (more on that in Chapter 7).

In a culture that assigns greater value to data, metrics, algorithms, and the technology that drives predictive outcomes, I strongly believe that we must fight hard to protect the other pieces of our consciousness that are not analytical, and learn to listen with curiosity, weaving the magic of our existence into the music of life like a good jazz musician.

An example of a man who straddles both quantitative and qualitative domains is Robert Green, a professor of medicine at Harvard Medical School. A geneticist and physician-scientist conducting large, multi-disciplinary and multi-institutional projects that have generated vast amounts of data that are being used to bring genomics into mainstream medicine, he's written over 400 scientific papers, advises national genomics programs around the world and has co-founded two genomics companies. Just thinking about his work makes my head hurt. Yet somehow this man sang semi-professionally for most of his career, including with a group that won five Grammys for choral recordings under Robert Shaw. Robert sings today with an all-men's a cappella group, the Sly Voxes in Boston, and credits this creative activity with providing balance in his life.

I reached out to get his perspective on how his creative life outside medicine impacts his work. He responded with this comment. "Singing well with others requires concentration and focus on rhythm, pitch and blend of a completely different sort than my scientific work," says Robert. "But the reward of channeling harmonies, whether motet or Motown, provides joy that I cannot find elsewhere and that I always intend to make time for. Singing with largely the same guys in an all-men's group over the past decade, we have created music together that expresses the spiritual longing in a Randall Thomas composition or the giddy free-dom of a Beach Boys medley. This kind of bonding is quite different than watching sports or playing poker. For one thing, it is deeply participatory, and you can't bluff your way into a minor seventh chord. But more importantly, there is vulnerability in the inevitable mistakes that we hear each other make, pride in the performance that is ultimately created together and the profoundly satisfying personal loss and redis-covery of self that occurs when we give ourselves over to the exquisite flow of music through our minds and hearts." Important lessons that we can weave into our lives.

Men can greatly benefit from removing the stigma that they attach to creativity and clarity of expression. We have much to learn from femi-nine wisdom here. I would encourage every guy reading this book to take up some form of creative activity or personal expression. It will not only advance your professional work but your personal well-being. And share your practice with other men. If nothing else, walk for pleasure, not exercise, with no expectations of an outcome. You'll be amazed.

NURTURERS AND CARETAKERS

As we noted in the opening chapter, during the final days of the 2020 election, several pundits observed that the nation was making a choice as to which form of masculinity we prefer in our leaders. In an op-ed for the *New York Times*, the journalist and author Susan Faludi observed that the choice presented by the media—whether we prefer "old-fashioned machismo" or a "a more complex 21st-century version of masculinity," defined by "compassion and empathy and care and a personal narrative of loss" in the Oval Office—was a misrepresentation of the decision before the nation. She carefully pointed out that prior to WWII . . .

"The masculine archetype of the 1930s and '40s was the anonymous common man who proved his chops through communal building, not gunslinging. . . . New Deal America championed a manliness of usefulness, demonstrated through collective service and uncelebrated competence. . . . The '30s ideal of heroic civil servant carried into World War II . . ."

She goes on to observe that this ideal was very evident in the grunt ethic of the men fighting the war.

"This service-oriented prototype of manhood—tending to the needs of others, providing protective support, spurning the spotlight—was essentially a maternal masculinity, all the purported qualities of motherhood, recoded for the Y chromosome."[45]

Despite these precedents set by the Greatest Generation, after the 2020 election, Gen X-er Josh Hawley and millennial JD Vance are waving the "traditional" masculinity banner as a rallying cry for Republicans in our culture wars, arguing that the progressive left is attempting to "deconstruct" the American man.[46]

I think framing the debate as an "either/or" choice is a mistake, both counterproductive and a misrepresentation of a fundamental truth. As men, we are both warriors and caretakers, and always have been. That said, I do also believe that our culture of masculinity does value and reward strength and aggression over the qualities that are required to be nurturers. The question is that if being an empathetic caretaker was perceived as a valid expression of masculinity until World War II, what has changed in the interim so that younger generations are leaning into the power-aggression side of masculinity? I have a hunch that the chain of logic goes something like this.

A sacred cow of our culture of masculinity is that men are expected to be good providers, even if we are stay-at-home dads, while the burden of attending to the day-to-day physical and emotional needs of the family continues to fall more heavily on the shoulders of women in many households, even during COVID. This division of labor is deeply ingrained. Old habits die hard.

Furthermore, with the strong economic expansion that occurred after WWII, being able to provide for the basic needs of one's family morphed into a completely different value: the vast accumulation of wealth. The result is that today your bona fides as a "real man" is now very much determined by how great your financial success is. Although this glorification of money has been a fixation in the American dream for a very long time, now it is trumpeted as a virtue. The French intellectual Raphael Liogier has traced this evolution in our thinking in his book, *Khaos: la promesse trahie de la modernité.* [47] He believes that Americans are so in love with large numbers—the vast accumulation of wealth, data, fans, votes, likes—that we have deified them to the point that they are now a substitute to the transcendent, the reality of our experience beyond human knowledge.

Some of today's dads, who realize that this way of thinking is a trap and harmful to their families' well-being, have tried to find a better balance. But in a culture that considers men less manly if they choose not to compete for prize money (and encourages women to do the same), it's a difficult challenge.

The sacred feminine across many ancient wisdom traditions takes a different view of wealth and how it is best acquired and deployed to make sure that all creatures thrive. Indigenous cultures around the world, and some ethnic communities within our own Western culture (particularly people of Celtic descent) attach great value to an "Earth Mother" force in nature that assures the well-being of all creation. Feminine wisdom, like much of the recent thinking of physics, biology, neuroscience, and environmental studies, sees the material world as an interconnected, interpenetrated system in which all creatures, animate and inanimate, are interrelated.

A litany of goddesses come to mind who personify this wisdom. A couple that have been front and center in the environmental movement include Gaia, who in Greek mythology "nourishes all life. Everything arises from her and returns to her. Gaia is more a power than an entity. She is life itself."[48]

A second image that has gained much public awareness is the Native American concept of Earth as Mother (in the Lakota tradition, Unci Maka). This widespread belief goes much further, deeper than the strong connection to the natural world that conservationists promote. All life flows through her. As she is our Mother, we cannot own her, and it is our responsibility to take care of her.

As a scholar of world religions, Starr observes that Our Lady of the Guadalupe is actually a "fusion between Earth Mother and Mary, Mother of Christ." She is "the Mother of All People" whose task is to "love, shelter, comfort, and protect us."[49]

She is an important figure among the Spanish-speaking Andean peoples who "see the universe as full of lavish abundance," "reciprocity," and "balance." Their impulse is to share, not hoard, as we are taught in Western European (and more "masculine") cultures.[50]

From this perspective, it is our responsibility to be caretakers and conscientious in the way that we utilize and replenish the resources that we have been given. This belief arises out of a fundamental understanding that the Universe is a source of abundance, instead of the scarcity mindset that haunts the hyper-competitive thinking inherent in our dominance-based culture of masculinity. I believe that both mindsets are valid, but unfortunately, our culture of masculinity completely dismisses the opposing view instead of finding a blend or balance between these two mindsets. Our exploitative, fear-driven attachment to a scarcity index may be the undoing of the human species.

As men, we need to restore the nurturer/caretaker in us to its proper place as standing equal to the warrior/provider model that we are taught. This is not a difficult task, but it requires focus on the many pieces of the male psyche that Americans have chosen to ignore over the past 150 years, including male archetypes that have been deeply embedded in us for centuries, as Matthew Fox so brilliantly depicts in his wonderful book *The Hidden Spirituality of Men: Ten Metaphors to Awaken the Sacred Masculine*.[51] These archetypes include Green Man, the Blue Man, the Earth Father, Grandfather Sky. An appendix in Fox's book offers ten pages of exercises showing men how to develop these capacities within ourselves. (Note: Our ability to take on these roles is greatly enhanced when we restore our connection to our inner emotional lives, as we'll discuss in the next chapter.)

I am happy to say that there are many guys in my network who embody both strong/aggressive/warrior and softer/nurturing/caretaker mindsets. A great buddy of mine, Peter Hasapis, is an example par excellence of what it looks like. He is a general practitioner whose patient population includes many high-powered men. All see in Peter a man who is strong (mentally and physically), robust, fit, Hollywood handsome, and extraordinarily effective in his position. His gifts for taking care of others go well beyond his practice. He is a wonderful father and husband, devoted brother and son, a great friend to many. An active member of the community, and a singer-guitarist in a rock band, he's the kind of guy you would want with you in a foxhole, when you are going through a rough patch in life. You know that he will do everything in his power to hold you and your loved ones together. He has been there for me and my sons, time and time again.

TAKING BETTER CARE OF OUR BODIES

I wade into this topic that has been the focus of much public commentary with some hesitation. Men's health and fitness publications have given guys so much advice about how to take care of their bodies that it would seem that there is little else to say. There has been so much deserved focus on how men misuse their bodies as "assault weapons" that to enter into a discussion about how to take better care of our bodies is tantamount to advocating for building better heat-sensing missiles for state-of-the-art drones.

My purpose in shining a spotlight on the vast amount of feminine wisdom regarding the human body in this section is to isolate how the feminine lens differs and might be useful to men.

In her book *WILD MERCY* Mirabai Starr calls our attention to several insights about the human body and the role that it plays in contributing to our well-being when properly utilized and nurtured. She suggests that we consider what we can learn from Mary Magdalene, a central figure in Jesus of Nazareth's inner circle, who some people think may have been his paramour, and quite possibly the de facto leader of the Apostles.[52] In Starr's view, Mary Magdalene offers a vision of what it means to celebrate the holy sweetness of the human body, not just for enjoying sex, but for savoring a vast array of sensual pleasures in life that are so critical to our physical and mental health, including food, exercise, and rest. Starr asserts that Mary Magdalene's physical proximity to Jesus demonstrates a way of being present with the divine—the way of the heart, devotion—using our bodies,[53] for it is through the body that we deeply connect with the divine incarnate in another human being. (Not all physical encounters need to lead to sex. I know, I know that's a new one for many men. We'll talk about this further in the next chapter.)

This is a very different view of the body than most men that I know possess. In a culture that values output and instant results, we tend to treat our bodies as a high-performance sport utility vehicle that offers us quick, adrenaline-charged, endorphin-releasing thrills at the gym, outdoors in the wilderness and on the streets, in the office, and yes, of course, in bed. On-the-go, in search of adventure and profit, we fail to make the time to savor the regenerative power of food, exercise and rest, their ability to reset the course of our direction, and open us up to a new, more highly charged way of being male, so that we might experience even greater heights, inwardly and outwardly. Instead, we engage in quick-fix diets, cleanses, ten-minute app-delivered meditations, massages to remove the toxins and the stressors in our system. In doing so we miss the opportunity to increase the pleasure that our physical bodies can provide. We forget to take joy in the material present as a wellness practice that is more likely to prolong our lives than any cardio workout.

We cut ourselves short by not expanding our relationship to our bodies. Think of the difference as the repetitive pleasures of fast food versus the diversity of experiences in fine dining. As Paul Newman once famously said when asked whether he had ever stepped out on the focus of his own libido, Joanne Woodward, "Why would I want a hamburger when I can have steak?"[54] We are missing the range of intense flavors that we could savor when we fail to appreciate the innate joy that can be had in treating our bodies as though they are a precious, holy commodity. A sacrament that can be enjoyed by others.

I realize that for many men reinventing our relationship to the body along these lines sounds so girly that you can't imagine taking a step in this direction. I do understand. I, too, was a gym rat for thirty years before I began to loosen up and explore new ways of getting in touch with my own body. I can only tell you that in my golden years I am experiencing as much if not more pleasure than I did in my turbo-charged, testosterone-fueled twenties, thirties, and forties.

Joschi Schwarz is the picture-perfect model of what this can look like. Joschi is former dancer who grew up in Germany and has multiple degrees in anatomy and sports medicine, as well as numerous certifications in yoga and other mind-body practices. Over the years he has attracted a long list of celebrity clients, as well as a loyal following of male millennials because he's located in Hell's Kitchen. His experience working in hospitals as a medical professional drilled into him how incredibly burnt out so many people are (employees and patients alike), and how we all need to develop a much better relationship with our bodies long before disease and illness sets in. His gifts for understanding the unique psychology of men and its relationship to the male body has made him into an oracle for these times, as men struggle with an inordinate amount of stress and the competing expectations of how to be a man. It is his view, from years of direct observation and his own personal experience, that our bodies can instruct us how to live a good life in these times. But we need to learn how to listen to our inner depths to get in much better touch with our body's wisdom and language. Having studied the body-mind-soul connection with him now for many years, I can tell you that he's a Jedi master on the topic.

"I work with a lot of men in their late 20s and early 30s. I'm surprised by how much anxiety and stress this age group is experiencing, and how that plays out in their physical presence. Young men have very complicated relationships with their bodies. Part of it has to do with the amount of medication that they are taking to cope with life (or the weed that they're smoking for the same reason). They are having little sex—some go for a year without it. The messages that they absorb from social media, and the time that they spend gaming and looking at porn, further cause further disconnection. It's a destructive cocktail that is causing a great deal of physical and emotional trauma. The body does keep score."[55]

I urge you within the context of whatever personal commitments you have made at this time to throw aside the cultural constraints and the self-limiting mindset that prevent you from enjoying the full scope of your physical presence. Take a walk on the wild side, whatever that is for you. Give yourself permission to explore the sensual wisdom of your body. I guarantee that it will take you places beyond your wildest dreams into the heart of the fire of desire. You won't regret it.

(Oh, and by the way, you may even discover that women find your "soft" side sexy.)

GIFTS OF INTUITION

Inherent to all the wisdom figures described in Mirabai Starr's remarkable book are the gifts of intuition. These gifts are not gender specific, of course, as all cultures offer mesmerizing tales of both men and women who possess the uncanny ability to form insights with no data, knowing what is right in a given situation without having to do heavy analysis. This is a key gift that many mystics possess, famous or ordinary, in most wisdom traditions.

The research base as to whether intuition even exists is not robust, however. It's an area of pop culture fascination and current scientific investigation. Is intuition merely pattern recognition or sensory integration at lightning speed? Is there a yet-to-be-identified collection of neural pathways that we all can learn how to fire up? We will have to wait to see what researchers determine.

I don't know why but it is my observation that at least in our culture women seem to develop a greater ability to suspend judgment or disbelief and feel their way into solutions in a flash. I suspect that it is a matter of conditioning, as Richard Rohr, the great Franciscan author and mystic long ago observed in his 1990 bestseller *Wild Man to Wise Man: Reflections on Male Spirituality* that he wrote with Joseph Martos. Based on the legions of men that he has counseled over the years, Rohr asserted that we live in a culture of masculinity that emphasizes the rational, analytical components over other ways of perceiving reality:

"A man without his feminine soul is easily described. His personality will move toward the outer world of things, and his head will be his control tower."

Rohr goes on further to explain how damaging a purely rational lens can be, limiting our experience. When we hold too tightly to a purely rational view, our lives lack depth and dimension, knowledge of the inside of things.

"He will build, explain, use, fix, manipulate, legislate, order and play with whatever he bothers to touch, but he will not really touch it at all[.]"[56]

A handful of goddesses across all faith traditions embody this way of knowing. In Starr's book, she directs our attention to Saraswati, the goddess of creativity, expression and insight. A second lesser-known goddess is Hecate, of ancient Greece. Often depicted with three conjoined bodies, her three-way perception allows her to see the connection of the past, present, and future at the same time. She is believed to stand at the crossroads of our lives, bearing silent witness at critical junctures.[57]

In Chapter 8, we will take a much closer look at how men can recover and begin to listen to their inner voice as we make important life decisions. For now, I would like to flag this gift as one that many women in my network possess—my mom, my sister, my wife, their friends. Indeed, so universal is its distribution among the women that I know that I have come to the conclusion that it is unwise for any man to think that he might be able to hide something from them. She knows, she just plain knows what you are doing, gentlemen, and it's not worth taking that risk, unless you are willing to deal with the consequences. (For an amusing afternoon of idle entertainment, conduct an Internet search as to whether women or men possess greater gifts of intuition. You'll see that the prevailing view is that women do, despite the many protests of men. The stated reason for women's gifts in this department is their ability to suspend rationality as the only basis for framing perception, a debatable notion itself. We will have to let science sort this one out.)

What's intriguing to me is how the gifts of intuition can be used in our professional lives. I have had the privilege of watching several men, who in the words of a private equity friend, have an "extra set of ears" or "a sixth sense" in action. They are excellent listeners, curious about people, and store vast amounts of information about individuals in their memory. As we will explore further in the next chapter, they are also heart-centered men, who have cultivated that sensory organ as a second brain. They can literally feel what people are thinking without them saying a word. They are unusually successful at forming strong business relationships. We can all learn from them.

Having made much comment about how the women I know are conditioned to use this way of knowing more than men in my network, I should acknowledge that one wise male intuitive I know, Rick Moss, literally changed my life. As a young father in my 40s, I spent each week on the road away from my wife and two sons for nearly a decade. Rick helped me to separate and clear the pain of my past life history that resurfaced along with the current heartache of being so far away from my current loved ones. He literally "saw" the possibilities in me that I did not and gave me the inner tools to unlock their power to make my current life situation work. I will be forever grateful to him.

POWER OF COMMUNITY AND CONNECTION

One last piece of feminine wisdom.

It is tough to stomach that forming relationships is perceived as a power that women uniquely possess, as it is so central to our success as a human species, male or female. Yet, because this wisdom runs counter to the teachings of our dominant culture of masculinity, has been gendered as "feminine," and is seemingly hard-wired into the DNA of most women, we need to accept that (at least for now) one essential component of who we are as human beings has been typed as belonging to the opposite sex.

You will hear repeatedly throughout this book about the negative impacts related to the fact that men are taught to be autonomous and independent as we grow up. There are clearly positive impacts, too. Indeed, our culture considers these characteristics to be a sign of maturity for both genders. Unfortunately, as Niobe Way so brilliantly articulates in her book, *Rebels with a Cause: Reimagining Boys, Our Culture and Ourselves*, this virtue of being self-reliant that our culture so adamantly extols is only half the story of what we need to be successful adults. The other half is the set of skills required to be social, relational beings. It is these capacities that most differentiate us from most of the other species on the planet, and according to many researchers like Frans de Waal[58] and Matthew Lieberman[59] it is the reason why we occupy the top of the food chain.

While decades of psychologists and sociologists (Daniel Goleman, William Pollack, Dan Kindlon and Michael Thompson, among others) have noted that emotional intelligence is important to social interactions and overall success in life, and have highlighted the consequences of a culture that teaches boys and men to detach from the emotions, there is little research on relational intelligence. Indeed, according to Dr. Way:

"In the field of child development, there are no studies of interpersonal curiosity. That should floor you. In the study of human development that is not even seen as a topic [for investigation]? And that's the root of our ability to connect? So guess what? We have a crisis of connection!"[60]

Relational intelligence is the set of skills required to form healthy relationships; emotional intelligence is the capacity to perceive the condition of our own inner world, and that of others. While both intelligences are essential in social animals, the body of evidence is growing that relational intelligence is the important driver of the interpersonal interactions upon which professional success in most work environments occur.

Think about this. As men we are conditioned to prize individuality, self-reliance, independence, and autonomy. Yet reams of research now indicate that individuals succeed in life because of their networks, and their ability to form and build relationships.[61]

You may counter that competitive sports teach us how to build and leverage relationships, and that is why many businesses actively recruit athletes. In response, I would submit that teamwork, as practiced on the playing field and at war by men and now women, is a form of relational intelligence that is a distillation of "feminine" sacred wisdom into highly targeted outcomes. Using the sports as a useful shorthand for the way our dominant culture perceives relationships, we can see that men are trained or hard-wired to:

- Compete with maniacal focus on a specific goal.
- Form teams (hierarchical structures) that protect our backs/flanks in order to win, survive, prosper.

- Be linear, temporal, sequential, and output oriented in a quantifiable way.
- Optimize performance, keep score, achieve results/victory, with material spoils as our reward.

In our highly transactional business culture, relationships are often a means to an end. Indeed, in America, we generally form relationships if first and foremost there is a deal. (I know that everyone will say that we're relationship driven, but formation of relationships is always with the end goal of making a deal.)

As an international television executive in Hollywood in the early 1990s it was my great pleasure to experience another way of doing business in Europe, where there was only a deal if there was a strong relationship first. I can't even begin to count the hours/days/weeks that I spent wining and dining executives and producers in London, Paris, Rome, and Cannes. It seemed to take an eternity for the relationships to be sufficiently developed so that a flow of deals began to come through.

The entertainment business back then was primarily conducted by men conditioned to make a ton of money, with a few important exceptions—women running networks (literally) at the time: Gerry Laybourne (Nickelodeon), Kay Koplovitz (USA Network), Pat Fili (Lifetime), and Judith McHale (Discovery Network). Nevertheless, as relationship driven as we thought we were in Hollywood, and we indeed were, as men we had to raise our game considerably to do business abroad. And that experience has utterly convinced me that men are certainly capable of integrating this "feminine" wisdom into their lives.

Now contrast this focus on making deals with how women understand the importance of forming networks, building community and connection as a critical component to not only their own success but also the well-being of those around them across all aspects of experience, emotional, mental, spiritual, as well as physical. Women understand the extraordinary power of community and collaboration that goes way beyond the transactional and material outcomes that most men worship. In addition, from observing the women I know like Gerry Laybourne and Judith McHale at work, I would conclude that women are gifted at working several power structures at the same time, activating multiple communities to get stuff done (GSD). They seem to be much more natural systems thinkers.

To help cement what real networking looks like (and for what reasons), Mirabai calls our attention to two wisdom figures that demonstrate the power of networks: the Spider Grandmother, a Native American figure, and the lesser-known Indra, a Hindu male deity.

Spider Grandmother is cocreator and sustainer of the world in the Hopi tradition of Arizona. (She is Spider Woman in the Diné tradition throughout the American Southwest, Ix Chel in the Mayan tradition of Central America.) Her task is to create life to clothe the naked planet. She molds all living things from the ground with her spit and covers creation with the mantle of her wisdom. She sings the web of the universe into being. She represents the power of interconnectedness.[62]

The rare male deity who understands this truth is Indra who maintains the web of interbeing that connects all beings. He literally holds the universe together, creating an exquisite net in his heavenly abode that stretches infinitely in all directions. He places a luminous jewel at the center of each intersection that reflects on all the others. "So not only is the net infinite, but the reflection of the net extends to infinity."[63]

Unfortunately, unlike Indra, men do not learn the power of community beyond the material results that they produce until we are removed from the only network we experience (at work and in our personal life) upon retirement. Stripped of the jobs, money, status, and the colleagues that define us, we have a difficult time forming new support systems of purpose and meaning with often catastrophic consequences to our physical and mental health.

This brings us full circle back to where we started this chapter, the high mortality rates; the global increase in mental health issues, substance abuse, and suicide among men. We must ask ourselves whether the wisdom of women can be acquired and incorporated into the male psyche at any stage of life. I think the answer is yes. And why wouldn't we want to play with a full deck of cards?

Occasionally, I stumble upon a guy who has a strong network of buddies who connect in ways that go way beyond hanging out in bars, watching games, playing golf. In fact, I work out with such a guy, Brett D'Elia, a Gen X man who exited NYC long ago to raise a family and be surrounded by friends that have been together since kindergarten. It's a marvel to live his life vicariously. He's lucky, and he knows that having such a group of guys who have his back is unusual. That said, Brett feels like his band of brothers could and should make more of an effort. "We have a two-week threshold. Any longer than that without seeing each other and gut bust laughing, I get anxious. Because there's a growing realization among us that health and happiness are inextricably linked, especially as we age, and being together advances both. I mean the common denominator between all of us is time. If not now, when?"

■   ■   ■

I hope this chapter provides some insight into the ways that men can gain much from integrating feminine wisdom into their identities. Think of this chapter as a "new" frontier that you might find useful to explore further, an adventure of discovery that is best enjoyed, like Lewis & Clark, with a good friend. If nothing else, it will help you better understand the women in your life.

In closing, let me reiterate once again, I am not advocating for a change in behavior that makes us less manly. I am advocating that we take seriously the challenge of understanding the way in which our culture of masculinity is hard wiring some damaging habits of behavior into our identities as men and teaching us to dismiss those attributes that we associate as feminine. I do believe that reducing this inherent bias against "feminine" capacities and understanding that they are part of our humanity as well will make us better men. When a man stops feeling bound by society's definition of masculinity, and instead acts according to the desires of his own mind and heart, he will be transformed. By entering into the actual complexity of his thoughts and feelings, he becomes more capable of relating to others, a better partner, a better friend, a better father. He has more to give; he is better able to receive. He becomes a more stable and generative human being. *He becomes a real man.*

So, listen intently to what is calling you in this chapter. Ask a woman that you trust to be your mentor and guide. Don't resist, don't be shy, don't be ashamed.

Jump in.

GETTING STARTED

As you know from Chapter 2, I think there is much to be learned from viewing the body through a feminine lens. In this chapter we have taken this insight one step further, exploring the wisdom that women uniquely possess about the human body, including their deep, intuitive understanding of the importance of self-care.

All men would benefit from applying their intelligence. Unlike many of us who treat our bodies like machines that need to be tuned up to maximize output and performance, many women know that the body is a temple, a life-giving force, a sacred space that must be nourished and protected, not exploited.

Men need to give themselves permission to adopt some of the practices that women use to honor their bodies. (Don't worry, I am not proposing that you become a metrosexual male, a walking vanity show peacocking around town.) There are numerous wellness practices that can help us take better care of ourselves with measurable medical benefits— yoga; regular saunas, steam baths, massages, and acupuncture. The research on these practices is compelling.

You may think that your busy lifestyle does not have room for such nonsense. In reality, many of these practices can be added to your workout routines without a noticeable addition of time, as I discovered when our older son was born over thirty years ago. I did the morning feed at 5:30 AM, put him in a car seat for a quick spin to lull him back to sleep, then deposited him in his crib and was in the gym by 6:00 AM. After working out for an hour and change at our local YMCA, I sat in the steam room for ten minutes, then hit the showers. I was at my desk by 8:00 AM, no prob-lem. Should be even more possible now that many of us work from home.

While you are enjoying some quality time taking better care of your body, make a list of the guys that you would like to hang out with more regularly, and make a plan to do so at least once or twice a month. Can you assemble a group of guys who regularly come together for for no reason other than to maintain the close personal friendships that you enjoy? Your goal should be to create a space where you can let your guard down and be your authentic self while you're having some fun.

And finally, here's another piece of feminine wisdom that I am willing to bet good money you will want to take to heart. In her book *Reclaiming Rest: The Promise of Sabbath, Solitude, and Stillness in a Restless World*,[64] Kate Rademacher makes a compelling argument for observing the Sabbath. A women's global health executive and mom whose 24/7 schedule drove her to exhaustion, she describes in great detail how she developed the dis-cipline of going off the grid weekly, including setting aside time to make love in the afternoon when she was rested with her husband. I'm sure that you will agree that setting your intention to honor your body in this way is motivating and has some intrinsic appeal. It may also stimulate your think-ing about other behavioral modifications.

Start there. Set your intention to reclaim the sacred feminine that is within you and adopt those practices that call you. You may be surprised to discover that you possess a whole new set of gifts that will greatly enhance your life.

CHAPTER 4

ENGAGE AND EXPRESS YOUR HEART

*It was Thanksgiving, and as we often do, we were hosting one of our son's friends who could not make it home for the holidays. Earlier that fall, I had purchased tickets to see Anna Deavere-Smith perform in her one-woman show, **Notes from the Field**, at Second Stage in NYC. Luckily, I was able to buy an extra ticket at the last minute, so I was sitting by myself, one seat in from the center aisle, while my family and our son's friend sat together. As the lights dimmed, a very tall Black man dressed in a turtleneck and sport coat slipped into the seat next to me.*

"Sorry," he whispered, apologizing for his late arrival. "I'm so glad I made it. I just barely got in from LA."

"Wow," I replied, impressed. "That's great."

It was a simple exchange, hardly my consent for the deeply personal and intimate experience that happened next.

While Anna worked her usual magic on the stage, conjuring up all the individuals she had interviewed to illustrate what it means to be an inner city or rural student in schools that have become a pipeline into prisons, I heard my new acquaintance sigh. He then became very still, tense.

As Anna's dramatic re-enactments built layer upon layer of first-hand impressions and meaning, he began to sob heavily. It was clear that he had direct experience with the evidence of systemic racism that was unfolding before our eyes. Finally, unable to bear the pain that was surfacing, he thrust his hand under mine, jammed his fingers around my knuckles, and clenched my first. Startled, I took a deep breath, and returned his grip.

Ten minutes before the performance ended he stopped holding my hand. After the lights went up, he put on his coat, turned to me, and smiled, sheepishly. "Thank you."

I nodded. "It was nothing."

I had never had such an encounter before. It was if our hearts were communicating without words.

How many times have you been told that you don't share your feelings or communicate your thoughts, that what is going on inside of you is a mystery, that you are a sphinx? You've also probably heard your buddies complain about the same accusations, or worse, that "Men are from Mars and have stone-cold hearts."

Have you ever wondered why this complaint is so common, especially when you know that you have emotions that you express in situations that you feel are appropriate? Well, this is our culture of masculinity at work again, shaping the perceptions of women about men, and men about themselves. Unfortunately, part of this narrative happens to be true. But it's only half the story.

The ongoing disconnect between the way in which our society perceives men as unemotional and non-expressive and the actual reality of the more varied and nuanced ways in which men construct and express their identities is troubling. Although we are moving beyond some of these age-old tropes, far too often we still resort to worn-out

adages to shorthand our experience. In the absence of a clear acceptance of the more accurate models of the many different masculinities
that real men actually exhibit, and a shared language that describes and
nurtures them, we too easily revert to the old stereotypes that are heavily
conditioned into us from childhood on.

This chapter will take a different approach. We will try to dig deeper
into the male psyche to capture what is actually going on in us and shine
a light on how men might engage their entire being—body, mind and
soul—to create a new set of understandings of what it looks like to be
a "real man" who expresses not only a Y-chromosome vibe but also his
thoughts and feelings in the 21st century.

However, we must first take a closer look at the core component of
the current masculine construct that is holding us back.

MEN AND EMOTIONS

A key tenet of the Man Box insists that a "real man" is strong, silent,
stoic. We demonstrate our power, strength, self-mastery (and protect
ourselves from others) by never showing our emotions (which would
be considered a sign of weakness) and hold our thoughts to ourselves
(unless of course we are transmitting our knowledge and expertise for
the benefit of others. Yeah, right.) While this conditioning is deeply
problematic for men, it also shapes women, as our culture of masculinity
permeates their world, too. Women are allowed to share their feelings in
settings that are not dominated by men, but in many, perhaps even most
public settings, and especially at work, demonstrations of any emotional
force are considered unprofessional, sometimes even unacceptable.

Yet we know that our emotions are central to our decision-making
processes. In fact, some researchers assert that they form the basis of
our decision-making.[65] We need to ask ourselves: what do we lose,
women and men, when we consistently refuse to acknowledge that our

emotions drive so much of our thinking and are an essential component of our human nature?

A phenomenal amount of attention has been dedicated to answering this question, especially as it pertains to raising boys and young men in a culture that genders emotional fluency and imposes expectations of stoicism on men. The list of best-selling authors addressing "the Boy Crisis" over the past 20 years,[66] and the research on the importance of emotional intelligence to career success in life is compelling.[67]

Most recently, Richard Reeves contributed his excellent analysis in his book *Of Boys and Men: Why the Modern Male Is Struggling, Why It Matters, and What to Do About It*.[68] The data confirm that men are falling behind. It is curious to me that this is the case after two decades of investment in cultivating young men's emotional intelligence and helping boys adopt new behaviors that will serve them better in a global-knowledge economy.[69] That we are in the midst of an epidemic of social isolation, anxiety, depression, suicide, and substance abuse among men such as there has never been seen before is more alarming, even after making all these investments. (Can you imagine what it would be like had we not made such investments?) Why has there been no real forward progress in men's ability to develop and sustain healthy relationships? What is missing? In this chapter we will endeavor to find out.

In Chapter 3 we looked at how our culture of masculinity sets us up to dismiss many "feminine" parts of the male psyche that can contribute to our overall sense of well-being and success in life. Now we are going to do a deep dive into the role that our emotions, and our conditioning to be non-expressive, play. Our aim is to better understand the breakdown in our ability to express our thoughts and feelings and identify ways in which we can begin to close the gap, so that we can become whole as men, and make a cultural shift to the benefit of all.

I have to say that I am frustrated with the sweeping generalizations that men are not in touch with their emotions. It is not my experience that this is the case. Most of the men in my networks—a group that is not "woke" by a long shot—are basically emotionally literate. I think that we are more comfortable expressing our feelings today than we are given credit for. And there are now excellent programs, like EVRYMAN and the ManKind Project, that help guys get more in touch with their inner landscape and change our culture so that an ability to express those emotions in a productive way is valued, and not gendered as "girly" or "gay." (See *Getting Started* at the end of this chapter for a description of each program.)

That said, while attending a weekend workshop is an excellent way to begin to regain some emotional connectivity in a safe space surrounded by other men, not everyone can get away for a weekend workshop. And while online offerings and support groups are informative and helpful, changes in behavior often require the assistance of individuals or coaches trained to facilitate the development of new habits and mindsets, especially when there is deep-seated trauma or long personal narratives that are difficult to shake. Thankfully, there are both ancient and contemporary practices to guide us as to how we can get in better touch with our feelings and those of others.

For most of us, modern Western psychology is a useful tool, although one of the peculiar realities of psychology is that we do not yet have a single, unified definition of what constitutes an emotion. As a result, there are a wide array of ways in which therapists can help us get in touch and work with them. I am going to share some of my personal experience—not to recommend one practice over another, but to demystify the whole "mental health" issue and encourage you to spend some time truly getting to know your own emotional life, if you have not already done so. Ideally this work will be done while working with a professional for some period of time, as well as guided by your own inner voice. I also share my personal experience to demonstrate the variety of additional resources that are available, while engaging with a therapist specializing in cognitive behavioral therapy (CBT). CBT is a heavily researched practice that absolutely should be considered as the first line of treatment in many situations. But there are multiple body-mind-soul practices that can help to put us in better touch with our emotions that might be beneficial as well. (As in all forms of therapy, it is important to work with a licensed professional.)

As you'll see, it's not always about sitting on a couch and spilling your guts out, as pop culture portrays, though it can be. And working with an expert is not evidence to the world that you are unstable, weak, vulnerable, or an indicator that you've experienced major life trauma that requires professional treatment. Dump the stigma that our society attaches to mental health.[70] Sometimes doing this kind of inner work is just a good self-care routine to help you stay fit and optimize your life, like working out at the gym with a trainer.

In my own case, it has been a combination of both. Although on the surface it may appear that my life has unfolded with remarkable ease, in reality a long series of unexpected life events has required that I periodically reconnect with my inner landscape. Then, once I was engaged in doing this work, spending part of my week cultivating the man within became a form of maintenance work, like mowing, seeding, and fertilizing the yard, raking the leaves, weeding the beds, planting shrubs and trees to replace the old, dead wood.

My inner work got started shortly after college when I had trouble landing a job, despite the fact that I had just graduated from an Ivy League school with honors. A Jungian analyst who was a friend of my parents encouraged me to work with my dreams and attend a journal writing workshop given by Ira Progoff, introducing me to an important tool for exploring my inner landscape. At the same time, I regularly met with an Episcopal priest who had just returned from doing mission work in India and Sujiv, Fiji. I also continued to practice transcendental meditation every day, as another way to probe the inner depths, watch my thoughts/emotions surface and recede, and fantasized about moving to Pune. My dad and mom were *not* amused that their investment in a Harvard education had led to this.

After five years of taking jobs (that I had little passion for) to make ends meet, and then attending Columbia Business School, I finally landed on my feet and quickly made up for lost time. My career soared, first as a Hollywood agent, then as the president of an award-winning children's programming company. I got married and had two boys. Unfortunately, this sudden, positive turn of events was short-lived. After a decade of success, my professional life began to crumble, my employment was rife with uncertainty, I was traveling 24/7 away from the boys, and domestic discord ensued. My wife and I began to cycle through a contingent of therapists—a renowned psychologist who specialized in family therapy and wrote several books on parenting,[71] separate psychiatrists for each of us (with offices in CT and NYC where we lived), a second personal psychiatrist for me in NC (where I was working during the week), a child psychologist for the boys, an additional pre-cognitive therapist and spiritual guide from Carmel, CA working with me by phone, and an army of family members, friends, and priests who committed to helping us make things work. (It was a throw-everything-you-got-at-it moment, and it worked.)

Then, another unplanned career transition after the national education non-profit that I had helped Chuck Schwab develop imploded. (Yes, the $100 million that we raised went up in smoke almost overnight.) That led to another slate of therapists, a string of weekend retreats at monasteries, and other guides, all of whom were extremely adept at helping me process the personal and professional trauma, as well as the extraordinary spiritual growth that I was experiencing. Was I getting in touch with emotions? Hell yeah, I was.

Through it all I kept writing, journaling, keeping lab notes on my experience of the mystery of life. What I learned was that while talk therapy is helpful, the other practices that I engaged in were important, too—meditating, attending workshops, hiking, mountaineering, gardening. Journaling, with its firm insistence that I remain in constant contact with what I was experiencing and feeling, was especially powerful in forcing me to observe and stay in touch with my emotions. My "lab notes on life" kept me intellectually honest in my conversations with the various therapists and advisors that I was working with and provided a bit of detachment from the emotions that were surfacing. Those journals have also provided me with a lifelong record of my evolution as a 21st Century Male.

Recently I have found myself drawn to another practice that is both spiritual and psychological. I have worked with Br. Carl Sword, an existential psychoanalyst and Benedictine monk, as I went through yet another unplanned career shift late in life. Our work together has forced me to address life-long negative patterns of thinking, self-criticism, judgment, feelings of inadequacy, a tendency to play the role of the victim, anger, and anxiety. Over a period of eighteen months, Carl has been able to help me learn how to simply describe my experience, not repress or bury my emotions, acknowledge them and hold myself accountable for my behavior, without judgment. This way of engaging in the day-to-day interactions of my life has created some additional mental distance so I can observe both what's happening and my reactions. In the space that this technique opens up, I am both participating in and watching events as my inner life unfolds. While doing so, I've witnessed how quickly many of my emotions come and go. I'm learning how to accept reality as it presents itself; I'm also seeing how much I create what I'm feeling. This window on life[72] frees me up to not get bogged down by the narratives that I've developed over a lifetime of disappointments that have kept me from celebrating the huge successes and many blessings I have to enjoy.

The "descriptive method" that Carl and I are using seems very much akin to Buddhist views of the emotions that I have encountered in working with various wisdom figures in that tradition. As I understand it, although the traditional languages of Buddhism have no word for emotions, "emotions" are not "good" or "bad" in themselves in this system of beliefs and practices. Instead, it's how they affect our internal equilibrium that matters. Emotions that we perceive as "good" might create attachments that aren't positive for us. Emotions that we perceive as "bad" might provide the fuel we need to do great things. That said, there are also *kleshas*, destructive emotions that co-mingle with our thoughts to disturb our equilibrium internally, producing "afflictive mental states" that misapprehend the true nature of reality. The practice of meditation trains our minds to observe the rise and fall of our thoughts, just like the "descriptive method," acknowledging them as they are so that we can release their grip or defang their impact. The mantra of Buddhism is "As it is."[73]

A third approach to the emotions that has captured my attention of late is derived from an opportunity to spend some time with Catherine Shainberg, a kabbalist who is carrying the lineage of Isaac the Blind of Posquieres (1160–1235), an unbroken transmission spanning more than 800 years. In her worldview reality unfolds through images, the senses, and our bodies. Similar to the ideas put forth by Bessel van der Kolk's book *The Body Keeps the Score*, this tradition asserts that our experience is imprinted in our bodies, and that sometimes our memories are accompanied by emotions that (if not expressed or resolved at the time) become stagnant energies or blockages in the body. In her therapeutic work Catherine has been able to help clients retrieve a memory by going back to the location in the body where an emotion is felt, so that it can be released or replaced by a more positive feeling. The work clears traumatic memories by "correcting" the imagery that is lodged in the subconscious—the images, smells, and physical sensations—transforming the experience by replacing the old image with a new one. The result is a new sensation, a positive feeling whose energy radiates outwards in expanding concentric circles, instead of the constricting blockages that it replaced.[74] This practice also resembles the "descriptive method" in that it insists that it is possible to better manage our emotions by changing the way that we think about or perceive them.

A final system of emerging thought about the emotions that merits your further investigation is the work by neuroscientists at the HeartMath Institute. They posit that the heart, with over 40,000 neurons, operates like a little brain. Because the heart is the most powerful source of electromagnetic energy in the body, with an electrical field 60 times greater than the brain, the heart plays a critical role in bringing coherence, order and harmony between our psychological (mental and emotional) and our physiological processes. The Institute has researched techniques for synchronizing heart and breath rhythms through positive emotional shifts. They assert that the result is a wide array of benefits that "include deeper perceptual and emotional changes, increased access to intuition and creativity, cognitive and performance improvements, and favorable changes in hormonal balance."[75]

There are other body-mind-soul practices that you can explore. I want to underscore here that some of these alternative strategies should not be considered substitutes for cognitive behavioral therapy when we are confronted with serious, deep issues that require professional help. They should be used as an additional resource, an extension of your core mental health work, or a wellness program as issues abate. Choose a practice that speaks to you and dive in.

Regardless of what is happening in your life, you are missing out, dude, if you are standing on the sidelines, encumbered by the "show-no-emotion" edicts of the Man Box. You are not experiencing the full dynamic range of the positive energy that can enter your life if you choose to acknowledge that you are an emotional as well as a rational human being.

On this important point, I'd like to share the experience of a friend, Michael Banten, who had a 28-year career at IBM. He retired twelve years ago to spend more time with his wife and their two boys. (As an aside, he asserts that the best managers he "ever had were all women. They mentored me. Women see qualities in men that men don't see in men. I really enjoyed working with them. I got so much more out of it than working with men.")

Unfortunately, his wife died shortly after his retirement, nine years ago. When I asked him how he handled his grief from losing the love of his life, his response surprised me.

"It's very tough for me still. I went into therapy for six years and attended a support group. Forget it. It doesn't work for me. I still have a lot of grief inside of me. There's just a hole that will never go away."

I then asked him if he considered attending a men's workshop dedicated to helping him process his experience. "I don't know whether I could handle attending a retreat of all men to process some of this. That takes me back to high school when I was not secure. I did not play sports. I wasn't even interested in them. I would have to think about that."

He paused, then continued in short, staccato sentences that men use when they are speaking from the depth of their being. "The weird thing about this grief that is stuck inside of me is that I am able to express my emotions. Unlike my father who was never able to do so and raised me not to either. I finally allowed myself to cry at my grandmother's funeral. I was 26 or 27, married, and had a child. I went around a tree to hide. My mom was in and out of mental hospitals, so I grew up with my grandparents. It was very hard for me to lose my grandmother."

He went on. "You know, I know I did a good thing. My sons are good men. I showed them that it was okay for a man to show his emotions. When our son Chris was a boy, my wife Colleen and he used to dance around the room to Louis Armstrong's 'What a Wonderful World.' They said that they were going to dance to this song at Chris's wedding, but she missed his wedding. Chris danced with his mother-in-law and cried the whole time. It was deeply moving."

By the end of our conversation, I realized that Michael has been working through his emotions by engaging with his family and friends as his support group. Often our intimate relationships provide spaces where we men feel safe; they offer the healthy, loving environments that we need for processing our feelings. And since it is these connections that we most need to experience a sense of well-being in our lives, doing the work of healing our emotional trauma in the company of loved ones can be a wonderful strategy.

RELATIONAL INTELLIGENCE

Now that we have taken a closer look at how being in touch with our emotions can enhance our well-being, let's return to the observation that the last 20 years of investment in emotional intelligence (EI) has not solved "The Boy Crisis." It would appear that while building our EI is an important step in rebuilding our identities as men, it isn't the whole solution. Researchers are increasingly focused on the fact that men need to also learn how to share what is inside of us. That requires other capacities that have been conditioned out of men as well. The question is how can we develop all the "muscles" we need for building healthy relationships in a world where valuing the innate human desire for connection is low, gendered as feminine, and male role models are few? What are the verbal and non-verbal components of strong expressive skills in the emotional sphere? Is there a "gym" where this work can be done?

Fortunately, the answer is yes, and the "workout" that we seek can be found in our daily interactions with others—loved ones, colleagues, strangers, you name it. Every exchange is an opportunity to practice, and better yet, there are several resources worth consulting to build your relational capacities.

In the previous chapter we discussed Niobe Way's take on the differences between emotional and relational intelligence in her book *Rebels with a Cause*. To recap (and greatly oversimplify her argument), emotional intelligence helps us understand our own inner world and that of others. Relational intelligence is an understanding of the interactions that occur in the space that lies between individuals. In her view, and increasingly that of many others, relational intelligence's importance to success at work and life is vastly underestimated today.

This skill is so critical at the present moment that she devotes a chapter of her book to describing how we can develop it. She believes that her work studying boys for over 30 years confirms that an essential component of relational intelligence is "listening with curiosity," which for the cognoscenti in the room is different from "active listening." (For example, active listening discourages interruption. Listening with curiosity believes that interruptions are a sign of an engaged, curious listener.) Originally developed as an interviewing methodology for her research, Niobe has come to see the set of conversational tools that she has used for decades as a framework for developing the skills that we need for asking "real" questions "nurturing curiosity, building meaningful relations, connection, disrupting stereotypes, and encouraging thick stories."[76] She and Joseph Nelson (her former student, now a professor at Swarthmore) are teaching their "transformative interviewing" methodology to build relational capacities in many settings.

Their methodology has eight guidelines.[77]

1) **"Start with a meaningful or 'real' question."** The key is to begin the conversation in a place that establishes that you want to know what the interviewee wants, feels, thinks, values, believes. From there,

2) **"Ask open-ended follow-up questions."** This allows interviewees to elaborate and tell you what is important to them. Next,

3) **"Ask curated follow-up questions and stay on topic."** This is more difficult than it seems because most of the time we aren't really listening. "Curated questions" follow the speaker's flow of logic, which is key, because it helps the interviewee feel listened to and understood. Then,

4) **"Ask for examples of the topic."**

5) "Get the details or gold nuggets."
6) "Ask clarifying questions."

Guidelines #4, #5, and #6 are designed to help build a detailed understanding of what the person is trying to convey.

7) "Ask a contrasting question" because humans often understand each other more when given the opportunity to compare experiences.
8) "Ask why or how questions" to get a sense of how the story or experience that an interviewee is relaying has had impact within the context of their life, how it holds meaning for them.

Though most of Way and Nelson's work is primarily executed within school settings, Way does go on to call attention again to the growing research base that indicates that relational intelligence is important in the workplace. She cites research conducted by Blair Miller indicating that employees would rather have a good boss, defined as a talented relationship builder, than a raise.[78]

Picking up where Niobe Way leaves off on the importance of relational skills in the workplace is Saliha Bava and Mark Greene's *The Relational Workplace*, a step-by-step examination of how to build the relational capacities of employees that are so critical to the successful implementation of anti-oppression, diversity, equity, and inclusion policies in companies.[79] In this overview of their tools for developing a corporate culture that nurtures belonging and connection, Bava and Greene make a compelling argument that relational intelligence is essential to overall organizational success. The book is a follow-up to their earlier joint publication, *The Relational Book for Parenting*, a wonderful how-to guide for "children of all ages."[80] Produced as a graphic novel, it walks parents and kids through a series of games and activities that develop the habits of mind that lead to stronger relational skills in navigating daily life. These steps include: "Ask questions, consider context, reframe stories, listen with curiosity, stay playful, hold uncertainty." Both are quick, brilliant reads—an easy entry point for anyone interested in deepening their relational capacities. They offer a powerful, practical system for creating healthier personal relationships critical to life success.

For those who are interested in advancing their listening/communications skills by a quantum leap, a respected colleague, spiritual advisor, and psychotherapist highly recommends working your way through *Say What You Mean* by Oren Jay Sofer. Drawing on his depth of training in mindfulness techniques and somatic healing, Oren offers a set of insights and tools that will change the way that you communicate. His core message is that "*. . . communication is not about what we say . . .* To communicate well, to create understanding through awareness, begins and ends with what is inside of you."[81] This is not a book that you can breeze through. It does not yield immediate results, but it does reward patient practice, and effects a lasting change in perspective and behavior that unfolds from the depths within.

THE NEED TO BECOME FLUENT IN THE LANGUAGE OF TOUCH

Up until now we have focused on connecting to our emotions and developing the verbal skills that are required to build relationships. Of course, one very important "verbal" communication skill is an ability to pick up on non-verbal cues. This points us towards another form of communication that is an important skill that we need to explore, although its practice is much reduced in this modern era.

Let's revisit what we know from Carol Gilligan, Judy Chu and Niobe Way's research. Men (and women) are born with extraordinary relational capacities; we are by nature social animals. As young boys we participate in this understanding of our true nature—we even cherish it—we know how important it is to talk, to articulate your feelings, your thoughts, and share them with friends in a safe space. We claim that we would go crazy if we could not do so. Yet by sophomore year in high school, this behavior begins to be conditioned out of us.

Research confirms non-verbal communication plays a significant role in developing an understanding of our emotions.[82] In addition, it appears that boys as infants and toddlers are much more sensitive to environmental stress than girls who have a built-in resilience, and boys are in need of more physical contact and emotional care, i.e., we do not need to be "toughened up, buttercup."[83] Gilligan and Chu's research confirms that young boys are emotionally fluent and intimate, and enjoy physical, non-sexual contact.[84]

Unfortunately, a discomfort with touch sets in during adolescence, as our culture's uneasiness about same-sex physical contact kicks in during puberty, fueled by the underlying homophobia that still exists, despite the LGBTQIA2S+ movement's recent gains.[85] As a result, the experience of touch for many men is greatly reduced to consensual, sexual contact, if any experience of touch occurs at all, even though our desire for non-sexual contact continues undiminished.

There is much irony here. The first irony is that in late adolescence men are cut off from their prior, limited, and decreasing experience of touch and intimacy just as their hormones kick in. Accordingly, it is no surprise that research indicates that at this stage in our development, boys begin to initiate touch more than women.[86] (Although it may be unrealistic in our homophobic culture, it would seem prudent—at least to me—that we explicitly train young men in the difference between sexual and non-sexual touch at this age, introducing the topic in same-sex settings designed for this purpose. This would accomplish two objectives. It would begin to set better boundaries and norms between men and women from an early age, and destigmatize and reintroduce same-sex platonic touch among men as an essential component of the manhood training that is sorely lacking in our society.)

A second level of irony is inherent in the solution that contemporary norms have crafted to the challenge of differentiating sexual from non-sexual touch: the construct of "verbal consent." There is no debate as to whether "consent" is, or at least should be, a requirement before initiating sex. Yet, as practiced now, according to Peggy Orenstein and others, young males are tipping their hats to consent, and then repeating the bad behaviors of their fathers.[87] Complicating matters is that fact that in a world that is weary of the tsunami of litigation that has arisen related to physical contact (and the understandable caution that has arisen as a result), the practice of verbal "consent" seems to be interpreted to apply to every form of physical contact. The default assumption is that any and all forms of touch could lead to sex (or might be interpreted that way). As many pundits have observed, this new social norm forbidding casual, non-sexual touch could not be happening at a worse time, as we experience a level of disconnect because of our lives being increasingly intermediated by digital spaces.

This leads to a third level of irony for those who are linguists. The word "consent" is derived from an Old French root *sens* that has bodily connotations: "one of the five senses, meaning, wit, understanding"—12c.[88] Its Latin root words the verb *sentio, sentire, sensi*, sensus ("to perceive, feel, know") and noun *sensus* ("sense, sensation, feeling, meaning") have both cognitive and physical connotations. While these root words assert that the body—all five senses—is actively engaged in perception, communication, and the construction of knowledge, contemporary standards of acceptable behavior between the sexes have eliminated the "bodily" elements involved in human connection and making meaning, demanding that we ask for verbal "consent" before we can experience touch in a relational space of any kind, sexual or non-sexual. So, for now, it is almost impossible to imagine how young men and women will become fluent in speaking the many languages of touch, as "consent" has become the gatekeeper to a binary outcome—yes or no—to physical contact, whatever it may be.

Before I go any further, let me just state that I realize that I may be setting off a firestorm of protest by advocating for the need for responsible, non-sexual touch as part of the way we communicate with each other on a day-to-day basis. To be clear, I am not suggesting that men be allowed to exploit non-sexual touch as an access ramp to sex. I am all in favor of the concept of verbal consent as a key component of sexual assault prevention, and I support the culture of respect workshops that are attempting to counter and deconstruct the hyper-sexual, hyper-aggressive behaviors promoted by the Man Box. But I am advocating for touch as a healthy component of human relationships. We are sophisticated social animals with extraordinary powers of perception that are not limited to our brains and hearts. Our need for touch is profound. We ignore the necessity of touch in healthy, everyday relationships at our peril. We should be able to develop new acceptable norms, instead of interpreting all touch that is non-consensual as unacceptable, as we are now.

Why? Since the beginning of time we have known that touch is an essential tool for communication, connection, and healing. Alternative medicinal systems across the millennia whose wisdom Western science is only now beginning to appreciate have acknowledged the healing power of touch: reiki, ayurveda, tai chi, yoga, qigong, and ritualized dancing, to name a few. In a fascinating extended essay *Touch: Recovering Our Most Vital Sense* (Columbia University Press, 2021), Richard Kearney devotes an entire chapter to the emerging body of research regarding this primal, powerful role that touch can and should play in our lives:

"Recent epigenetic research shows that key alterations in our bodies are made not just by toxins and biochemical stimulants but by the way we resonate with our fellow beings. For all the good medication does for trauma sufferers, the most effective way of alleviating stress and suffering is, new research indicates, being 'touched, hugged and rocked': actions that quell excessive arousal and make us feel 'intact, safe, protected and in charge.'"[89]

So, I ask you: Given the evidence distilled from ancient and contemporary wisdom, is the best solution to the fact that we are not fluent in the linguistics or pragmatics of touch that we should forgo the experience altogether, except for when the possibility of sex is in the air, and then only by giving our verbal consent? Is it possible that the epidemic of loneliness and social isolation that we are experiencing is not because of social media or virtual reality but is due in part to our uneasiness with ordinary, everyday physical contact?

It didn't always used to be this way. In the not-too-distant past a wider range of non-sexual physical contact was acceptable. A peck on the cheek. A hand on a wrist or forearm. A slap on the back. An arm around a shoulder. A hug. As we matured as men, we became proficient in the language that athletes use with each other, the customs that our parents and families deploy, and the hand gestures/greeting that our friend groups view as acceptable. All distant memories now. I am deeply concerned that young men and women today are not conversant in the positive way in which some familiarity in speaking the language of non-sexual touch can greatly enhance their lives.

Shortly after the #MeToo Movement took off, a panel discussion on NPR featured three women, each from a different generation—a baby boomer, a Gen X-er, and a millennial—discussing their own personal experience of the microaggressions that men commit in the workplace and outside. It was their observation (at the time) that women have an innate sense, they simply know when touch is innocent or not. The three women went on to say that because of this innate sense and their personal willingness to set limits, they had been able to establish boundaries with the men that they had encountered in their lives. This perspective is consistent with the public statements that my own sister has made as a high-ranking oil and gas executive about the challenges of being a woman in such a macho industry still very much dominated by Man Box culture:

"I think the problem is that men and women know full well what sexual assault is, but we don't fully understand what harassment really is. It's not an isolated incident, or a poorly stated compliment. It's a repeated behavioral phenomenon. And then there is bias, which is a systemic challenge. Each requires its own set of responses.

"Harassment is pretty simple. When a man crosses the line with another man, he draws a line and stands his ground. If it's a one-time event, and the guy self-corrects the next time, it's over. The problem with harassment is that it's two-sided, and some women don't draw the line, because we don't like being direct. But you have to learn. A woman has to say, 'I don't like this.' Unfortunately, it seems to me that sometimes women are out to get guys on stupid stuff. We should not be on the lookout for gotcha moments."[90]

That said, the three women also acknowledged that they were very lucky, as so many of their women friends have been victims of assault. (14.8% of women and 3% of men have experienced sexual assault.)[91] My sister was not so fortunate. Neither was I.

This on-air conversation set me off on a quest to figure out what, if any, level of touch might be appropriate in this modern era, given what we know now about the behavior of some men. My sense from the very beginning was that we might throw out the baby with the bathwater if we were not careful.

Like many men, my investigations ranged from conversation with guys in my network to a fair amount of reading, and then some writing on the topic. A conversation with an older gentleman in my network stuck with me early on. Bob Whyte is a Harvard MBA and venture capitalist who worked with Jock Whitney, back in the day. Now in his 80s, a distinguished gentleman, banjo-playing bluegrass musician, and iconoclast who has always strummed to the beat of his own heart, Bob humorously shared that when he was an undergraduate in the '60s at Berkeley, it was absolutely customary for men and women to give each other back massages regularly without any expectation that something more would develop.

This was not unlike the behavior of our older son and his friends on field trips during high school ten years ago, shortly before #MeToo exploded. They used to cuddle up and sleep in a pile of bodies that mixed genders. As a concerned dad trying to raise two sons who were respectful in relationships, I had to ask, "Is there something else going on here that I don't know about? Are you sure that your behavior is being respectful???" Slightly offended and hurt that I would think other-wise, he responded with a definitive, "No!," and rolled his eyes as if I was an antediluvian lizard to believe that every physical encounter is inter-preted as a prelude to sex.

Later, in 2019, as more and more men and women began to talk openly about the need for a new way for men to roll, I remember sitting at a sold-out discussion of masculinity at the Alliance Française in New York. The talk featured the French philosopher Raphael Liogier and his American thought-partner, Mark Greene, about the current state of things. The space was absolutely packed, standing room only, as four times the planned number of attendees showed up. A grand dame of Gallic descent sat next to me at a café table. After an extended Q & A that went for a full hour longer than anyone anticipated, we gathered our things to leave. Perplexed, she pursed her lips, frowned, and leaned into my personal space. "But what is zis all about?" she asked rhetori-cally. "It's simple, no? Be a gentleman, have some manners, be kind. C'est tout. The rest will sort itself out." I pulled the chair out from under her, as she got up to exit. She gave me a kiss on each check before she did.

Towards the end of his 140-page "essay" on touch, Richard Kearney issues a call for the creation of a "commons of the body" to do the work of healing trauma at the communal level, in response to Van der Kolk's observation that "trauma is the greatest threat to our national well-being." Both men argue that we need to focus on the "lowercase traumatisms that tend to pass beneath the Big News grid": "domestic abuse, car accidents, neighborhood gang feuds, school bullying."[92] (To this list we can now add cancel culture, social media distortions of reality, COVID.) We tend to medicate these problems or pave over these potholes with therapy.

Kearney suggests that something more must be done. Reflecting on truth and reconciliation projects of South Africa, Rwanda, and Northern Ireland, he underscores the role that bodywork can play in healing.[93]

Citing Van der Kolk, Kearney enumerates many different practices that can rehabilitate the body and overcome psychic dissociations, including:

> "walking, dance, theater, sports, swimming, yoga, gardening, deep tissue massage, and various forms of hands-on art making . . ."[94]

I would submit that coming out of #MeToo we need similar societal reconciliation between men and women, along with a major re-evaluation of how important touch is to our well-being.

Another problem here, however, is not just figuring out what non-sexual touch is permissible without consent between women and men. As the movie *Close* directed by Lukas Dhont so powerfully articulates, the fact that all touch is viewed through a sexualized lens is problematic in interactions between men as well. Most physical contact between men is considered gay in the States, except for the drunken exchanges that sometimes occur on a guys' night out. How can that make sense? Especially when we know that touch is essential to our physical, emotional, psychological, and spiritual health?

What we desperately need is to create an entire generation of men and women who know how to use their minds, hearts, *and* bodies to express themselves in a healthy and positive way. This is a tall order, since our culture teaches us that guys who possess these gifts must hide or discreetly demonstrate their emotions and relational capacities.

The work of making such a shift in our touch-averse culture is too important to everyone's well-being, men and women, for it to be ignored any longer. We must lean in and get the job done.

GETTING STARTED

A good first step for every man who wants to explore the body-mind-soul connection is to attend an all-male weekend workshop. These programs offer a safe space for men to become vulnerable and share the emotional trauma that we have all endured in becoming adult males in a dominance-based culture of masculinity.

For guys who identify as traditional males, The ManKind Project (MKP) offers a workshop, New Warrior Training Adventure, that you might want to consider attending. Founded in 1985, the program has a long, storied history, including a period in the '90s where the weekends devolved into drunken orgies. (This is no longer an issue as alcohol and controlled substances are banned.) Created as an update to the men's initiating groups that were prevalent across America during the nineteenth century, the program offers a much-needed cultural experience: a powerful initiation rite for men. Leveraging the power of myth, stories, and the hero's journey, the three-day weekend leads participants through a set of experiences that enables men to do a deep dive into their inner landscape. Although critics (myself included) have observed that this process can reintegrate models of masculinity that need to be updated and expanded, the fact is that the leaders of MKP are reinventing their work to align the needs of today's men who are hearing the call of the wild man within, and know that they need help in dealing with their inner emotional pain. As we seek to reframe our understanding of what it means to be a 21st Century Male, MKP provides a strong foundation upon which to rebuild male identities from the inside out. The ManKind Project also offers opportunities for participants to join groups that meet regularly in person and online after their experience.

A second weekend workshop that I highly recommend picks up where the MKP stops. Created by EVRYMAN, which was founded in December 2016, the organization's Men's Emotional Leadership Training (MELT) equips men with the information and mindsets that we desperately need to better manage our emotions. Meeting together as a single body and then breaking into small groups and triads, the program does a brilliant job of introducing and modeling somatic exercises and psychological tools that are sorely lacking in our utility belts. The program's leaders have a gift for helping each man surface a core trauma and a related set of limiting beliefs that are causing harm in his life. (The acronym MELT is apt; every man in the program dissolves during the weekend.) Taking a page out of van der Kolk's book *The Body Keeps the Score,* they show participants how to use their bodies as guides to identify where past trauma is a stored and/or the place from which our current emotions are arising. Then they show men how to use their bodies to manage, release, and express that trauma or emotion. Much covered by the media, the program deserves all the accolades that it has recently received from the *New York Times*, *Men's Health, GQ,* and *Men's Journal.* In addition to their weekend workshop, EVRYMAN hosts Zoom webinars with thought leaders in a healthy masculinity space and offers skill building online programs as well as opportunities to join weekly men's groups.

I found both experiences to be transformative, each in its own way. They are definitely worth the investment. Both programs encourage guys to join a men's group that convenes regularly, a recommendation with which I heartily agree, regardless of whether you attend an MKP or EVRYMAN workshop. Pull together a group of guys that you feel comfortable sharing your "Deep Secrets"[95] with. We all need a squad of men that has our back, at every stage of life.

CHAPTER 5

OWN YOUR
FULL SEXUALITY

My wife, friends, and I walked to dinner at Coriandolo on via dell'Orso just across the square from La Scala, where we were enthusiastically greeted by the restaurant's maître d', whom Sarah and her friend Jocelyn agreed was one of the finest male specimens that they had ever seen.

A six-foot, blue-eyed, dark blond bell'uomo, he must have painted on his clothes, as every anatomical detail of his body was on display. Watching him move with an athlete's grace and devastating self-assurance, I realized that the restaurant had smartly hired a Milanese Apollo to oversee the room.

Sarah and Jocelyn were mesmerized. Even Jocelyn's big, burly husband Stan was affected, joking that although it was obvious to which side he dressed, he wasn't certain which way the guy swung. I was certain he was straight. His conspiratorial nods for me to check out various women around the room, as I tried to get his attention for some wine, were international code that every guy understands. I smiled back, then focused on my first family meal in Italy. It was the perfect way for a guy to enter his golden years.

We had a fantastic, three-hour dinner. Jocelyn declared her Veal Milanese the best that she had ever eaten. I thought that my osso bucco was of equal stature. Who knew by the end? We drank several bottles of wine, including some champagne.

Our evening was capped by a charming Italian custom on the occasion of my 50th birthday. Two seven-inch sticks of fireworks were jammed into an enormous dessert that our maître d' Adonis presented from the kitchen, leading a parade of young women to our table, each of whom planted a kiss on my cheek. As they departed, he wedged himself into the gap on my left and leaned over to place the plate in front of me.

Withdrawing his hand from the dessert, he bent over again, placed his right arm around my back, and his left hand on my sternum, bringing his face closer to mine.

"Buon compleanno," he beamed, obviously proud that he had brought so much unexpected pleasure into my life.

"Grazie," I replied.

He then slid his hand down my abs, across my lap . . .

I shook my head. When in Milan, I guess.

So far in our effort to rebuild our male identities from the inside out, we have taken three steps.

First, we have explored the need for men to get naked as a symbolic act that strips off the old, prevailing models of masculinity and creates an inner space where we can be vulnerable and transparent, willing to create something new. This puts us in a position to be open to change. Second, in an effort to express the full range of our identities as men, paradoxically, we have begun to reevaluate the qualities that society categorizes as feminine, seeing them as dormant capacities within men that need to be reclaimed and reactivated. Third, we have also begun to open our hearts, realizing that as men we have been conditioned to detach from our emotions. This is contrary to our own basic nature as human beings who derive meaning and purpose from the ability to form deep, meaningful connections with others.

In this chapter we will examine how Man Box culture prioritizes hypersexuality, preferably in heterosexual form. Over the past ten years, some social commentators have begun to question whether heterosexuality as it is defined by our culture of masculinity may be an oversimplification of the actual set of sexual impulses experienced by the majority of men. Unfortunately, many men, myself included, feel trapped into accepting the Man Box's edicts that in order to be a "real man" you need to be hyper-heterosexual. As a result, exploring a new understanding of male sexuality is very high risk for men. Not only does it require uncomfortable self-examination that shakes the very root of our identity, it also demands that we defy the precepts of the Man Box, and its glorification of a narrow definition of masculinity. Unraveling its impact is an almost impossible task. But we must try.

So, let's begin to discuss the forbidden topic of the actual sexual identities of men, not the stories that we tell each other in the locker room. You may be asking why on earth do I need to examine something that is so deeply embedded and fixed in my psyche that there is no reason to question it? Ah, well, in fact, things might not be as fixed as you believe. They just feel that way because there is such strong pressure to conform to the hyper-aggressive, hyper-sexual construction of masculinity in our culture that it is quite possible any variation in our impulses is submerged, remaining hidden from view (including our own), or simply conditioned out of us. In reality, as you will soon see, there is every reason to believe that much variation does exist. The point of this exploration is to expand the definitions of masculine sexual identities so that they better align to the realities of the population of men that present them.

To this end, we are going to explore the full range of male desires as recorded by today's researchers. Why? Because desire offers us an invitation to find the true self, the hawk or eagle within us that soars high in the sky not conscious of itself. When we shackle ourselves to conventions of masculinity that might not reflect our true self, we are actually limiting ourselves, clipping our wings, preventing ourselves from demonstrating our full capacities as human beings, and as men. Great care must be taken in these explorations, however, as not all possibilities, not all impulses, are in line with your true self. They may do harm or hurt others, by breaking our need to stay safe and be connected in healthy ways. So, I am not suggesting that we should race out and try new behaviors as some millennials are today. What I am proposing here is that getting in better touch with our actual sexual drives is an opportunity to learn and grow. Some impulses may be pure fantasy. Others may not, but they could do harm. And others may be wonderful additions to your routines.

If you have any questions about any aspect of the self-discovery process that this chapter proposes, please consult a therapist or ask for help. Most men don't seek help, so take this to heart. No one is objective, no matter how strong or fully developed he may be. We can all use a third party to discern what is authentic and causes no harm.

THE MYTHS OF HETEROSEXUALITY

Okay, now let's get started with the forbidden discussion of actual sexual identities of men, and let's start at the top of the hierarchy of men: the heterosexual male. I hate to break it to you, but there is good reason to question the qualities that define the "heterosexual male," since the word "heterosexuality" itself is a man-made artifact that was invented in the 1860s and has changed over time. Hanna Blank recounts in her book, *Straight: The Surprisingly Short History of Heterosexuality*, that the term is nothing more than an intellectual construct, a label, that entered mainstream thought because of its ability to shorthand certain aspects of sexual behavior. Hetero activities were contrasted with same-sex or "homosexual" behavior, another construct invented at the same time. Both of these phrases were coined to describe and label individuals expressing a particular kind of sex drive, which no one bothered to name before. Over the decades, heterosexuality, which in the early 1900s was understood as a "morbid sexual passion for the opposite sex,"[96] became associated with "normal" sexual behavior exhibited by the vast majority of respectable men and women. Blank contends that redefinition of the term occurred with the rise of the middle class, consistent with its need to avoid diverging from norms to protect social position.[97]

Like all constructs, heterosexuality has its strengths and weaknesses in illuminating the behaviors that it represents. While it captures some common elements of a form of male sexuality that is prevalent among men, it also establishes artificial boundaries or limits—a "box"—that real, live men may not fit. Nonetheless, we feel pressured to define ourselves in relation to the assumptions that this construct puts on us, whether we identify as heterosexual, gay, or bi-sexual. The very act of trying to fit any of these labels constrains our individual humanity.

There are serious consequences of performing up to the expectations set forth in the word "heterosexuality," as it is interpreted by most men, since our culture of masculinity encourages men to perceive sex on some level as an act of aggression. Executed in the extreme, this "norm" has led to sexual assault (of women and men), domestic violence, and partner abuse, which often also triggers mental health issues such as eating disorders, OCD, schizophrenia, and bipolar depression among women.[98] Separating what is real and what is myth about heterosexuality and our actual healthy sexual and romantic impulses is therefore an essential task for these times.

The narrow range of behaviors that the Man Box deems "normal male heterosexuality" is not inevitable. Nor is it biologically predetermined that men exploit other people. Given contemporary research on male sexual behavior, the time may have come for these terms to be reinvented, or perhaps even discarded to reflect our new understandings.

Before we dive into a discussion of the emerging research about what is actually going on inside of men, I should reveal my own biases and experience with variability in male sexuality. While I identify as primarily straight (in today's modern lingo) and admit that I have felt a diversity of impulses, I am not sure that I am unusual for my cohort, for two reasons. As a boomer, I came of age during the sexual revolution, and entered my twenties at a time when men and women exercised their libidos during an "anything goes" era that pre-dates AIDS. So, my outlook on sex is a bit more laissez-faire than the current, dominant culture of masculinity prescribes, and strangely more in line with millennial males' behavior today.

Despite my readiness to critique the traditional male macho code, I must also acknowledge that my views of male sexuality are still very much shaped by our culture's puritanical attitudes towards sex, and the culture of masculinity within which I was raised. We all know the basic rubric that is drilled into men from a young age, regardless of how we identify. We are taught that males hunger not just to have sex, but to be wanted specifically for sex. These twin needs are considered so central to being a man that some say sex is always on our minds, consciously or subconsciously.

While there's nothing wrong with a healthy sex drive when it's exercised responsibly, where it gets us into trouble is when we press our needs on others without their consent. That's when our conditioning by the Man Box to be hyperaggressive and hypercompetitive in all pursuits comes into play. Our non-stop drive to get laid, along with our need to prove our standing socially among men by getting laid, leads to the exploitation of women.

If you pretend that you don't know what I'm talking about, I ask you to be honest, at least with yourself. We've all been here. We've experienced that moment when we have pushed too hard, literally and figuratively, even in committed relationships. We obviously need to take a step back and reevaluate.

Finally, although I am not an expert on male sexuality, I have become conversant over the years with the work of several academics conducting in-depth research on our sexual behavior. I am impressed by their body of work. Getting to the core essential truth about men's actual behaviors is a very tall challenge. Most men are unwilling to reveal even to themselves the psychological realities of our sex. We are taught from an early age to boast or downright lie about our heterosexual exploits in order to gain street cred in the locker room or wherever we gather, and to deny any other impulses. We know from experience that any divergence from the rigid norms against which we are expected to perform is viewed with suspicion or condemnation that can have personal and professional consequences. We are taught that being "other" (gay or bi-sexual) is an aberration and that we cannot tolerate any "deviant" impulses or behavior in ourselves.

Because of the pressure to follow the rules, an authentic discussion regarding the realities of our sexuality as men, even in confidence, is difficult to achieve. Thankfully, a new generation of young men is more comfortable in their skin and is willing to speak up. Unfortunately, even for these more open men, underneath the surface of many a guy's hetero sex drive is a second, unspoken, darker preoccupation—the need to prove that we are not "other." As we've examined in Chapter 3, guys are conditioned by our culture of masculinity to define themselves by denying the "feminine" parts of our personalities, because they are "girly" or "gay." This mandate against any behavior that might be perceived as "not straight" has instilled an extreme homophobia among us that may be, as it turns out, a direct denial about our actual lower-level sexual and romantic impulses that more men have than we may think.

WHAT'S REALLY UNDER THE HOOD?

Several fields of research are now contributing to our new understandings of the variability in male sexuality, loosening up our deep-seated biases. We now know from the neurosciences that variability in male sexuality is likely. I spent nearly a decade as the founding CEO of All Kinds of Minds, a non-profit institute devoted to the understanding of the many different ways in which our brains are wired, so I have had an opportunity to absorb the early research that confirmed the rich diversity of minds and personalities that is normal among humans. (Although allegations against its founder Dr. Mel Levine later surfaced that cast a serious shadow over his career, there is no question that his pioneering framework for synthesizing and applying the emerging research on the the brain was the work of pure genius twenty years ago.)

In his celebrated book, *A Mind at a Time*, Dr. Levine advanced two core ideas. One, there is a great deal of neurodevelopmental variation in the brain that is normal, not deviant. Two, there is a great deal of "plasticity" in the brain. (Plasticity is the ability of the brain to change and adapt to external stimuli.) These two fundamental observations, derived by Dr. Levine from an in-depth study of 23 different disciplines of research, mean that while we may be born with certain genetic predispositions (due to the configuration of strengths and weaknesses of our neural pathways), our neurodevelopmental profile evolves—sometimes slightly, at other times radically, as a result of the interplay between our brains and external stimulus. Our minds, in other words, are more flexible than we think. It is also important to note for this discussion that higher-order cognition, or the mental processes that coordinate complex problem solving—reasoning, decision-making, creativity and impulse inhibition—are not fully developed in most men until we are ages 25–30, because the pre-frontal cortex in men don't fully mature until that age.

Genetics now shows that many more factors contribute to the determination of male sexuality than the standard, binary X-Y models we have been taught. Harvard historian and philosopher Sarah Richardson contends that there is a high degree of variability in sexuality in the human species and that the field of genetics' earlier focus on the X and Y chromosomes as drivers of sex determination is too narrow and simplistic. "Scientists now understand sex differentiation . . . as the result of numerous interconnected genetic 'switches,' some on the X and Y and others on the other 22 pairs of chromosomes." These switches aren't so much the determinants of sexual orientation or of gender-related expectations as "sex-linked variables" that are related to the determination of sex. They don't decree sexual identity in a mechanistic "if-then" way. They present possibilities. This fluidity is, of course, challenging for scientists and societies who want to categorize, label and predict phenomena.[99]

A group of researchers studying current adult male sexual behavior no longer view heterosexuality as a fixed set of neurological impulses that leads to a narrow, rigid system of sex-related behaviors without any deviation. In their view it turns out that sexual orientation is most likely not a pre-determined, steady state but a reflection of multiple sexual and romantic responses that may shift over time. As evidence, these researchers report that some young straight men are increasingly confirming that they experience (and under some socially acceptable circumstances execute on) their same-sex impulses even as they settle into predominantly straight behavior.[100] Other studies indicate that straight men in rural America are choosing to respond to their same-sex impulses even though they are married for a range of reasons—sexual, romantic, or social.[101] (A close buddy who had epic sex with his wife— she is also a friend and vocal about his performance—decided to switch it up after his divorce after 25 years of marriage. When I asked why he made a shift, he responded, "You know, when you boil it all down, I think orientation may be a function of who we fall in love with. The rest takes care of itself.")

All these findings are consistent with Alfred Charles Kinsey's breakthrough studies of human sexuality in the '40s and early '50s that confirmed that men and women in the real world demonstrate a spectrum of sexual behavior. His Heterosexual-Homosexual Rating Scale ("The Kinsey Scale") seems now prescient in these gender-fluid times, as his research not only presented human sexuality as a continuum on a seven-point scale from 0 (exclusively heterosexual) to 6 (exclusively homosexual), it also showed that sexual behavior, thoughts, and feelings towards the same or opposite sex were not always consistent across time.[102] Nevertheless, a group of social scientists who are "lumpers," and the population at large, continue to categorize men as heterosexual/ normal and other/gay-bi. (I suspect that Man Box culture, homophobia, and binary thinking, which are so deeply encoded in the male psyche, have a lot to do with this.)

Because of today's millennials' openness, our understanding of male sexuality is becoming more nuanced. One researcher, Ritch C. Savin-Williams, is particularly on it. In his insightful book, *Mostly Straight: Sexual Fluidity Among Men*, Savin-Williams offers rich, intimate portraits of young men who "report that they have same-sex attraction even as they identify as straight."[103] Through a series of detailed profiles, he presents the complex spectrum of behavior that forty heterosexual young men use to acknowledge and express their attractions, however limited their same-sex impulses may be.

He confirms that defining "mostly straight" men and boys is difficult:

"He knows that he's not gay, but straight with a touch of gay-ness. But how much gayness? Not much—a relatively small percentage, say around 5 percent to 10 percent, of his sexual and romantic feelings . . . expressed in various ways, from erotic fantasies to actual behavior."[104]

The poster boy of the mostly straight man in Savin-Williams's book is Dillon, a college hockey player who is sexually active, exclusively with women, having engaged in a series of long-term relationships, and casual bar sex when not committed. Despite his strong straight sex drive, Dillon admits that he has a romantic infatuation with men. He goes out to clubs with gay friends, has kissed strangers, and has even been in a relationship with an older man with whom he makes dinner and cuddles. No sex. Pupil dilation confirms that he is way more attracted to women than men, but it also affirms his low-grade, same-sex romantic attraction.[105]

So how large a population is the group of men who identify as "mostly straight"? Savin-Williams asserts that the numbers are difficult to pin down due to underestimation caused by self-reporting. In one study of 8,000 men, 20% of youth ages 18–25 report that they experience same-sex attractions while being straight.[106] In another group of studies, 60% of today's young adult men who have had sex with another man identify as straight.[107] (One study hails from Down Under, ultra-macho, hetero-friendly Australia.) In the end, Savin-Williams pegs the incidence of "mostly straight males" in the US at around 10% and argues further that if you remove this group along with their gay and bi brethren, the "heterosexual" population represents 80% of men. This is very different from the prevailing view that hetero men represent 90–95% of the U.S. population. Given the expanding numbers of men who are willing to admit some same-sex attraction in the younger population, it's entirely possible that a generation from now we'll see numbers that are even larger and more accurate in the actual incidence of these lower-intensity impulses.

Jane Ward takes Savin-Williams's line of thought one step further. In her book *Not Gay: Sex Between Straight White Men* she examines men's same-sex behavior in hyper-masculine settings: adult male circle jerks, hazing initiation rites in the military and fraternities, man-on-man sex in prisons and public bathrooms. Instead of categorizing the men who engage in these behaviors as homosexuals in denial (as so many of her gay and bi critics contend), Ward asserts that sometimes men have sex with other men for heterosexual reasons. In her view, "deviant" sexual acts, like the infamous elephant walk that straight men perform in fraternities, are not signs of homosexuality but "ways in which men use homosexual acts to authenticate their heterosexuality." Same-sex contact in these situations is often seen as meaningless, however much it may reveal and confirm the complexity of masculine sexual and romantic desires.[108]

Strangely, the incidence of this same-sex behavior among heterosexual males across the entire socio-economic spectrum seems to reinforce homophobia instead of eliminating it. For some reason men want to have it both ways—we want to acknowledge our varied interests yet remain safely within the Man Box. As Ocean Vuong states in his article for the *Paris Review*, "Reimagining Masculinity," the phrase "no homo" gives men permission to do things that might be considered gay while still maintaining our straight identity.[109] It seems that this phenomenon confirms the existence of a strong masculine culture that discourages or perhaps even defies variability and change.

Despite articles to the contrary, millennials are no exception in this regard. While millennials may appear to be more fluid and transparent in expressing their masculinity, new studies also confirm that strong heterosexual norms persist even among these "woke" young men. Peggy Orenstein's disturbing book, *Boys & Sex: Young Men on Hookups, Love, Porn, Consent, and Navigating the New Masculinity*, reports that the exploitation of women by straight "woke" men continues, with a mere nod to consent.[110] To wit: Reflecting on the 100 young males between sixteen and twenty-two that she interviewed, she observes, "When I asked them to describe the ideal guy to me, [they] appeared to be channeling 1955. Emotional detachment. Rugged good looks . . . Sexual prowess. Athleticism. Wealth . . . Dominance. Aggression." She asserts that her interview subjects were trying to live out more modern ideas of gender, but were unwilling or unable to let go of the old ones.[111] Much as we would like to believe that the new generation of men is behaving better than their fathers did, the evidence that she gathered is not encouraging.

A doubting Thomas, I am always curious to confirm the findings of researchers with my own informal field investigations, securing personal anecdotes from real men sworn to tell the unvarnished truth. In writing this chapter, I consulted a range of men representing a broad spectrum of sexual identities and experience across the generations—several younger male straight friends in my network, an urbane, Harvard-educated internist whose practice is 65% men (increasingly millennials), a suburban, Columbia-educated general practitioner whose patients include young adult males and their fathers, a venture capitalist on Wall Street, a retired but sexually active and single architect, my very macho haircutter and through him his three straight twenty-something sons, a real estate broker, a yoga instructor/massage therapist and life coach, as well as a bunch of guys in my cohort of men in their "golden years." I also listen closely to conversations among guys in the bar or in the locker room when traveling, gathering observations.

A buddy who is an aspiring actor and bartender in Santa Monica reports, "I work with a guy who's 26, a model, lives in West Hollywood,

and doesn't put a label on himself. He has hit on me many, many times."
My friend is a tall, well-built, former college basketball player, with a
square jaw, gravelly baritone, thick dark hair, and blue eyes that the camera loves. Being hit on by men is familiar territory for him, but he was
surprised by his colleague at work. "At the same time he's working on
me, he's hooking up with women right and left, more than I am, and is
constantly telling me to check out various babes who come into the bar.
Finally, I said to him one day, 'I thought you were gay. You also sleep
with women?' He responded, 'Yes. I like to dip my toe in the other pool
now and then. It just depends on the person.'"

The aspiring actor moved on to talk about non-traditional male sexual behavior as exhibited by straight men. "There's a bunch of bulked-up,
hetero guys at the Y that lounge around in the sauna without a towel,
hoping to get blow jobs from the gay men in the gym. They are always
hitting on my roommate. It's uncomfortable. Gross, actually." This is
similar to reports I've heard from guys in New York City and other metropolitan areas where there is an understanding that what happens in
the steam room stays in the steam room.

Then he mentioned the "Burning Man" factor.

"A really good buddy of mine and his girlfriend go to Burning Man
with a bunch of friends every year, now ten in a row, but they attend
separate parties. He sees a lot more action. There's the sex tent, which
starts off hetero with a partner. Once you're inside, anything goes."

"You mean?" I replied.

"Yes," he responded.

While this anecdotal evidence confirms the existence of fluid behaviors among young men, the Harvard-educated internist I know offers
the following cautionary tale. Now in his 70s, he's been a physician and
friend to hundreds of young men due to the close proximity of his practice to a major university. As a result, he's had an up-close-and-personal
view of several generations of guys in their late teens and early twenties,
and the institutions and culture of masculinity that shape us.

"The hetero-orthodoxy is all pervasive, including in the practice of medicine. There has not been a push in med schools to acknowledge and respond to the spectrum of sexual behavior that adult males present. A few years ago, I began to ask my younger patients 'Are you gay or straight?' to normalize the orientation issue. All the young males in my practice, even those who identify as straight, respond without comment, as if the question is perfectly appropriate."

I suggested that his "review-of-systems" protocol might need to be expanded in light of the current research, as self-reporting into big broad categories—straight, bi, or gay—might not capture what is really going on. He agreed and observed that young men are much more comfortable talking about their emotions these days, but almost never discuss sex. He went on to say:

"I have a patient who came to me as a college sophomore. He has been with his girlfriend since high school, or possibly even junior high. He is deeply in love with her, they are sexually active and happy together, but recently he's developed an anxiety disorder because he has a new attraction to men. He's actually OCD about the issue, won't go to the gym anymore, even though he was a swimmer until he went off to college. His girlfriend knows what is going on, is remarkably supportive. He's open, willing to talk about it. But for now, he's on an SSRI for anxiety."

I asked why he thought this young man who has identified as heterosexual, and has much confirmation of the same, was so freaked out by the issue.

"That's simple. Our society is so black and white about this stuff. He's not comfortable being a little bit into men. We have to normalize the fact that there is some variation that is normal. We have to validate his experience as with the range of acceptable behavior. Males, from a very young age are terrified of being 'other.' If what is normal, or even acceptable could be expanded, you would get rid of so much suffering among men."

Conversely, my suburban MD friend in CT confirms that it's tough for him to pop the "gay or straight" question with younger men. He lives in a community of Wall Street execs and corporate titans that is known for its emphasis on conformity. It's strange that it should be hard for him to ask the question, as he's a man's man, willing to crack dirty jokes with his male patients to advance healing. Yet even he, with his many manly virtues and his gift for talking to men, worries that straight young males will take offense and think that he is challenging their carefully constructed hetero identity, when what he really needs is an understanding of their sexual behavior so he knows what underlying health conditions he should be on the lookout for. He concedes that men's reluctance to confess their actual sexual experience illustrates the challenge of getting an accurate read. Men typically don't come clean until they have a sexually transmitted disease that requires treatment.

It wasn't until I connected again with Joschi in New York City that I got a more complete picture of what might actually be going on. He's the yoga instructor, healer and life coach that I mentioned in Chapter 2.

I asked for his perspective on the findings of the emerging research on male sexuality. Amused, he looked at me as if I could not be serious.

"This is news? I guess the fact that we're talking about it is. I've never understood why American men are so inhibited. There is so much homophobia here."

I told him that a former colleague, now a beloved high school math teacher in Connecticut, adamantly asserts that none of this "fluid" behavior is going on, because if it was, he would have heard about it.

My friend laughed. "Do you really think that in this culture young men are going to have sex with their buddies and tell their teachers or parents about it?"

He continued, "You know that, besides a handful of clients who come to see me when they are in town, I mostly work with men in their twenties and thirties."

I nodded. I also knew that after a yoga-massage session with him, most of his clients stay around to talk, and suspected that after being naked in his presence for two hours, most guys open up. So I was hoping that he would share what he was hearing. He did.

"Millennials are expressing a ton of confusion. Some are married, some have girlfriends or boyfriends, or both. There is enormous pressure on them to follow the rules about what it means to be a man. I'm not sure why. I think it's fear that drives them. When the topic of their sex life comes up, I never ask them whether they are straight, gay, or bi. Labels are irrelevant. What matters is who the person is and how the energy flows between individuals. Guys usually come to me when their life is not working, their mind-body connection is blocked somehow, and they're stressed, tired, experiencing some pain, or need to relax. We talk about what is going on in their lives, and that includes sex. If it's not satisfactory, we discuss how to make it better."

He went on. "There is a level of trust in the work that I do. I get to know my clients pretty well, so when a guy's sex life isn't working, my radar picks up a signal that he isn't acting on his impulses. I ask him whether he has tried sex with another man. Surprisingly, many of the men who are straight and in a relationship say yes. They feel comfortable acknowledging their fluid desires. Single men almost always say no . . . unless they are gay or bi, of course. As the conversation continues, many of the straight single guys open up, so I ask whether they have ever thought about having sex with another man. Almost every single guy admits that he has these days. My impression is that guys think about it, but they don't actually execute."

He paused, then went on. "The question is why? Why can men only talk about their sexual fluidity from the vantage point of being heterosexual? What is holding them back? I think it is the current social structure that men are forced to operate in. It prevents guys from being who they are."

Confirming the view that fluidity exists even as social pressures are forcing a fierce adherence to contemporary hetero norms, it seems important to note at this point that same-sex behavior by straight men isn't exactly new. Every generation has had its squad of straight young men "sowing their oats" indiscriminately. Scotty Bowers's memoir, *Full Service* (and the Netflix Series *Hollywood* that it spawned), provides an entertaining, eye-opening account of extraordinarily randy straight men returning from World War II who accepted pay for straight and gay sex in Hollywood while hotly pursuing and eventually marrying a beautiful woman. Not unlike hundreds of straight male strippers all across America today. Men who have attended boarding schools in America and England can also confirm that some boys go through a phase of experimentation with other boys. (A male head at a prestigious co-ed school in the '70s famously called a meeting of all the male faculty to allay fears about the extraordinary level of same-sex activity that the sophomore boys were caught exhibiting. Descended from a legendary patrician family that is a household name, he declared, "Look, this is normal behavior. It happens in boarding schools among boys this age all the time, and it's been going on for generations. I did it. It's a phase. We go onto other things.") And finally, we know that prior to the Victorian Era, generations of men formed intimate relationships with other men that were considered normal in their day.

Before we leave it here, I should probably make an important distinction, one that causes a great deal of confusion among men: a homosocial relationship is different from a homosexual one. Without knowing the details of the encounters between young men discussed above, it's hard to know how to characterize their relationships. Were they primarily homosocial with benefits, as sometimes young men exhibit when they begin to become sexually active? Or were they homosexual? Homosociality is defined as nonsexual attractions held by men or women for members of their own sex (Lipman-Blumen, 1976). For the record, much ink has understandably been spilled against vertical homosociality, which is hierarchical and strengthens bonds between men (and between women) to maintain and defend power. I do believe, however, that horizontal homosociality among men is healthy and important and surprisingly absent in today's world. Men need the emotional close-ness, intimacy, and friendship that homosocial relationships provide.[112] Young men especially need this form of connection, bonding to other young men in their lives. Unfortunately, this aspect of boys' experience is groomed out of them far too early, especially here in the United States. By contrast, I feel most fortunate to have a lot of close male friends, some of whom you are meeting in this book. In my opinion, we would be much better off if this element of men's lives was socially accepted in the US, as it is in other cultures around the globe.

A NEW REALITY?

So, given the possibility that we may experience some fluidity in our desires at some point in our lives, what would the new normal in male sexuality look like?

First and foremost, men need to accept that the full spectrum of their own sexual and romantic impulses is authentically male, and should be embraced, enjoyed, and celebrated. While the vast majority of us on the bell curve will be fixed or constant in our orientation towards women as the object of our desire and affection, it is a lie to deny that other impulses might exist. We need to become more open and honest with ourselves and each other. This may be as simple as acknowledging a bro's level of fitness, his ageless vitality and devilish charm (or whatever captures our attention) with some word or gesture of appreciation. For example, a buddy of mine—straight, former high school running back and wrestler, All-State—likes to tell the story of attending a barbeque where his friends—a couple contractors, sales rep, a factory worker in their mid-30s and early 40s—noticed that he had dropped a few. They made him stand in the middle of the group and turn around so that they could appreciate his new physique. They then gave him a nickname "GILF," "Grandfather-I'd-Like-to-Fuck" (which they still call him to this day).

Instead of teaching boys to boast about their sexual conquests, real or imagined, we need to help young men explore and celebrate their authentic sexual identities in whatever configuration they may be taking shape. This means much earlier, more honest, and ongoing discussions about sexuality at every stage of their development, so that they are aware that it's okay if they are feeling a range of impulses at any given time. Cara Natterson's *Decoding Boys: New Science Behind the Subtle Art of Raising Sons* is a wealth of information, a pediatrician's how-to manual on parenting young males. She confirms that "The Talk" should actually be a series of talks that starts early, best conducted while driving so that a parent and child do not have to look at each other.

Knowing what I do now, I wish my wife and I had had more talks with our two boys about sex as they were growing up, so it became as second nature to them as brushing their teeth and discussing healthy eating habits. We started talking about sex early, were careful to express our support of whatever set of sexual or romantic impulses they might feel, and we made sure that they were surrounded by both straight and gay role models. I even had a conversation with them when they were in high school and college about the variability in impulses that they might feel that wasn't as awkward as I expected. But I wish we had done more.

Men also need to develop a much more nuanced sense of touch. Although we all know that physical contact is essential to our health, as noted in the prior chapter, we live in a world where we experience the therapeutic benefits of non-sexual, consensual touch less and less. This is a huge sociological mistake, and especially damaging to men as a result of touch deprivation we experience growing up. Just as we have seen that men need to be role models for their sons in order to help boys reconnect with their emotions, so fathers must demonstrate the fine art of touch, not only with the objects of our romantic attraction—women or men—but especially with our buddies, and with their consent, our female friends. More fluency in the language of touch will go a long way to reduce society's rampant homophobia, and help establish new norms for non-sexual touch between men and women. Boys also need to learn the new boundaries for interacting respectfully and in friendship with women. Athletes have a good feel for this—we need to export their knowledge and make explicit their learned wisdom.

A friend who has spent most of his professional life traveling back and forth to Hong Kong reports that despite what we have read about touching, hugging, or showing affection being uncommon in Chinese families, his interactions with Chinese men demonstrate the opposite. He tells stories of men in his professional network, many of whom were from the provinces, who were quite comfortable being physical in a non-sexual way and vocal about their feelings of connection. He asserts that his experiences changed "my idea of what male relationships are and could be. Maybe the Western model of masculinity is not the only one that is available to us." Perhaps we can learn from other cultures as well. When in Milan . . .

As fathers parenting young men, we need to challenge ourselves to have authentic conversations with our sons about the role of sex in building healthy relationships. The locker room chatter, its demeaning attitude towards women, and its homophobia, will never go away unless the current generations of men band together to eradicate the exploitation of women and the dismissal of individuals who identify as "other" as a mark of manhood. I suspect that means that each of us who is a father, grandfather, uncle, or elder needs to go through some training about how to do this work. This type of sexual education is different from sexual violence prevention courses that are currently being offered in higher education and corporate America. This work is more about giving dads the tools they need to raise sexually healthy boys to become men who have the internal capacities to acknowledge and express their desires in a responsible way.

Finally, we need to move beyond labels and tackle the homophobia that persists among men to this day. Young men need to know that having a same-sex experience doesn't make you "gay," and that, further, it's okay if you prefer to have sex with men. But it's not okay in any way to denigrate or dismiss an individual for his, her, their orientation because, as it turns out, we all have more going on under the hood than we think. Millennials seem to have integrated these understandings into their MO. Perhaps they can help us all see beyond labels that are so damaging to our common humanity.

A redefinition of male sexuality along the lines outlined above will provide the gunpowder we need to blow up the Man Box. It is my firm belief that when a man fully integrates his personality to include all aspects of his being—the full range of his thoughts and feelings in a complete way—he becomes a more stable human being, capable of relating to the hearts and minds of his partner and his kids in ways that men defined by the Man Box cannot. Such a man is more desirable as a husband, as a colleague, and as a father. He has more to give and knows how to receive. Nothing less than the happiness and well-being of future generations is at stake here.

I'm optimistic that some version of the scenarios depicted above are emerging with one caveat. While it is tempting to believe that younger generations' instinct for this level of ambiguity might help men make some advances, they are no less caught in a culture that still expects and rewards conformity to existing models of masculinity.[113] On the one hand, millennial and Gen Z males understand that in place of the rigidly defined heterosexual male of Man Box culture, we must now build a new set of masculine identities (plural)—whose profiles are no less strong, tough, vigorous, and virile—as we fiercely protect the right to create a new set of expectations and sexual behaviors that more accurately express the dynamic possibilities for love, romance, connection, and partnership that all men possess. On the other hand, even among "enlightened" younger generations, there are entire tribes of young men following thought leaders who advance the patterns of behavior that are central to our dominance-based culture of masculinity. And many young men are hanging on to the old stereotypes. So, evolving into a fuller range of masculine identities is going to be a long, multi-generational process.

Closing this chapter, I find myself reflecting on the words of Terence: "I am a man. Nothing human is foreign to me."[114] This way of thinking about male sexuality—as a spectrum of impulses—is liberating. The additional awareness of the range of possibilities within you will most certainly deepen the connection that you feel with women, but it may also affect your interactions with men in your orbit. It may come as an awkward surprise that opening oneself up to the full range of desire may unleash a rush of physiological, emotional, psychological, and spiritual responses that seem alien at first. Do not be dismayed. You probably will not have sex with another man, but you may find a new level of bonding with your bro. It will nourish your soul. As men, we experience the awakening of male consciousness when we allow our understanding of ourselves to arise within us and enable its physical and emotional connection to others in love.

GETTING STARTED

At the "Women Teach Men" conference that I attended in July 2018, Esther Perel challenged each man to make a list of the women that they had mistreated in their lives and place a phone call to apologize for their behavior, if they had not already done so. In the following days and weeks, we did.

Using her suggestion as a springboard, I offer the following questions to help you begin to get in better touch with your actual sexual identity.

1. Write up a short, bulleted list of experiences that captures your real sexual identity (not the myths that you tell yourself and your friends).

2. Ask yourself whether there were any partners that you exploited. If the answer is yes, write them a note of apology. You need not send it. But you do need to get in touch with the trauma that you caused and its impact. It may still be lodged somewhere inside of you. As you read and re-read your note, ask yourself where you carry the pain that is attached to your memory of this experience inside your body. Can you feel where it is located? Does it intensify or release as you acknowledge the trauma? If you feel unsettled by this exercise, you may want to talk to a therapist.

3. If you were a victim of coercion or assault, write a letter to the person who violated your boundaries to help them understand how much they hurt you. (Again, you need not send the letter.) Follow the same procedure as in question #2 to identify where the pain is lodged and get in touch with it. Breathe into it. (Once again, if the feelings of anxiety or distress that surface are overwhelming, you may want to seek professional help.)

4. Finally, make a list of the sexual fantasies you have not enacted or the impulses that you have not responded to. Identify one or two that you can safely explore and do so, mentally. Write out what it would feel like to act out your forbidden desires, however significant or insignificant the act may be. You may discover that your inhibitions are misplaced. And be aware that a profound liberation can sometimes occur simply by acknowledging and accepting your own desires without acting on them.

There may be good reasons why you choose not to act. Your desires may not cohere with your true self, or they may cause harm to yourself or others. If you do choose to act on your impulses, please do so wisely, consulting a professional, if necessary. Use your judgment, be safe, and act with due consideration of others.

This exercise or practice of acceptance is designed to expand your enjoyment of the impulses or fantasies that you do respond to. So be bold, be brave. Ask your partner to jump in with you. Role play. Have fun.

CHAPTER 6

PRACTICE STILLNESS

I was a college freshman when Herbert Benson published **The Relaxation Response***, initiating millions to the basic principles of transcendental meditation. A lonely, stressed-out young man 2000 miles away from home, I would go deep within for an hour every day, sometimes two.*

After college I desperately wanted to complete my escape from reality and live in a newly established ashram in Pune, India, but I did not end up going there. The desire to be on a path of purpose and meaning continued to burn deep inside me, however. As I continued my meditation practice without anyone to guide me, strange disassociations occurred. I heard voices. I watched the world from an elevated place. I flew in my dreams. I thought I was losing my mind.

I prayed for these experiences to stop, but they did not. Finally, no longer able to function like a normal person in the real world, I asked for forgiveness for not being able to take the next step into whatever awakening was occurring. I became an advertising exec in New York, then eventually

a husband and father, and I confined the deepening of my spiritual prac-
tice to the Judeo-Christian traditions that I had known since childhood.

Thirty years later, because I would not go to India, India came to me.
A series of strange encounters occurred. After the dust settled, it became
clear that a soul cycle of great consequence had been completed.

Y ou may have noticed that this book is taking us on a journey deeper
and deeper into the male psyche. We started our expedition in search
of healthy masculinity by first exploring the shame that we men attach
to our bodies. We also confirmed the importance of stripping ourselves
to our bare essentials and becoming more vulnerable. In the second
chapter we reclaimed the "yin" (or sacred feminine) within men as our
birthright, a set of capacities that are inherent to our being that rounds
us out as men. We then dove deeper into the male psyche to explore the
many different ways that we can get in touch with and express our emotions. Finally, we went one more level down to acknowledge and own
the full range of sexual impulses that we experience.

In this chapter, we are going to take our investigation of the male
psyche down one more notch to the region where we experience the
substrate of our being that is core, elemental, foundational, the root of
our existence.

POWERING DOWN, REVISITED

Since time immemorial religions and philosophies around the world
have developed systems of thought and practices that attempt to capture
and engage our relationship with the transcendent—that quality of life
that lies beyond our ability to know it. Because we live in an aggressively secular age when all faith traditions are being held to account
and made to atone for their sins, the entire world is engaged in a

massive redefinition of our relationship to the divine. Thankfully, this re-formation seems to be less about differentiation as in ages past, and more about finding common ground.

Nonetheless, despite the chaotic deconstruction and reintegration that is going on, we Americans, at least, remain deists, much like our Founding Fathers. According to Pew Research Center, 9 out of 10 of us still believe in a higher power or purpose, and a majority of us still pray to some omnipotent presence.[115] This is most surprising when you consider the fact that several generations are now "unchurched." It confirms that deep inside of us there is a great hunger or desire for connection, meaning, and purpose.

I also think it affirms that, at our core, we sense the existence of a presence that is somehow connected to that same presence within others as well as the higher power that we bear witness to. The Self.

Our dominant culture of masculinity trains us to believe that we are in charge of our lives, and that independent of our relationships and impact on others, it is within our power to determine whether or not we will succeed. On some level this belief is accurate. We are blessed with free will and the ability to make choices, work hard, and apply our gifts to achieve the specific outcomes that we desire. There are periods in our life when this guiding principle produces the results that we seek. However, our relentless focus on our own individual needs and our mistaken belief that we are the sole determiners of our destiny (despite Malcolm Gladwell's summary of the research to the contrary)[116] eventually catches up with us. Our self-centered, overachieving attack on life falters, and we are left to our own devices to pick up the pieces.

Most of us do "hit a wall" sooner or later. We (or someone we love) experience an unexpected job transition, a personal loss or a catastrophic illness that is not part of our carefully crafted plans. Hopefully, this wipeout occurs early enough in life, so that we are forced to make a shift in our behavior and acknowledge that we are not the masters of the universe that we think we are. My father-in-law was privy to this knowledge. A very wise man that enjoyed a beautiful life as a Fortune 500 CEO and Congressman, he sat on the Boards of IBM, P&G, Citibank, Genentech, B.F. Goodrich, New York Telephone, Owens Corning; and was also a Trustee of the Brookings Institute, among other non-profit organizations. He often observed that the problem with many of the extremely powerful and wealthy members of the financial professions, and other industries where quick money is possible, is that they achieve far too much early on, so that they have the audacity to believe that they were the authors of their own success and are blind to the limitations of their experience and knowledge.

I was not so lucky. I had some early successes, but then hit a wall many times traveling at 200 mph, as I tried to provide for my young family. Along the way, I had to navigate a series of major, unexpected setbacks. Picking up the pieces is very familiar territory for me.

I'm either a slow learner, or the Universe is trying to drive a lesson into my soul so that I never forget it. Over and over again, I discovered (and rediscovered) that in these moments of creative destruction, a great reckoning occurs. We are forced to do some soul searching, and we often spend an enormous amount of time looking for the whys and where-fores of our experiences. (I once spent two years recording every bit of information about my past and present in order to determine whether there were any data points that should shape how I should move for-ward as a new man into the future.)

THE NEED TO SURRENDER

Having been through so many unplanned transitions, I have discovered that the best way to survive is counterintuitive. We must surrender to it. Time and again, when I tried to muscle my way through and forge a new path, mobilizing networks at a breakneck speed that left me in a state of high anxiety and physical exhaustion, I learned that our lives unfold with new direction and grace at their own pace. We do not enter a new, sustainable chapter until we have done the inner work that we need to do to advance the life lessons that we came to learn. (Otherwise, we set ourselves up to repeat our mistakes.) That said, I am *not* advocating sitting on your ass while your world is falling apart. Responding to your survival instinct and reflexively throwing yourself at creating a solution is essential. But life is a dance. We are partners in the mystery, and we need to learn how to follow someone else's lead. This is especially hard for men.

Through trial and error, I have learned that it is essential to develop a contemplative practice—in my case several—to navigate these life-changing transitions. Otherwise, at least in Western societies, we tend to medicate our traumas as a solution. The earlier we begin to develop our skill at exploring our inner landscape the better, as the space that opens up deepens and expands over time, making us increasingly able to weather the storm with some equanimity and patience.

To be clear, I am not recommending meditation apps or mindfulness techniques that are currently all the rage for this purpose. These can be helpful in the zig and zag of our day-to-day challenges, reducing stress, increasing mental alertness, enhancing energy, boosting productivity and performance, and firing up your sex life (as you will read at the end of this chapter). However, they can sometimes encourage us to focus on ego-driven personal, psychological, or physiological outcomes, distracting us from the most important lesson that we need to learn during these times, which is how to be open and receptive to the larger picture that is developing in the depths within us. We need to learn to surrender to what is trying to emerge anew.

Mindfulness apps can sometimes lead us to the contemplative practices that we need. They can instill a discipline that helps develop some of the inward-facing perspectives that we need to thrive and help others do the same. But a real contemplative practice of some depth and scope is life altering—not a stress reduction routine or output enhancer—that completely rewires our inner landscape. Some practices don't require huge amounts of time. Others do. What is most important is that time is spent in silence, solitude, and inner stillness, so that the mind shuts down, our sense of time disappears, and our inner adaptive capacities can do their work unimpeded by distractions. We need to learn how to get into a dead space, the Zone,[117] the place where you experience a state of flow, and stay there.

Cultivating this inner space takes commitment and dedication. It requires self-discipline. It leverages the "make-shit-happen" yang of your being. But it also requires an ability to release our need to be in charge or control, and trust the inner process that unfolds when we take off our mental armor. (Yes, that's why we discussed getting naked in the first chapter.)

Curiously, like the gift of our emotions, we are born with the capacity to do this work. It is the natural state of our minds when we are at rest, when we are in the Zone.

You may ask why. Why is it important to develop this gift, especially if we are born with it and it's our natural state? The answer is that we live in the Age of Reason. From our very early childhood we are conditioned to use our rational minds to "overcome" our base instincts, to "manage" our emotions, to solve problems, to interpret our experience. We are trained to believe that the mind can discover the answers we seek and create the success we crave. We spend vast amounts of money and time educating ourselves to enhance our reasoning capacities to be able to analyze and respond to the people and life events that we encounter. Some parents will spend over $500k educating their children to give them a leg up, increasing the probability of their financial success, since there is a high correlation between educational achievement and income.[118] The problem is that when the mind runs the show, when we use *only* our rational capacities to intermediate and direct our understanding of our life experience, we cut ourselves off from a vast array of inner resources that are important to our success in life. Our emotions.

Our gifts for forming relationships. Our intuition. Our creativity. Our sixth sense. Our peripheral vision. And most significantly, our ability to acknowledge and allow a higher power in our life to guide us.

Men, conditioned as we are to detach from our emotions, to be self-reliant and live independent of others, are especially prone to believing that the rational mind should govern our behavior. (Remember the Richard Rohr quote at the end of Chapter 2 on the sacred feminine?) The direct result of our insistence that the left brain is in charge of our being is that we are often at a loss as to how to respond when the world does not operate in the way that we predicted, when there is no logical connection between our input and the outputs that occur, when the sequencing of events that we have so carefully constructed goes awry. Eventually we learn the limitations of our rational minds and that we are not in control.

It is therefore essential that we develop our inner adaptive capacities, the set of skills that allow our lives to unfold without our direct intervention; that we learn to listen carefully to the movements of our inner presence and its appearance in those around us; and that we acquire an ability to enter into the void, sit in awe, and dance with delight as our lives unfold against the infinite blank, flat screen of the eternal present.

MINDFULNESS VS. MEDITATION

A long list of men and women credit their meditation practice as providing the engine for their professional success. They note its ability to help them maintain a high level of functioning and increase the clarity, focus and innovation in their thinking, while also reducing stress, boosting their immune system, and improving sleep. The roll call of luminaries who acknowledge contemplation as giving them an edge runs the gamut from business billionaires to professional athletes and Hollywood celebrities: Jeff Weiner (LinkedIn), Ray Dalio (Bridgewater Associates),

Bob Stiller (Green Mountain Coffee), Steve Jobs (Apple), Melinda Gates (Microsoft), Bill Ford (Ford Motor Company), Bob Shapiro (Monsanto), Marc Benioff (Salesforce), Oprah Winfrey, Arianna Huffington, Paul McCartney, Ringo Starr, Lady Gaga, Hugh Jackman, Russell Simmons, Katy Perry, Madonna, LeBron James, Derek Jeter, Michael Jordan, Carli Lloyd, Serena Williams and the late Kobe Bryant, to name a few.

In offering this list I do not want to create the impression that the primary benefits of meditation are performance enhancement. Affirming contemplative practices' ability to optimize our output only reinforces our attachment to one of the mantras of masculinity, one whose influence on our thinking we need to reduce in our culture. We are not what we produce, despite the fact that our society tends to see both men and women in that way. (We will discuss this at length in Chapters 7 and 8, so let's put a pin in that conversation here.)

Every religion in the world has a different method or set of practices for suspending or keeping the rational mind busy so that our inner capacities can develop. And thankfully, the planet is filled with individuals who understand that our greatest accomplishments arise from the depths within guided by a self-organizing principle.

I should note here that I have no interest in entering a debate about which system of thought is best able to guide deepening understanding. As a lifelong practitioner in several systems, I can attest that they all work. There are many options here, so try a few, pick one, and stick with it. Too many men are wasting their time dabbling in multiple systems, hedging their bets, diversifying their portfolios. These practices are not slot machines. Yes, there are a few moments when you hit the jackpot, but that is beyond your control. It's better to think about these practices as inner ellipticals, equipping you with the cardio conditioning you need for a healthy and long inner life. And because there are no quick fixes, it's best to choose a path—it generally chooses you—and stick with it, sooner rather than later, because this is an essential piece of the journey of rebuilding our identities from the inside out as men.

I also strongly encourage you to work with an accredited, trained spiritual advisor (or within a contemplative group) that will hold you accountable when your mind and ego take over and want to run the show. Working with others will put some rigor into your practice and give you a support team that helps fend off the tendency to treat meditation as either a gateway drug that will help you get what your ego wants (as many followers of "The Law of Attraction" believe), or an escape hatch from your current travails, blissing out. It will force you to dig deep and be patient, which is when you will begin to see a shift occur.

I want to give you an illustration of how this process works and the impact it can have by sharing the story of a soul brother, Joel Serino. I sometimes wonder whether we are twins separated at birth, except for our twenty-two-year age difference. His journey is a beautiful example of how stillness creates the space out of which new things emerge.

Joel had a near death experience at age 14 that left him with a chronic spleen condition. I'll let him tell his own life story in his own words from here.

"I almost became a Navy Seal. I actually got into the program but broke my ankle and the pain refused to go away even after the ankle healed. It was very weird.

"Then I almost went to seminary—I wanted to study religion—but decided to go to art school instead. We had Lily when I was 25. When we moved to Nashville, I took a job working with a cell phone company that provides insurance for all the cell companies in the world. We had lots of teams in India and the company decided to relocate some to the US, which I became very involved in, as I directly reported into the number two person of the company. That's when I fell in love with Indian culture, yoga, methods to attain a better sense of reality.

"By age 27, the alchemical process had begun. I was at the company, causing a bit of trouble, as you might expect. At the same time, I was working with a 'spiritual sherpa,' you know, a psychologist/therapist who was also a chiropractor that spent eleven years in Nepal and became a

Buddhist. He suggested that I get off the grid. He said, 'I know that you think you have this under control, but you don't.'

"So I followed his advice, and went off the grid, by myself for three weeks. It totally blew me away. I came back with a huge experience that completely changed my life, grounded my life. I healed my body through ayurvedic science when I was told by Western medicine that I would have to live with my spleen illness for the rest of my life. And I was connecting with the divine in ways that I had never before.

"I still use this experience to this day. It got me on track. I took ownership for my own stuff. Not accepting what is on the surface, I keep going deeper. My spiritual sherpa saw what was coming and prepared me to do that.

"And it created a pattern that is still with me to this day. Moments of stillness and silence that almost always starts with a quest for truth. Yeah, I think that's been the constant through it all, the desire to know the truth about everything.

"I'm still working on a lot of stuff. I have repressed a lot of anger, so sometimes my life is an emotional joy ride. One of the things that is curious about my life is that I was being guided by deeply empathetic, feminine archetypes at the company molding me into something less abrasive and straight edged. They were teaching me why to be quiet, and that led to me to the understanding that contemplation is actually the space where the integration of change occurs, in daily practice, daily life."

Joel has gone on to launch a string of tech companies focused on social and environmental impact.

MEDITATION AND MOVEMENT

Contrary to popular perception that contemplative work is *always* about sitting on your butt for hours on end while emptying your mind, it is also true that dance and other forms of movement can put us into a meditative space. Stilling the mind is the main objective, and many contemplative practices do not require that you remain inert, which is good news for restless men and women like me. It is okay to have a couple of practices in motion simultaneously, if your schedule permits, so that if one well becomes dry and dusty, not bringing you to life for the moment, another can reanimate your core. (That said, nota bene, it's important to focus on digging ONE very deep well, not fifteen shallow ones.)[119]

A contemplative, "on-the-go" practice that speaks deeply to a lot of men is walking. For ages, faith traditions around the world encourage pilgrimages, meditative walks, and labyrinths as a way of engaging the body and stilling the mind as an individual is going through a life transition. Neuroscience is confirming that walking or hiking may fire up the synapses in much the same way that seated, stationary meditation practices do, while also delivering a host of physical, mental, and emotional benefits. Shane O'Mara's excellent, easy-to-read book, *In Praise of Walking*, offers an in-depth discussion of the neuroscientific research on perambulation, including the ways in which mindlessly meandering without an objective frees the mind to be creative, realigning old patterns into new shapes and forms, creating innovative solutions that seemingly arise out of nowhere . . .[120]

Many other wonderful practices teach individuals how to focus their attention and still the mind while engaged in some form of movement. Unfortunately, these practices often tend to encourage individuals to power up instead of power down, reinforcing our mistaken belief that we are masters of our own destiny.

For example, an ability to move with deep inner perception while letting go of thoughts is prized by many martial arts traditions across all societies. Present not only in Eastern traditions, but in the West as well, these practices tend to reinforce the perception among men (and increasingly women) that the body-mind-heart connection is a combat weapon, reinforcing the flashpoints that Man Box culture has created about the male body, more specifically the penis, and the well-justified criticisms of the #MeToo Movement. Indeed, the Russian military trains its recruits in Systema, which utilizes breathing techniques derived from Hesychasm, an Eastern Orthodox mystical tradition that uses breath and prayer to enable control of physical faculties and mental concentration. All too often Chinese, Japanese, Korean, and Southeast Asian martial arts programs in the West train men and women to achieve a similar mindset or level of fitness as well, teaching individuals to be fierce warriors in life without conditioning the contemplative components into the practice. While there is nothing wrong with these training regimens—centuries of men have benefited from their self-discipline—they can be a barrier instead of an aid in getting across the gaping void that sometimes opens up, encouraging us to persevere and try to force the Universe to do our will, when what is required is an ability to let go. So, proceed with a humble spirit knowing that your goal is something more than self-mastery and self-aggrandizement.

There are many other benefits to learning how to power down that are important to our everyday lives. The inner qualities that stillness nurtures are critical to developing our relational skills, enabling us to listen with curiosity and suspend judgment, instead of immediately react and "jump to concussions," as a beloved mentor of mine used to say.[121] As we learned in Chapters 2 and 3, connection and community are key to our physical health and emotional well-being, as well as our overall success in life, another reason to look within as we continue our journey.

I want to comment on another situation that you may find yourself in at some point for which there is no remedy except contemplative practice. In addition to enduring unplanned job transitions, catastrophic illness, and the loss of a loved one, there are times in life when we are put on the bench for no explainable reason. It just happens. No matter what we do to make a shift, nothing happens. Since the duration of these periods is not known at the time, you can go mad waiting, and waiting, for the Universe to do its thing. This can be an extremely challenging experience. You must throw yourself at every opportunity in the hopes that it might be the next big chapter of your life even as you are sitting still inside, biding your time, watching for the leviathan of your inner depths to surface and be revealed.[122] A contemplative practice (and perhaps therapy) is essential during these times. There simply is no other way to get through it. Go believing!

ON DISCERNMENT AND THE EMERGENCE OF SOMETHING NEW

The good news is that centuries of wisdom experience from all around the globe confirm that when we learn to listen to our inner voice and that of others without anticipating outcomes, the results are astonishing. Sometimes groups of people are moved to tackle extraordinary tasks. (In the lingo of spiritual pros, this practice of listening to the inner voice at both the individual and communal level is called "discernment.") It is important to be patient and not pre-game or direct the process, because it can be manipulated to encourage disastrous, damaging outcomes. Careful attention should be given to testing and verifying the ideas that arise, as you would in building any enterprise. That said, discernment, moving with the Spirit, works.

One of my favorite examples of how the Universe organizes at the community level if we allow it to do so was relayed to me by a great friend, Courtney Cowart. In her book, *An American Awakening: From Ground Zero to Katrina | The People We Are Free to Be*, she tells a harrowing tale of her own near-death experience on 9/11 when she was saved by a building contractor who whisked her off the street into an air-conditioned trailer as a dust cloud blew through Lower Manhattan. Eager to be of service in the aftermath, she volunteered at St. Paul's, "The Little Chapel that Stood." Her book describes in vivid detail the "self-organizing system that . . . materialized [that] was stunning in its scope and effectiveness." Her verbatim accounts from relief workers and volunteers provide significant supporting evidence that when we step back from thinking that we need to direct the show, "diverse self-organizing mobilization" occurs on a scale that we very rarely witness.[123] As if that were not enough to prove the point, she offers a second example of this principle in the second half of her book which outlines the way relief efforts unfolded after Katrina in exactly the same manner.

She asserts that leaders in a time of crisis must learn to operate with a level of openness and trust. This includes allowing people to take ideas and run, letting them rise and fall on their own merits, and being okay with failure. Enabling a self-organizing system to mobilize people into action ultimately produces triumphs, along with misfires, that sometimes hit the national headlines. It also engages and builds a community of practice that is more connected, experienced, and alive on the other side of disaster.[124]

She admits that there is some "tension" in adopting this leadership style, as it is often at odds with the structure and discipline that is necessary to survive in these situations, and she has a high respect for individuals who maintain order. But she insists that a leadership group must be "creative and adaptive, as well as directive, at the same time, because you cannot control all the grassroots responses that occur," and the situations that arise. In the end, "you need someone who is a risk-taker with a big vision working with someone who can impose structure. That's why it's a team sport. You have to go into it with a deep collaborative heart. The scale of response is always way beyond what one individual or group can execute."[125]

Her observations should make us pause. In a world that tends toward command-and-control decision-making, with endless major and minor power plays as a result, she is calling for a new form of leadership, whose qualities are strikingly similar to the new forms of masculinity that are emerging—open, heart-centered, collaborative, and relational.

Unfortunately, these capacities are still in short supply at a time when we need them the most.[126]

As a humorous aside I should make note here that Courtney also reports that many of the men "in charge" of relief efforts at 9/11 and Katrina did not believe that letting things unfold as the Spirit moved was an adequate response to the situation. They demanded a much more structured approach, with plans, org charts, flowcharts, and tables detailing how relief efforts were being managed. Although the documents were helpful in capturing the scope of the need in a moment in time, they were obsolete within minutes. As the need for a multi-faceted emergency response continued to evolve, the carefully thought through plans were often insufficient to the demands that arose, which required many imaginative, creative, and spontaneous responses.[127] Much research on managing VUCA (volatility, uncertainty, complexity, and ambiguity) in industry and areas of business where uncertainty and constant change is the norm has been conducted since these times.[128] To that literature I would add my own point of view drawn from personal experience that we need to trust the wisdom of the Universe in these situations.

Lest you think that outcomes driven by a higher power are unique to the spiritual world, any number of writers, artists, inventors, and entrepreneurs have attested that their ideas, their work seemingly arises out of nowhere, as if their body-mind-souls were merely a portal or door enabling a creation to come through. For excellent discussion of this phenomenon, watch Elizabeth Gilbert's TED talk[129] or consider Einstein's philosophy of the importance of doing nothing as a way to generate new ideas (a philosophy that as a society we must seriously take to heart).[130]

It's ironic that the ways things seem to work is that our ability to produce our greatest output occurs when we don't pretend that we are in charge of doing so. Yes, we have some personal agency in the process, but it appears that we are just a partner in the dance.

Deepening our inner capacities is also an essential task in developing our ability to address the social issues of our day. The Rev. Dr. Martin Luther King Jr. spells out the necessity of prayer and looking within before taking non-violent action in his eloquent "Letter from a Birmingham Jail" (1963):

> In any nonviolent campaign there are four basic steps:
> collection of the facts to determine whether injustices are alive,
> negotiation, self-purification, and direct action. . . . We were
> not unmindful of the difficulties involved. So we decided to go
> through a process of self-purification.

In a world that is so completely polarized, Dr. King's words should make us stop.

As I reflect on the urgent need to address the dominance-based culture of masculinity that is wreaking havoc on the world, I have often wondered whether the appearance of COVID was divinely timed to arrive shortly after the #MeToo Movement exploded on the scene, so that the universe could deliver a powerful one-two punch, essentially forcing men to rethink our professional and personal lives. As the days turned into weeks in our national solitary confinement, the lessons of corona began to emerge.

Without our busy, distracted schedules, we experienced a deep hunger for authentic connection that was always present beneath the surface of things. We began to realize how interdependent we are. We encountered the inequities that are inherent in our social and economic systems, confronting the reality that our hyper-competitive paradigms are flawed, and our "Winners and Losers" race is handicapped.

More than anything, we learned that we are not in control.

These were tough lessons for everyone, but they were especially troubling for men. They called into question the beliefs around which we organize our daily lives. We have been taught from a very early age that if we are strong, independent, emotionally detached, aggressive, and energetic, we will ultimately prevail. And because we achieve some success with these behaviors, we are afraid to break their overwhelming influence over us.

It's ironic that it wasn't until the world threw us a major curveball that we were forced to acknowledge the flaws in our own assumptions, our weakness, our vulnerability, our inherent need to be in healthy relationships, our deep-seated desire to heal our own pain and that of others. Our secret wish to rediscover the joy and beauty of simply being alive.

We were afraid for our own lives, and for the well-being and financial security of our loved ones. Men are not emotionally equipped to deal with personal failure, and the loss of personal agency. There is no assurance that things will ever return to normal. And perhaps, they should not.

I am increasingly convinced that our current suffering will continue until men learn how to reframe our MO, our definitions of happiness and success at work and at home, and the methods by which we pursue them, becoming more invested in lifting people up instead of putting them down in order to thrive.[131]

By now the necessity of developing a contemplative practice to undo the way in which our culture trains us to prize rationality over other aspects of our personality should be self-evident, *especially* for men. Not only are we conditioned to aggressively pursue our objectives in the mistaken belief that we are engaged in a zero-sum game of life, we are also encouraged to express only two emotions, rage and lust, as Mark Greene so often observes.[132] All the more reason to develop a practice that enables us to use other forms of engagement and response in meeting the challenges we encounter. Dr. King's approach to resolving conflict and addressing social injustice is the perfect antidote to the combative, hyper-aggressive conditioning of Man Box culture.

Through the ages, the stories of the men and women who are masters of a contemplative practice that guides their life have become legends.

Their exploits sometimes defy reason, and are retold for generations, taking on mythic status. Frankly, I wonder whether these stories do us a disservice at times, as they can make us disbelieve our own power to have similar experiences as well. The truth is that ordinary people, everyday mystics, have experienced moments of grace and ease thanks to something arising from their inner depths. You probably have, too.

I would be remiss if I did not share my father-in-law's entire story, including the events of his life as a contemplative. Despite his amazing success as a CEO (whose vision is seldom given the credit it is due—his company invested heavily in fiber optics for seventeen years long before the use case had emerged), Amory Houghton Jr. was at heart a humanitarian—a humble, self-effacing man with a gift for listening to others, lifting them up. Not content to hang up his cleats upon retirement, he spent a year in deep discernment, consulting spiritual advisors in his beloved Episcopal Church. After much prayer and thought, he decided that he wanted to spend the next chapter of his life in *service* to others and that he would become a missionary in Malawi. Many thought he had lost his mind.

Then, over the Memorial Day weekend, the phone rang. We were on the Cape with my wife's parents, so I picked up the receiver on the rotary dial phone and tried to respond to a local reporter who wanted to know whether my father-in-law was running. Perplexed by such a strange question, I explained that my father-in-law was a golfer, not a runner, and that he was out on the course at Kittansett at the moment. After some back and forth to clarify his question, the reporter informed me that Senator D'Amato had commented in a press conference that he thought "Amo Houghton was the best person to run for Stan Lundine's seat." (Congressman Lundine had declined to seek reelection because he was running alongside Mario Cuomo for Lieutenant Governor.) Amo "ran" and won in a landslide with 87% of the vote, *serving* the constituents of his beloved Upstate New York district for 18 years, exactly as he had desired after his discernment process.

My purpose in telling this story is to underscore how the Spirit works at the individual level. You do your inner work, embrace an intention to move with the Spirit, act to the best of your ability on the findings of your discernment (in his case renting a house in Malawi), and then you learn what the plan is. It may not be what you think. It may be better.

If you would like to live a life of wonder, joy, and deep satisfaction, it is vitally important to begin early to develop your contemplative muscles, your inner adaptive capacities to remain open and receptive, so that your life can unfold with the imprint that is written into your soul's DNA. Exploring the spiritual aspect of your being requires a giant leap of faith in this secular age, but I assure you that plunging into this adventure will be the trip of a lifetime.

Go for it and see where the Spirit leads you.

GETTING STARTED

We live in a universe where increasingly people are using mindfulness apps for anxiety, stress reduction, attention issues, and sleep. So, you may think that you already have the tools you need to create the stillness within that you require to be able to empty out, opening up the inner space from which new things can emerge. Having practiced transcendental meditation and powerful forms of prayer for over forty years, I thought I was well-equipped, too.

Turning fifty, however, I discovered that my contemplative work was way too much in my head. My daily meditations had become dry, stale, and brittle. An extraordinarily gifted young contemplative, Matthew Wright, who is also an Episcopal priest and Sufi practitioner, showed me how to move my practice lower to my heart center, which grounded me and put me in touch with my body as a component of my meditation discipline.

Around the same time, I began to practice yoga. Its focus on breath and developing an awareness of how energy moves through the body spoke deeply to me.

When this fundamental shift in my routines was in place, I stumbled upon two practices for cis men that I highly recommend. (I suspect that they appeared because I was more open to them, as I became more comfortable in my body.) Both practices help men harness our sexual energy to maintain and increase our vitality as we age. I enjoy exploring both practices daily, taking advantage of the last of the many erections that I still have every night.

One practice comes to us from the Tao tradition and has been introduced to Western men by Mantak Chia.[133] It trains guys how to refrain from ejaculation as we reach orgasm so that the energy that arises can be moved up the body, into the head, and back down into the pelvis (following the Microcosmic Orbit which is indeed cosmic).[134] It also has the additional benefit of enabling men to make love for a longer period of time. (Many Silicon Valley executives have proven this claim be true, as they all revealed on our retreat in Ojai.)[135] Those who are truly masters of the method experience multiple orgasms without ejaculation.[136]

The other is an esoteric practice that I learned from my German friend a yoga instructor who was taught how to use his breath to move energy up through the body from his perineum (root chakra) to his third eye (sixth chakra) and crown (seventh chakra), while bringing himself to a heightened state of arousal. I find this practice particularly invigorating as it oxygenates the blood, and also intensifies and channels my sexual energy so that it animates my entire body. It really revs me up for the day. Better than coffee.

There are many online resources that can help you master this meditation technique as well. Unfortunately, they focus on this practice's gift for enhancing sexual performance. If you decide to engage in this discipline, I recommend that you challenge yourself to refrain from ejaculation and direct your attention to the breath work and the way in which it enables you to move energy throughout your body and expand your consciousness.

When these exercises are combined with my morning meditation, I enter into a significantly expanded space within that is both alive and still at the same time. I feel more grounded, present, and connected in my body and to others.

The great thing about these contemplative practices is that they can be self-taught and are available to all men, regardless of what your personal circumstances may be. You have everything you need to become a master of these meditation techniques (and an incentive to do so as you respond to your biological impulses). It's a win-win situation that you may find will become a cornerstone of your daily routines.

Try them out for yourself. You won't regret it.

CHAPTER 7

IMPOSE RETREAT

I found the house where we were gathering for a meditation retreat with some difficulty, as it sits high in the headlands above a community of closely packed houses with breath-taking views of the Pacific. The waves crashed miles below among the rocky crags that guarded the sequestered beaches that lined the bay. Not another sound could be heard.

I parked among the gigantic conifers along the driveway that stretched past a garden. Buddhas were placed at focal points among long exotic grasses. A ceramic red, pink, black, and white totem pole stood in their midst. Two elevated metal lawn chairs on spring-like ladders stood sentry, from which I guessed many a soul had attempted to catapult onto a higher plane. Arrows jutted out of the top of the chairs confirming blast off, a cosmic union.

I was early and entered the house in silence, taking off my shoes as a sign requested. Once inside, I walked through a study where a Chinese chair with ornately carved dragons on its arm rests sat in front of a desk.

On either side were chairs with shirtless, hunky cowboys depicted on their pillows, contemplating their inner silence. Eventually, I found my way to the great room where others would gather for meditation. A twelve-foot, red wooden dragon was suspended above a huge stone fireplace on the far side of the room. I sat at the back by a cracked window where I could feel the wind and hear the pounding surf below.

We meditated for ninety minutes, beginning at 9:30 AM. I was overcome by a sense of stillness that I had never known before. My mind darted around in the beginning, then went blank.

Devaji, our teacher, joined us, spoke for fifteen minutes, then answered some questions. The same process was repeated in the evening, beginning at 5:30.

I can't remember what Devaji said on either day, but what was important was that I was off the grid. The crashing waves, the gentle breeze, the occasional motorcycle provided enough mental distraction for me to go deeper and deeper within. It was so still. I was surprised at how quickly our sessions were over.

In between meditations and teachings, I hiked Sobranes Canyon and Point Lobos for hours, went for a daily run, soaked up the salt air and sun, and read by the fire in the evening. Immersed in silence, the tightly coiled spring of my hard-charging male identity unwound, revealing a gentler man at its core.

After the first day, I slept soundly. I awakened from a dream in which my cell phone was busted because one of its small parts was missing. The dream was so vivid that when I woke up I checked my phone. It was fine. I laughed. Clearly, the dream transmitted a couple of messages. One was that I needed to really disconnect on the retreat but wasn't doing so. And the dream was also telling me that someone or something was trying to get through to me but couldn't because I was missing a key piece. I had all the basic equipment that I needed in order to connect with the divine but was missing one small but essential part. Later on during that retreat, that small part or connection was plugged in and it blew my mind. In essence, I had to disconnect in order to connect. So the dream was both an accurate depiction of my current state at the time, and presaged what was about to happen.

THE MYTH OF PRODUCTIVITY

Another key tenet of the Man Box is that men are output machines. I've often wondered whether some of our full-frontal attack on life may be hard-wired, as our bodies are biologically engineered to pump it out, take a brief break, and go at it again. So, some of our modus operandi may be in our wiring as men. I believe that most of our hyper-aggressive, hyper-competitive behavior, however, arises from our culture of masculinity that prizes and rewards these qualities in men, and more recently in women as well. The damage that we do to ourselves by not taking breaks and pacing ourselves better is enormous, as study after study increasingly confirms that our around-the-clock work habits are truly killing us.[137]

We sometimes think that our attack on life is something new, a by-product of living in a digital age. There are, however, many longstanding forces underlying our workaholic culture that are increasingly out of control around the planet. They are rampant especially here in America, as we export our culture around the globe. The values and beliefs that shape and drive our focus on work and material success as a benchmark of overall success in life is persistent and powerful. Our Protestant work ethic and the scarcity/land of opportunity mindset passed along to us by our immigrant ancestors who founded this country. The enormous economic advances that have been made by individuals generation after generation (though not by all). Our obsession with the vast quantification and accumulation of things.[138] The possibility of crafting a decent standard of living limited only by our imaginations and the energy level that we possess. The deification of our give-it-all-you-got mindset (which has led to the demonization and dismissal of those who struggle to earn a living, even when inequality of access or a reversal of fortune occurs).

Indeed, our work-focused culture so dominates the global knowledge economy that it literally has no boundaries thanks to the Internet, personal computers, cell phones, and a host of technological advances. We all lament how difficult it is to unplug and disconnect from work even as we check our texts, voice mail, and email messages over the weekend out of fear, anxiety, or addiction.

There is another cultural force for men operating here, however, that specifically drives men's behavior and the work habits of women competing in a man's world. A core component of our Man Box culture is the notion that "you are what you produce." This mindset, when coupled with the expectation that men be great providers, puts enormous pressure on both men and women. We know that where we sit in the hierarchy of men (and our access to networks where our families might thrive) is determined first and foremost by our productivity, output, and financial success; and second, by the power and prestige that accrues to our identity by virtue of our work.

It doesn't take a genius to figure out that this attack on life is problematic. As the "providers and protectors" of our families (at least in our own minds),[139] men have often convinced themselves that their work is so vitally important to the family unit that we have to sacrifice our relationships, our health, and our need for play on the altar of financial stability.

In a state of awe as a young man, I distinctly remember watching my father and his peers commit every waking minute to this single objective. I am also grateful to every individual who has been a partner or a member of my team—male or female—whose work ethic is strong. The valor of those who apply themselves with so much dedication and discipline, whatever their station in life, is worthy of our admiration. Work can give our lives meaning and purpose, connect us to others, and expand our horizons. It is our call as human beings to care for a universe that requires us as its creative partners.

I am hesitant to criticize our tendency to overwork too sharply, as I have many, many times been guilty of working day and night on projects that I love and truly believe in. Such work can be energizing, restorative.

However, we also know that a single-minded devotion to work has a host of negative downstream consequences, particularly in a culture whose pecking order, despite our democratic principles, is determined by the spoils and the correspondent status that we are able to generate by applying ourselves. Our work-first mindset can lead to an unhealthy obsession with wealth, celebrity, and power. This obsession can also lead to burnout, fractured relationships, isolation, infrequent sex, and addiction to alcohol and various controlled substances to fill in our hollowed-out lives.

As we enter into our older years, we cease to exist when we are no longer working or when we are temporarily out of work in a society that defines you by what you do and encourages us to organize our social networks around work. No one is there for you when you are unemployed, as you are no longer of use to anyone professionally. For men whose networks are primarily work-oriented, this is especially a problem. Is it any wonder that we are experiencing an epidemic of suicide among younger men getting started in life who have yet to establish their professional networks and older men as they retire into oblivion?[140]

We need another approach, a new mindset, a different way moving headlong through life. A mindset that can help us avoid the downside of our "give it all you got" culture and the negative impacts that can occur at work, at home, in the gym, even when things are going well and we're in "the Zone." This book proposes an alternative.

This cultural phenomenon is not unique to American men, or these times, though its current virulent form is very much an American export. A band of rebels in the first century BCE tried to turn the tide against this mindset, asserting that human beings are not "justified" by their work but by grace.[141] Two thousand years later in a culture that traces its roots to this rebel group and prides itself on its ability to embrace and embody new ideas, the Latin dictum *Laboribus Iudicamur* ("We are judged by our deeds") are the words around which many of us still organize our lives. (It also happens to be the motto of the boys' school that our sons attended.)[142] Its power over us has created a culture that worships heroes—political figures, actors, athletes—and narrows our view of what constitutes success in life.

OUR QUIXOTIC ATTEMPTS TO ACHIEVE WORK-LIFE BALANCE

So, what does a more balanced approach to life look like? Let's examine how we take a break from the action now, in order to figure out what's missing.

Our typical reflex after a day, a week, a month of "leaving it on the field" is to chill out. This is the right instinct but in our frenetic pace of life, we typically engage in mind-numbing activities when we get home from work—quick fixes that stimulate (or simulate) the release of dopamine, endorphins, or oxytocin—like watching sports, surfing the Internet, binge-watching films or a TV series, strolling through YouTube videos, having a few drinks, looking at porn, masturbating. Cheap thrills that take the edge off and reduce some tension. Often alone, we take care of our immediate needs to hide our . . . exhaustion, and shame. It's easy and only a click away. It prevents us from transferring our anger and frustration onto others. A little bit of this stress release behavior is probably healthy and a good thing. We need to dump the tensions that we often carry home from work and enjoy the temporary sense of restoration that occurs, a reward for a long day of putting ourselves out on the field of sometimes brutal, depleting play.

On the other hand, we are now learning that our digital media habits, and some of our other sketchy behaviors, when conducted in excess, may be causing as much harm as good. In particular, porn and mind-lessly scanning through videos on social media can encourage unhealthy perceptions regarding our bodies and how they perform. In addition, the social isolation that occurs when we pursue these activities in the dark corners of our homes can exacerbate our sense of loneliness and impact our physical and emotional well-being.

Fortunately, there are other day-to-day options. It doesn't take much creativity to learn how to unplug and do something more worthwhile with our time. Things that get us up on our feet and moving or give us a mental break from the torrent of non-stop emails from work are a good start. We can exercise with a buddy or a trainer, go out for drinks with colleagues after work, search for connection with friends and intimacy with lovers, or participate in community service. This mixes things up and relieves some of the tedium of our work routines. But sometimes we go at these activities so hard that they become burdensome, instead of energizing, achieving the opposite of our aims. And, unfortunately, even these strategies are not the entire answer to the problem that we are trying to solve. They provide balance in our lives, but we still sense that something is missing. We crave rest, an extended period of relaxation and restoration.

In search of a reset and reconnect with family and friends, when we can afford it, we often go on vacation. I should probably note here that this was not often the case for many Americans, except for the leisure classes, in prior generations. Growing up in a farming community in Ridgeville Corners, Ohio (population 300), I was well aware that it was virtually impossible to ever take a break. I watched my dad transfer and apply that mindset to his work as a teacher, coach, administrator, college professor (and bus driver) in education in "Smallville," OH and the Hill Country of Texas, then in his second career as a financial manager and civic leader in suburban Houston. As a child I heard stories of guys who *never* went on vacation for years told with great pride. I also watched the women in my life—my mom, aunts, grandmothers—work themselves into a state of exhaustion, never getting a break from the action, even when they came home from the classroom, the store, or the office. All were cited as examples of selfless dedication to family and the community. And all too often I watched the pillars of strength in my parents' generation suddenly drop dead of a heart attack. My dad had one at age 30. (I remember because I was age eight at the time. Thankfully, he survived.)

The problem with vacations, as we all well know, is that they, too, are a temporary fix. We relax and unwind, if we are not packing too much in, but we return to the same rat race and routines that depleted us in the first place. Thinking that shorter, regular escapes might be the answer, men who can afford it schedule weekend circuit breakers: retreating to a remote second home or cabin; ski trips, fishing trips, hunting trips; surfing, kayaking, sailing, hiking; walking in the woods or along a beach nearby. These weekend jaunts can be therapeutic and restorative. They can also become testosterone-fueled marathons devoted to excessive consumption of food, alcohol, sex, and drugs. They seldom alter the patterns of behavior that have gotten us into trouble, because many of us take our hard-charging mindset with us. Indeed, these weekend breaks often become extensions of our deeply ingrained patterns, brief refractory periods, if we are able to refrain from being active for a bit, as we slow down and recharge. They still remain biochemical reboots so that we can go at it hard again.

Recently, some men have taken up the practice of going to wellness spas with a spouse or partner, increasingly with less teasing from their buddies for doing so. Who doesn't like a massage? Unfortunately, again, the same dynamics apply here. We only temporarily exit our workaholic mindset and quickly return to our default mode, resuming our bad habits unless some serious behavioral modification program accompanies the experience. The problem with weekend breaks, vacations and spas is that they don't permanently rewire our operating systems. They also aren't affordable by all.

THE POWER OF RETREATS TO RESET THE BODY, MIND, AND SOUL

So, what is the solution? I would submit that what men, like women, need to do is give themselves permission to go on retreat at regular intervals. Indeed, we should force ourselves to do so.

I really didn't fully understand the difference between a vacation or weekend escape and a real retreat until I accidentally attended one in my early 50s. My sister convinced me to go to a workshop on grief with her at Holy Cross Monastery on the Hudson River in West Park, NY, and then bailed on me when she got hit by a dump truck. (It's a long story that I will tell you sometime.) In a brace and unable to fly in from Oklahoma City, she insisted that I attend without her. When a series of events occurred that left me with no choice but to show up, I went, prepared for the worst. It made no sense for me to be there. I'm not the kind of guy who would ever bare his soul to strangers, or at least I wasn't back then. And, I didn't have any major life events to grieve. Or so I thought. When it became my turn to share my life trauma as our small group went around the circle, I slowly spilled out a very full tank of woes, failures, and disappointments that was fueling angry outbursts and bouts of anxiety and depression, and was wreaking havoc on my wife, our sons, and family and friends. Under the gentle, loving guidance of Mirabai Starr,[143] I was taught how to grieve and how to let go. It would not be an overstatement to say that my life was transformed that weekend, as it began to unfold in a strange series of events whose outcomes have yet to be revealed.

I have gone on a dozen or more retreats since meeting Mirabai—co-ed, single sex, solo. More often than not, except on men's retreats, I am the token male in attendance. I don't care. I need to regularly be in the space that has opened up and expanded within me by virtue of my regular commitment to sit and face the guy inside of me that I would rather not have to deal with. Slowly, but surely, we are becoming friends. I know his strengths and weaknesses. I am learning his tricks, the way in which he deceives me into taking action that is not aligned with who I really am as human being. I can now call him out on his bullshit and tell him to back off. I know his trigger points—good and bad. I know him much better than I have been able to achieve through psychotherapy.

As a result of my investment in getting to know a man whose behavior I would rather not own (yes, I do prefer the avatar that I present to the "real" world as well), I am better able to connect with others in a genuine way. Or so I'm told. So, I'm just fine being the token male. It's working for me.

At this point, if you have never been on a retreat, you are probably wondering what the heck is the difference between a retreat and a weekend escape. Let's talk about what a retreat is, and what it is not . . . for one thing, it is not a boondoggle with your buddies. (Sorry.) Although the experience does not need to be solitary—some fellowship or social interaction can be beneficial—the real objective is to enter into a space where you are present with your inner self (we talked about that in the last chapter), not the guy that you have created as your representative to the world. Going on retreat with men that you know well can reinforce the bad habits that you're trying to shed. It's probably not a good idea, unless they are willing to "get naked" and shed their avatars in front of you, and then not go back to using them in their private, personal interactions with you going forward.

We also need to suspend our tendencies as men to pack in as much activity as possible, and absolutely must check as much of our mental baggage at the door. Less is more here. While doing something physical is important to trick the mind into letting go, far too often a retreat can become a yet another high-octane endurance sport, instead of slowing down, taking a break, and truly unwinding. It would be far more beneficial to go on a quiet walk, read a book, take a nap, listen to some music, or wander aimlessly for a couple of hours, days, weeks, than turn it into a physical fitness test. It is also essential that there is no expected outcome from your activity beyond expanding your horizons. The point is to do something that occupies and engages all aspects of our being— body, mind, and soul—to allow something new in your life to emerge.

In my view there are three crucial components of every great retreat that I have attended.

Physically, this may seem obvious, but it bears underscoring in our non-stop, ultra-connected universe. There must be a total separation from the world as you daily experience it. You need to remove your bodily self from your routines. Force yourself to detach. Let go. Be still inside. Otherwise, you are wasting your time.

That said, a retreat for men usually needs to provide an embodied experience that involves movement. Although it may be a cliché, the vast majority of men that I know are hyperactive, tactile learners. Because it's very hard for us to sit and pay attention for long periods of time, we need to be in motion using our bodies as we attempt to construct our own knowledge, mastery, and skill. So, some form of activity that keeps the executive, task-oriented mode of the mind occupied is in order here. We have to silence the "monkey brain"[144] or keep it busy, so it can't constantly pull our attention down rabbit holes. This physical activity should not be so demanding that it prevents the default mode of our brain from doing its inner work. Walking, hiking, swimming, yoga, any activity that requires a lot of boring, repetitive "tasks" that keeps the body and mind busy will do.

Mentally, a retreat should also prevent our minds from running its normal routines and replaying all the damn narratives that we have created about life experience. We need to shut down the playbook that we run day in and day out. That's why traveling to a distant corner of the world is ideal, but any destination that disconnects you from your day-to-day priorities can work. This does not necessarily need to be a remote wilderness experience. I have found it possible to disconnect by engaging in an extraordinary range of spaces—weeding the flower beds in our backyard, hands in the dirt for seven hours at a time, walking for hours through the streets of New York with no destination in mind, sitting before a magnificent painting for long, silent stretches. Even sitting in an empty church on a frigid winter afternoon while the wind howls through the rafters can still the mind. Mine sometimes goes blank for long periods of time just looking out a window.

Finally, although you may not identify as a spiritual guy, I hope that the last chapter may challenge you to acknowledge that although we live in a secular world that is sometimes aggressively hostile to the notion, there are spiritual aspects to our beings as men. As we saw in Chapter 6, neuroscience has now confirmed that there are component parts of the human psyche that want to align to a sense of a higher power, to the transcendent,[145] however we experience and express that. That part of our brain needs to be nurtured whatever your belief system is. You need to let the spiritual guy inside of you stretch his legs, and a great way to feed your soul (or reset your intention to do so) is to go on a pilgrimage or retreat.

As I close this section of the chapter, I want to underscore that cost is not as big a deterrent as you may imagine. In prior generations, men's groups run by religious organizations and other fraternal orders offered opportunities for guys to remove themselves from the world to engage in a period of restoration. While it is true that in this post-feminist, secular age, some of those programs for men have disappeared, they do still exist and often have funds to help subsidize attendance, so be sure to ask if cost is an issue. And check for local retreat centers. You'll be surprised how many may be in your own backyard.

A NEW HERO'S JOURNEY

To me, the place where all three requirements are best met—physical, mental, and spiritual—and where I experience the greatest sense of restoration and renewal, is when I go on a retreat to a destination that also enables me to get outdoors, preferably to a remote place where there is no wireless to tempt me to check in. As the Judeo-Christian tradition has recorded through the ages, the wilderness is not only a place where we are tested and defined; it's also a place where we experience transcendence and encounter the divine. It's the natural equivalent of a men's wellness spa.

Neuroscience has recently confirmed that cultivating a sense of wonder and awe is one of the best ways to promote our own well-being. (People are publishing lots of books about awe these days, I suspect a by-product of the millions of people who took up the habit of walking outdoors for exercise during COVID.) A terrific book on the topic is Dacher Keltner's *Awe: The New Science of Everyday Wonder and How It Can Transform Your Life*.[146] In its sixth chapter, "Wild Awe: How Nature Becomes Spiritual and Heals Bodies and Minds," Keltner makes a moving argument for the power of even the smallest encounter with nature to change our lives. He asserts that "it is hard to imagine a single thing that you can do that is better for your body and mind than finding awe outdoors." He then goes on to list a host of medical and physiological benefits.[147] Later in the chapter, he discusses his own research that suggests "mean egotism" (narcissism, self-focus, arrogance, sense of superiority, entitlement, and the consequences of these attitudes) can be reduced by wild awe.[148] Last, but not least, he shares his experience connecting to a benevolent force that is larger than ourselves while hiking around Mont Blanc, processing his grief upon the loss of his brother, Rolf. Oriented to everyday awe, he saw the "new directions his life will take now lacking [his] younger brother."[149]

A lifelong hiker and lover of poetry myself, I am predisposed to all this stuff, but it wasn't until I met Mark Kutolowski that I learned the scientific and spiritual technicalities of how being in nature moves us to experience the divine. A Division 1 hockey goalie in college, Mark went on a kayaking trip in Northern New Hampshire during his freshman orientation week that set him on a path toward becoming a wilderness guide and instructor of survival skills at Dartmouth for over fifteen years. After recovering from a severe back injury through holistic methods, he took a year off to heal, which led to a deep immersion in Qigong in Malaysia, a year of solitude in South Texas, and a contemplative practice that is centered on nature. I have now spent hours with Mark happily spellbound by his talent for guiding individuals inwardly while they are completely absorbed by the intimate details and expansive presence of the world around them. He has a unique gift for enabling people to experience the awe and beauty of nature simultaneously within and without.

Sitting by the fire pit on the deck behind our house on a spectacularly still fall evening, Mark told a wonderful story of what happens when individuals return from a solo wilderness survival expedition. It was October, so I was expecting a terrifying ghost story, but I never quite expected one like this to unfold.

"You know I've led many immersive wilderness trips. Almost every participant comes back into camp from their experience with a story. Even the most confirmed atheist, as she or he sits by the fire upon their return, opens up about an encounter that they cannot explain—an event, an unusual or mysterious appearance of an animal, an uncanny moment of serendipity, a piece of information, food source, water that is essential to their survival that suddenly appears at just the moment it is most needed. They don't know what to make of it, but you can see on their face that it left them in a state of wonderment as to whether there might be something going on out there in the wilderness that we do not understand."

The euphoria that we feel when we are outdoors can be addictive, and in a good way. In middle school, my nephews took up rock climbing at a local indoor wall for exercise and to blow off steam. They eventually got really into it—at one point they were ranked nationally. The passion for the sport determined which colleges and grad schools they eventually chose: the University of Tennessee-Knoxville, the University of Georgia, the University of Colorado, and Arizona State University. All techies who can work remotely, and two with PhD's in engineering, they continue to spend weekends climbing. It's become a way of life for them that keeps them sane and balanced (or as much as our hyper-kinetic, high-strung genes will allow).

As often is the case, a passion for the outdoors can take people to great heights, physically, emotionally and within. It can also lead to many other unexpected surprises. I was a walking train wreck when I left the non-profit world in my early 50s. After an extended holiday in Italy with the family, my older son and I continued for another week to go mountaineering in the Swiss Alps. The experience was so extraordinary that we returned for a second summer. These were peak life experiences that I had dreamed about since I was a child, because my grandfather's family was from Bern, and I had absorbed many fables about life in the Alps from him. It was amazing to reflect on how far this young boy had traveled from the small farming community of 300 that he was born into.

Our guide was a Scotsman, Brian Farquharson, who (at the time) was the only licensed mountaineering guide in town who spoke English as a native language (though arguably his Scottish brogue was only barely more intelligible than his German). Like my nephews, our guide had become enamored with the mountains while on holiday during his studies in the UK as an engineer. Unlike my nephews, he decided not to return to finish his degree, but remained and undertook the arduous task of completing the formal training that is required to become a licensed guide. On our trek across the Aletsch Glacier moraine, we learned that Brian was deeply steeped in geology, botany, meteorology, zoology, and human anatomy, in addition to being a mechanical engineer. All subjects are required to be a licensed guide and EMT in the Alps.

An inveterate journal writer, I recorded this list of insights that arose in the Alps right after our second trip with Brian. "We are learning many lessons from Brian in the mountains that may prove useful to us both in the coming years. The most challenging is the notion that while getting to the top of the mountain is nice, it isn't the goal. The goal is survival, and enjoying the journey, whatever it may turn out to be." Other insights that I thought worth jotting down include: "Because most ascents are difficult and steep, you need to break them down into "bite-sized bits." (The only safe way to the top is taking "Himalaya steps," as Brian says.) "It is important to be in the zone while you are climbing—a meditative state that makes even the most difficult ascent mentally manageable." "Mountaineering requires self-discipline, practice and conditioning. So it is in life." "Look for the moments of synchronicity. Indeed, expect them. They often occur when you are lost or in conflict." "Sometimes you get what you want and you don't even know it."

At the time, I remember marveling how life, in strange, mysterious, and inexplicable ways, gives us lessons just before we need them, and was deeply grateful that my son and I were so blessed as he was embarking on his own first, solo ascents in life, about to go off to school. What I did not realize then was how much I was going to need these lessons as well in the months and years ahead.

I share this remembrance because I want to make an important observation here. Pop culture makes it seem as though going on retreat involves participation in a bunch of navel-gazing exercises or baring your soul in an emotional trauma center so that deep inner work occurs. It can be. But that deep inner work can also occur if you fiercely disconnect from the world and open yourself up to a space to watch what happens. Your body-mind-soul is perfectly capable of structuring the time to provide you with the information and lessons you need. You only need to let go of running the show and be observant while your "BMS" does its work.

So, I'm guessing that at this point you are thinking something like, "I can see why retreats may be helpful, even necessary, but what are the immediate benefits going to be realistically speaking?"

Physically, of course, assuming that we sleep when we are away from home, we experience a level of rest and relaxation that is difficult to achieve when we are surrounded by the ongoing demands on our attention and time. If we engage in some form of physical activity that involves exercise, we activate many biochemical systems that restore health. The improvement in our well-being is almost immediate.[150]

Mentally, I can attest that giving the mind a break can also have deep psychological benefits that trigger a reset. The mind can and does shut down when it needs to. We recently traveled to the West Coast to spend the holidays with our two boys. Though we weren't in a remote corner of the world far from civilization, we were definitely dropped into an alien environment that was very different from our own: Santa Barbara, a glamorous "Hollywood getaway" since before there was Hollywood. (Silent pictures of the 1920s were produced by Flying A Studios here.)

Typically, the holidays are exhausting for me as we entertain and party as though we were still thirty years old while I continue to attend to whatever tasks arise at work that won't wait until my return. This holiday I gave myself a total break. I did nothing for ten days besides cook an occasional meal, and then only for my personal pleasure. Released from any responsibility professionally or personally, I slept ten hours a night. It turned out that I wasn't physically exhausted so much as I was mentally drained from years of being such a hard charger. I returned back east completely re-energized with an elevated mood that has lasted for months. I'm still sleeping eight hours each night. It was a double lesson for me regarding the need to pace myself better, and the need to take a break mentally.

I should probably comment here that rewiring your brain while on retreats is where meditation comes in. As we discussed in the last chapter, it's a discipline that forces your brain to shut off, if only for a few minutes, and that has significant benefits to our well-being mentally. There is also a spiritual component that we should discuss now, as it is best activated while on retreat.

Practicing meditation while on a retreat is like establishing a new lawn. First you strip the soil of any ground cover it may have (yep, here we go with "getting naked" again), then you rake and aerate the earth. Then you spread seed as profligately as you can, but evenly, with care. (Responsible men know how to do this innately.) Then you fertilize and cover the area with hay, pray for rain, and water if necessary, for a month. You do not walk over or disturb the area. You let it grow, of its own accord, on its own timetable. You can't rush it. It just happens, according to the laws of nature.

Going on retreat to deepen your contemplative practice is exactly like that. Six months to a year after you have established your lawn, you may decide that the lawn needs to be reseeded, or overseeded, to get the results that you want. So, you begin the process again, go on retreat, with the benefit of knowing that you don't have to start from scratch. You fill in the gaps, or overseed for denser growth, fertilize, cover and wait. A year later, you probably still have some spots that need attention, so you repeat the process. Later, you may decide that your lawn wants to be a meadow of wildflowers and perennials so that it becomes a pollinator garden or a haven for wildlife. Or it may want to become an apple orchard. You may want to expand it or add a vegetable patch. Add a border of blackberries and raspberries. Once again, you strip, plant, weed, feed, and wait. It's that simple.

What you will find if you give yourself permission to go on retreat regularly is that the recidivism into your old ways of being begins to diminish. In fact, you are returning to the world not quite the same person. Your body-mind-soul has been rewired. You will witness that some of your really bad habits will begin to change. They probably won't go away, but they will cease to be your default, your knee-jerk response to the trigger points that bedevil you.

You may also discover, as I did, entirely new capacities that you always possessed will begin to emerge. This is especially likely to occur when you return home and meditate daily to support however the Spirit, or whatever you may call your higher power or sense of purpose, animates your thoughts.

There are many stories across all faith traditions about how these kinds of personal transformations occur. I have already shared a couple of my favorites, recounting the life experiences of Joel Serino and Courtney Cowart. A consistent theme across all these stories is that we discover that we have unique gifts that are much needed when we are called to the work that arises during a time of trial or transition, and the self-organizing principle of the Spirit takes over from there.

So how does this personal transformation occur in our normal daily lives, not just when triggered by the need to respond to a crisis? The technical term for the slow, unfolding process making a fundamental shift in your interior landscape is kenosis—emptying out. That is what happens to you when you meditate. If you're lucky, you empty out so much that you sometimes feel as if the old you, the avatar that you have created, may cease to exist and a new person has begun to appear. You may also begin to sense that there is a great void, or a great light, or a power source at the heart of the universe that you can connect with. People who experience this void/light/power talk about it as a deep awareness of the presence of Love. Such an encounter can be blissful or terrifying, sometimes both. When it occurs, you know to the depth of your being that you will never be the same.

Over time, as you meditate more, you become aware that your inner space is growing in its own unique way. If we stick with the practice, and we're lucky, we eventually get to watch the ego begin to surrender, allowing our true Self to be seen and become more accessible. We become more vulnerable and naked, stripped of the protective narratives that we wrap around our souls. We also begin to tap into the extraordinary strength that is buried within us, exactly as I discovered when I posed nude for Bek Andersen. As this space deepens and expands, it enables the Spirit to move through us, so that the self-organizing principle that animates the universe can get behind the wheel and drive the car, while we ride shotgun in the passenger seat, helping to give shape and form to what is emerging from our depths.

Although this is a way of being, a way of experiencing life that is available to everyone, sadly, only artists, poets, innovators, and mystics seem to truly understand and trust it. It is extremely foreign and sometimes uncomfortable terrain for most men. However, if you wish to live a life that expands and goes beyond the limits of your own abilities and imagination, this is the lesson that you must learn. Going on this journey is best accomplished by daily devotion to some spiritual discipline, a rule of life. And going on retreat to receive guidance from a trained, spiritual director who is familiar with the terrain you will be traveling is advised.

If we're paying attention as our practice unfolds, we begin to see a shift in which fundamental changes in our lives occur—physically, mentally, and spiritually. Part of the reason this happens is that by removing ourselves from our day-to-day experience we can get enough distance from our lives to allow new possibilities to arise, things that we cannot entertain when we are in the trenches and fighting to hang onto the status quo or advance in a dog-eat-dog world. There's a liberation that occurs in these moments that is almost impossible to replicate in other settings, and it is transformative.

A second reason why there is a shift is because of our increasing ability to focus on optimizing the body-mind-soul connection, fostering wholeness and well-being, clearing the detritus and enabling a reset, so that we can take stock of where we are and encourage new personal growth to take root and be nurtured into being. If we commit to making that happen and get out of the way of it doing so, enduring changes can occur. But we have to trust the process and go believing that they will.

If we happen to be on retreat with other men, we have the privilege of learning from their stories, their perspectives, and their life experience as well. Given the harm that Man Box culture has inflicted on us and those around us, I think it is especially important for men to engage in this activity regularly, and I hope that we'll see more of the Y-chromosome in these settings.

A final parting thought here. People often say that they cannot meditate. "It's simply not true. Learning to meditate is like learning to ride a bike. Everyone can do it," says Will Duncan, a lavender farmer in Skull Valley, Arizona, who flies around the world offering weekend meditation workshops in corporate settings, conventions, and retreat centers.[151] It can be helpful to think of meditation as an experience of stillness that is available to all.

Because, at our core, all men aspire to be Superman/Clark Kent (or another favorite superhero), taking care of our family and friends in some superhuman fashion, I thought it might be useful to close this chapter with a line from the television series *Superman & Lois*. It's fascinating to me that in this modern era, our mythological archetypes—like kind, reserved, somewhat nerdy Clark Kent—have decided to move off the grid and return to the family farm in Smallville, with Lois and their two sons, just as many of us did during COVID.

That tells us a lot about the times in which we live. But of course, things don't work out as expected.

JOHN DIGGLE: So, this is where you and Clark moved the family.
LOIS LANE: Yeah, we thought a slower pace of life might be good
    for us.
JOHN DIGGLE: Well, looks like that didn't go quite as planned.

Retreats might not provide us with the exit ramp from the hamster wheel of life, the never-ending rat race that we run as men. There seems to be no escape from the epic battles that we will fight. But going on retreat and developing a contemplative practice does offer us another set of tools that might be very useful in winning the war within and without between the forces of good and evil.

And that's good enough for me.

GETTING STARTED

The main roadblock to getting out the door on retreat is carving out the time. That can be tough, especially when there are so many competing priorities at home and work. But it is not as difficult as you might think. Like many things in life, the obstacle to getting off the grid is in your head. If you actually set your mind to do it, you can definitely figure something out.

If you are like me, you will postpone this part of your journey into healthy masculinity until you are going through a major life shift. I will just tell you that based on my experience, it would be a better idea to get in the habit of taking a solo mental hike long before you hit a wall. It's harder to develop the self-reflective skills you require to navigate a tough turn of events when your mind is in crisis mode, addled by fear and anger. Better to train your brain now how to take a break, relax and empty out before you need it to do so while experiencing some trauma.

I got my sons out the door early. First, we started spending a week or two in the summer in the Adirondacks. Then our older son and I raised our game in the Alps when he went away to school. Later, as a 21st birthday present, he and four of his buddies trekked the High Sierra Loop hut to hut with a US Ranger/*pleine air* painter ("the Fishslayer") and me. Then, I summitted Wheeler Peak and traipsed around the high culture hotspots around Taos with our younger son when he turned 21. I guess it should come as no surprise that the boys' idea of a great family vacation is to sit quietly, journal, think, and read on the Finger Lakes for a week, surrounded by silence, and hike.

Wanting to know how other guys' retreat habits got going (and double check that our experience is not unique), I asked a buddy who has entered my life recently, Thomas Benton, how on earth he arrived at the conclusion that he wanted to do the Camino. I mean, who in his right mind decides that hiking 500 miles over 45 days is a thing he should do . . . ???

While hiking the Camino might not seem within the reach of most men, due to time and cost, I should point out that for centuries hostels have supported pilgrims of ordinary means on this journey. Indeed, Thomas somehow figured out how to do this pilgrimage on his inconsistent income as an actor. So, making these kinds of trips is not as impossible as it may seem.

"Yeah, well, the thought of it scared the hell out of me. But then, I saw a book whose title spoke to me on Facebook. I read it. The author talked openly about how she processed her divorce and a death of a loved one while hiking the Camino. Then I read Shirley MacLaine's book. Her experience was also transformative. Then I went to caminoways.com. They sent me an itinerary. And the next thing I knew, I had booked the trip."

"So it was an impulse decision?"

"No, I felt drawn into it."

"Were you going through a rough patch?"

"No, I wasn't really in a major crisis. I just went to gain some perspective on my life, insights on where I wanted to go next. You know, to answer the question of what I wanted my next chapter to be."

"So you were going through a career or life transition?"

"No, not really a major shift. I'm an actor. I had just moved from Boston to the New York metropolitan area for a bigger market, hoping that I would be able to land more work. Sporadic assignments are the nature of the game. So I'm used to that. I was anxious about how things might work out and wanted to think through what I wanted to get out of it."

He paused, reflecting on his experience:

"You know they say that everyone has their own Camino, and I think that's true. It's hard to explain, but doing the Camino is so big that you can't mentally, emotionally hold it. I mean, it is 500 miles, I had never been to Spain, and I don't speak the language. You very quickly realize that whatever is going to happen is going to happen. You can't cover up your anxiety, but you can't hold onto it either. The first thing you do is walk straight up the Pyrenees. That forces you to let go.

"The first two weeks you fight your demons—all sorts of emotions, negative voices come up—and then you have to surrender. You kind of get into a groove, you learn what your pattern is because you are doing the same damn thing every day, day after day after day. I discovered that for the first three miles my mind was going to say, 'This sucks, you're sore, you're tired, what the hell am I doing . . .' Then after the first three miles my mind would say, 'I really love this.' Eventually, you get into a flow state."

"At the beginning of the day, I started out with the group, but then I would stop to take a picture and walk the rest of the day alone, because everyone was chit-chatting about stupid, inane things.

"The Camino became a journey of self-reflection. A question would come to me every morning that would lead to something—another question, or a thought. Most of the time I wasn't thinking, I was just processing."

"What do you mean?"

"I was too busy walking and absorbing my surroundings to think, but underneath it all some deep internal work was getting done—clearing stuff out, sorting—because every once in a while an observation about my life would pop up."

"Really, out of nowhere?"

"Yes, and you begin to develop a sixth sense. When you are at a rest stop, you start feeling other people's energy. I always knew where I wanted to sit. I was careful to protect the bubble that I was in."

He paused, reflecting.

"The Camino becomes a very grounding experience that you can take back with you. By entering a meditative space—every day—you create an internal space within yourself that you can bring back from Spain with you.

"I discovered that for me acting wasn't about getting a job, it was about getting important, meaningful work. I discovered that what was important was being happy about my work. I came back with a different internal dialogue about what acting meant to me.

"I also discovered that doing the Camino had a direct impact on how I approach doing my work. Arriving on a set can be a nerve-wracking experience. I always get anxious, and I have to try to find peace and let go. The Camino taught me how to do that. Instead of being anxious, I let go.

"The experience was totally transformative. It keeps growing on you. It calls you back.

"It's all transferable to your day-to-day life. During COVID, I applied the lessons of the Camino all the time. You have to chunk things down to something you can hold: 4 days, a month, whatever it is . . ."

I was struck by how much Thomas's experience mirrored my own on the retreats that I have gone on. You will be, too.

CHAPTER 8

REFRAME SUCCESS

Life sometimes has a funny way of forcing you to face unpleasant truths. The pursuit of happiness often first entails going through some dark places.

While I was reeling from the reality that the startup I had poured everything into was going to crater, creating a financial hole that was going to take years to fill during my golden years, my older son also went into the pit. He had graduated from college without landing a job in a training program at an investment bank or consulting firm and was convinced that his prospects were now forever diminished.

A couple of years later, he did not get into one of his top choices for business school, and I no longer had a paycheck, that benchmark that defines every guy on the planet. I watched in horror as my son went into an even darker emotional space. Why was he being forced to endure these hardships, he asked, when he had been a bright shining star up until these recent setbacks?

I had no answers for him or for me, but I tried to reason with him, pointing out that compared to so many others, our lot in life was pretty good. He wasn't having it.

It was perhaps providential that he went through this professional meltdown early in his career, as it forced him to dig deep, think hard about his priorities, and construct a more solid foundation from which to estimate his own self-worth (rather than relying on status symbols and perceptions of others).

Ironically my deep concern for his well-being and my insistence that he clarify what's important was also a timely reminder for me to reframe my own perspective as I entered the final chapters of my professional journey. More than once the young man that I sired had the balls to tell me to take my own medicine.

For his brazenness, tenacity, and youthful courage, I will be eternally grateful.

We have now reached the last leg of our journey and are entering into some of the toughest psychological terrain for us to navigate as men. That territory is how we define and experience success.

BREAKING THE MOLD

Our culture of masculinity maintains its stranglehold over us because the consequences (real or imagined) of not following its standards can have a significant impact on our access to the networks and opportunities that determine success. In a nutshell, on a material level, the hierarchy of men that Man Box culture protects also rewards those who play by its rules by opening the doors to wealth, power, status and fame, while encouraging bullying, coercion, and exploitation of those who are lower in the food chain. It is impossible to overstate the insidious ways in which the distribution and hierarchy of wealth plays out in men's lives.

The rewards that are apportioned out according to the edicts of Man Box culture vary by stage of life and socio-economic position. At younger ages, for many men, status may be defined as a hot girlfriend (or the amount of sex that you have), the car you drive, and your clothes. Later in life, status may be defined by your job, where you live, the size of your house, your personal net worth, your hot wife, your children's academic success, your sports car or Jeep, your Rolex, etc. In a society that prizes the vast accumulation of things, and a culture of masculinity that controls who gets the biggest rewards, size matters. (Please note: I personally object that women are viewed as status symbols and objects in our culture. But I'm also learning from my single women friends that men are viewed in a similar way.)

As difficult as it is to stomach this system for distributing material benefits, it is the physical and psychological impacts of Man Box culture on "others" that are the most disturbing. Its odious exploitation and degradation of women who endure men's derogatory remarks and sexual harassment, as well as women's plight as individuals further down the pecking order, should condemn the men who participate in the hyperaggressive, hyper-sexual behaviors that this culture of masculinity conditions into them.

The rejection, the sense of isolation, and the ridicule that men who are lower in the hierarchy experience is equally troubling. It turns out that to be that this might be another dangerous and downright lethal impact of this culture. Chronically deprived of some form of affirmation that builds healthy self-esteem, in addition to hungering for basic relational connections that we all require as human beings, men who are on the lower levels of the hierarchy often lash out at "others," typically women and gay men, who are even lower on the totem pole. Of late, these men deprived of affirmation are banding together to form their own support groups, in person and online, and rehearse or reify their societal grievances. Stoked by each other's rage, they act out. Time and time again, we have witnessed the deadly impact of their anger, as they often make the news with their mass shootings or other acts of violence.[152]

Men who identify as gay have a more complex path up and down the hierarchy. Since I identify as mostly straight, I cannot pretend to comprehend gay men's experience, but I can bear witness to what I have observed about the challenges that our many, gay, life-long friends, and our own beloved younger son, have encountered. As a younger man I remember well how my gay friends were rejected by their straight peers. As a media executive and entrepreneur, I have also watched several gay men rise to the top of the Man Box hierarchy, if they were willing to adopt some of the bad behaviors of straight males, boasting about their sexual prowess, exploiting others, and spending a boatload of money earned from a status-oriented job. Some even contend that gay men work harder than straight men to achieve success because of the deep shame that comes from living in a homophobic culture.[153] Unfortunately, I have also seen several young gay men go into a tailspin of depression fueled by a sense of shame and a lack of acceptance. Is it any wonder that there is higher risk of suicide and substance abuse among this group of men?[154]

It appears that race hands out as a wild card for non-white males who follows the rules of Man Box culture. Similar to their white brothers, men of all races are sorted by their level of dominance, sexual orientation and prowess, and all the other behaviors that our culture of masculinity conditions into men, both within and between racial groups. Non-white males get knocked down a level in the overall hierarchy of men, unless they demonstrate extraordinary skills that males generally admire, as professional athletes, musicians, actors and entrepreneurs sometimes do. Material rewards—earning a ton of money, getting a lot of sex, and buying a big home—are the currencies that all men, whatever their background, appreciate, respect, and covet.

Curiously, while men are no longer thriving as they once did,[155] our dominance-based culture of masculinity is. That raises the question as to why. In part, this culture that is so damaging to all survives because of the fear it generates; it is a system of sticks and carrots that is perfectly set up to resist change. And underneath that system is a deeply embedded cultural belief, a mindset that we live in a world of scarcity where a finite set of resources are distributed unevenly to those who are the most aggressive, combative, and assertive.[156] This ideology can be summed up as "My gain is your loss." Though scientifically debunked, this survival-of-the-fittest, Social Darwinist view of life has had many negative impacts of vast consequence over the past 150 years: first eugenics, then Nazi Germany, now serious income inequalities. Underneath it all, to this day, Man Box culture, animated by a scarcity mindset, holds us in its hypnotic sway.

It is my firm belief that this scarcity mindset is itself a direct result of the culture of masculinity that we live in, and the behavioral patterns that it conditions into us. That is, we experience scarcity because we believe that we live in a world where we must conquer others to secure our material and emotional needs. A society that promotes less inequality of access and more sharing of life's rewards would eliminate our fear of being left out. We might even discover that we live in a world of abundance with enough to go around. Recent research by evolutionary biologists suggests that humans are more genetically similar to the nurturing bonobos with their supportive social structures than the hyper-aggressive chimpanzee (and their dominance-based culture). In the world of the bonobos, there is enough to go around.[157]

Man Box culture causes further psychological damage that affects almost everyone. It tends to encourage us to take on identities—in work, relationships, and play—that do not match our profiles in order to be successful. Aiming to land on top and prove our self-worth to ourselves and others, we often pursue careers, enter into partnerships, and join social networks that are ill-suited to our personality traits, talents, skills and/or interests. Recognizing that the odds of success favor a handful of individuals, we bend, twist, and contort our body-mind-souls to fit paradigms that are often a mismatch for who we are. We mistakenly believe that if we could amass a ton of money, hold a high-status job, marry a catch (male or female), or travel in high circles, our lives will be fulfilled, and importantly, our position in the hierarchy of men will be secure.

This is, of course, pure madness. The only constant in life is change, and no one, not even billionaires or presidents (all white males with few exceptions), is immune to the ups and downs of fate. Indeed, the more you have to protect, the harder you have to run to stay in place. As Mark Greene and others observe, this becomes increasingly challenging as younger generations of men come up through the ranks and start to vie for your position. This fight not to be replaced is real, of course, on some level, but it is exacerbated in a culture that does not respect elders and the wisdom that only age and experience impart. (And yes, elders need to respect the expertise and skills that only younger generations possess.)

In addition to encouraging us to take up occupations and form relationships to which we are ill-suited, our blind obsession and pursuit of the material goods that our society unevenly bestows can often wreak havoc on our lives. We absent ourselves from loved ones and adopt other unhealthy behaviors that fuel several, multibillion-dollar industries dedicated to helping us clean up the damage: failed marriages, broken relationships, and unhealthy bodies.

Believing that there is no way to change the system, we become super achievers in order to claim our portion of the pie.

Of course, there are times when we can and must choose to do whatever it takes to survive and feed our families; however, adopting these choices for the long haul often has negative long-term consequences. More often than not, we reach a point where we realize that the game that we play cannot go on forever, and that no amount of money, status, power, or fame is ever going to be enough to secure our position in the hierarchy, much less make us happy. We hit a wall that forces us to stop, take stock, and figure out if there is a different way to move forward through life—one that addresses all our needs in this moment in time, not just those that are financially driven, focused on survival, and the ever-receding horizon of our "best state" in the future.

Having grown up in a family that placed an inordinate value on making money to the detriment of other priorities—and having been surrounded by families of great wealth for most of my life—I am painfully aware of money's limitations. While a minimal level of financial security is liberating,[158] the vast wealth to which many aspire can have crippling effects. Wanting to avoid these toxic impacts, I have spent decades exploring how to accumulate a basic level of wealth *and* live a balanced life in our materialistic and consumerist society. This is no easy task.

DESIGNING YOUR LIFE

My fascination and eventual disaffection with money came to a head during the go-go eighties. As I watched my peers make fortunes on Wall Street while growing increasingly disenchanted with their lives, or cynical about their work if they stayed in the game, I set off in search of fame and fortune in Hollywood, which I soon discovered was an equally soulless place. I realized that however exciting and fulfilling being part of a creative community was, I would never have a balanced life and be the father/husband that I promised myself and my wife I would be in this 24/7 work environment (which was also, to my great surprise, even more focused on money than Wall Street was). So, I cut loose from a very promising career that I had always wanted, in search of an authentic life more coherent with my values.

Because my journey predates the current tsunami of scientific research on happiness and contemplative practice, I was forced to be a trial-and-error experiential learner. With only philosophers and contemporary elders as my guides, I learned to follow my inner voice. I think it is fair to say that after twenty-five years on the hunt, I have taken most of the personality and aptitude tests that there are, have worked with multiple coaches, and have explored so many wellness practices that I have more information and tools than I can reasonably use. In fact, I have the burden that digital "idiot savants" have today—Too Much Information. While these outside inputs are invaluable as they have consistently challenged and expanded my thinking, at the end of the day I have learned that the answers that we seek lie within.

The problem with external inputs is that they have no power unless you are forced to understand them through direct experience. They also tend to reinforce the dominant cultural understandings of the day, when forging a new life requires close examination of your own personal situation—honest self-assessment and self-awareness as you dig deeper and connect to the real, inner drivers of your personality and behavior. This includes developing greater familiarity with the false narratives and beliefs that we have adopted to survive and succeed in Man Box culture.

It is for this reason that I have spent a chapter of this book describing the contemplative practices that clear the mind and empty the inner landscape so that that new possibilities can emerge. And I have stressed the importance of detaching from the world and either going on retreat or attending weekend workshops where we can disarm the narratives that hold us in their vise-like grip—a restoration to our natural state that we need as men, individually and collectively. It is only through self-immersion in this work that we can release ourselves from the harmful cultural narratives that have been conditioned into us, and come to truly know who we are, while we simultaneously develop the inner adaptive capacities and resilience that we need to thrive.

Through this work we come to recognize and ultimately trust our inner voice (as opposed to the ego-driven wishful thinking that so dominates our younger years). Steven Spielberg spoke eloquently about this voice in his commencement address at Harvard in 2016, during which he urged that listening to the whisper of the Universe was the most important skill one could develop in life. This voice is hard to hear in our communication-saturated, distracted world. To awaken to its call, we must commit some time to solitude, separation, and stillness, in small doses and for extended periods of time.

Once we become familiar with the "sound of the genuine,"[159] its power to guide and transform us is enormous. You may be surprised to know that the quiet inner voice within sometimes senses what is about to occur long before there is any outer tangible evidence or pattern that would predict it. I spent several months recording this phenomenon in journals, taking notes with scientific objectivity so that I could not be accused of selectively shaping the data that prove this to be true.

When connected to this voice, it is possible to begin to discern a set of options for moving through life that responds to the full set of our needs as human beings. This includes our need for work which provides for us and our loved ones financially, while at the same time giving our lives purpose and meaning, however we choose to define that. It also includes our need for love and connection, as the social animals that we are; our need for play and other ways that we might experience joy; and finally, our need to maintain our physical, emotional, and mental health so that we can enjoy the lives that we are creating.

The world is filled with self-help manuals recommending steps that we can take to optimize our lives to meet these needs. The list of titles worth reading is literally endless. They all have a common weakness, however. They require that the reader invest some effort to adopt new behaviors in order for their recommendations to be implemented and become successful.

There is one book, however, that I believe can really change your life, in part because it harnesses and gives some structure to a set of practices that most people are already doing: self-reflection. The book is titled *Designing Your Life: How to Build a Well-Lived Joyful Life*. Developed by Bill Burnett, executive director of Stanford's legendary "d.school," and Dave Evans, adjunct lecturer at the school, a management consultant and a co-founder of Electronic Arts, this program has taught thousands how to apply design thinking to design their lives. Its genius is that it gives you "tools, ideas, and mindsets" that are useful at every stage of life, enabling individuals to re-invent their lives over and over again, ensuring that every chapter is fulfilling, no matter what their life circumstances may be. Practical and rigorously researched—the professors are at Stanford after all—the program delivers "statistically significant" outcomes. ". . . [Individuals] who took our class were better able to conceive of and pursue a career they really wanted; they had fewer dysfunctional beliefs (those pesky ideas that hold you back and that just aren't true) and an increased ability to generate new ideas for their life design (increasing their ideation capability)."[160]

The book offers a set of exercises that readers execute in collaboration with a design team chosen among their "supporters" (often friends), "players" (often a co-worker), and "intimates" (people who are the most directly impacted by your life choices). This network is an invaluable resource as the reader implements the design principles and tools that the program offers, developing new behavioral habits that impact the balance and vitality experienced across four dimensions of life: work, play, love, health. What I discovered in utilizing their program is that even if you don't execute every exercise to the level of detail described, the book's wisdom and insights, along with some of the initial tools offered, are enough to change your life.

I first implemented their model to discern the career path that I am on now. It revealed latent interests so deeply buried that I did not see them, uncovering among many other things a desire to begin writing a set of essays on healthy masculinity that were eventually published by *The Good Men Project*, which led to writing this book. To be honest, ten years ago when a highly gifted intuitive predicted that I would publish a ton of essays online, instead of the novel that I had just completed, I stridently responded that she was wrong. I had no f'ing interest in writing a blog. Later, when an agent who edited Sam Keen's *Fire in the Belly* read my essays and offered to represent me, if I would write a book similar to his for today's generations, I also told *her* that I wasn't interested. And yet, here we are. I have since applied various elements of design thinking to other life challenges with the support of lots of friends in my network. My conclusion: it works.

The beauty of Burnett and Evans's approach is that it relies not only on listening to your own inner voice but also the voices of others who know you well. This provides you with honest, direct feedback that prevents your ego and false narratives from running the show.

Another reason why I recommend that you check out the *Designing Your Life* process is that it dovetails beautifully to the work that you have been doing in *Getting Naked*. Our explorations—developing a healthier relationship with our own bodies, unearthing the sacred feminine components of our own personalities, getting in better touch with our emotions, deepening our relational capacities, owning the full set of sexual and romantic impulses that we possess as men, learning how to be still, taking breaks to rest and restore—all these investigations provide a rich amount of material that can be integrated into your life plan design. Working together, the two systems should tee you up to pursue an expanded definition of success that is more aligned to who you actually are, not the mythical male avatar that you have created for yourself thanks to Man Box culture.

LIVING A GOOD LIFE

So, what does a successful life look like? It's impossible to respond to this question in a generic way, as it very much depends on the individual. (Like Burnett and Evans, I resist the notion that there is one right option for moving forward with our lives, and that a one-size-fits-all set of sweeping recommendations sometimes offered by pop psychology have the answer. They generally don't. That said, there are certainly behavioral patterns that demonstrate ways in which we can find a feeling of contentment and success as the current happiness craze asserts, but it's up to the individual to craft their own solutions.)

Within the context of the need for individuation, I will venture one observation, however. A successful life is one in which there is a sense of coherence—an alignment of body, mind, and heart—around a set of priorities for the chapter of life that we are in. These priorities are unique to the individual, though certain aspects of them might be related to our stage of life. For example—it's entirely possible that focusing on work and placing less emphasis on health and play may make sense early on as we build our careers. It may also be the right move later on, if we are fortunate enough to experience the full flowering of our gifts, as "late bloomers" often do.[161] (This does not imply that it ever makes sense to completely ignore any category of needs for an extended period of time, because such a sustained imbalance usually leads to neurotic behavior and major negative impacts downstream.)

The point is to remember that change is the one constant in life that you can count on. It therefore makes little sense to clutch tightly to the dream or vision for your life that you once held. Holding onto your prior plans as to how you will achieve happiness and success prevents you from realizing the possibilities that are right before your eyes in the present moment. What I discovered in letting go is that the dream doesn't entirely vanish. It is often hiding an underlying desire that begins to surface and come into focus. And we're drawn or led to achieve our dream in another way against an ever-changing set of life priorities.

I recently had to learn this lesson myself the hard way, when I refused to give up on my dream as a twenty-five-year-old that I would someday become a wealthy humanitarian. (It's okay to laugh. It does sound ridiculous, especially for a small-town guy. What can I say? I always was a dreamer who thought big.) Stubborn and persistent by nature, I struggle with letting go a lot, so I can give you endless examples of the harm that I have caused to myself, my family and others because I did not revise my vision in regular five-year intervals. Instead, I stuck with my original plan, as tenacious entrepreneurs sometimes do.

However, not succeeding in my plan after 35 years, I did some careful self-analysis. I observed that I have always been interested in projects that have societal impacts at scale, as for three decades I took on leadership responsibilities in organizations focused on the issues that I cared about. I began to realize that I need to shift out of high profile, high impact, high stress jobs focused on a single issue, into a portfolio of projects so that I am better able attend to a very full set of current priorities. Over the decades my love life shifted from its exclusive focus on my wife and college friends during my "student" phase, to a split focus on her and our boys along with a few close friends during my "householder" phase.[162] And now that the boys are adults, my love life is shifting once again to my wife, the boys and their children (if they have any), my parents and siblings, and the broad network of friends that we remain close to. My exercise regimens have shifted from the high-intensity, adrenaline-pumping thrills of my youth to routines that are respectful of current physical limits but still charge me up. I am still learning how to play.

This notion that we need to periodically revisit our understanding of what is important and revise our thinking about how to build a life was underscored very recently. Because our older son and I recognized that we were each going through yet another major life transition, we decided to work through pieces of the *Designing Your Life* process together—he in the early stages of his career as he contemplates getting married and having a family, and I as I enter my "third chapter"[163] (a time for giving back that Rosabeth Moss Kanter, founder and director of the Harvard University Advanced Leadership Initiative, once joked that I actually began when I was 41—I just didn't know it at the time). It was fascinating to be a thought partner to our son as he evaluates his options designing his next steps and charting his own path through life. On my end, I was astonished to reaffirm how much my work remains constant, even as how I do the work and allocate my time to other priorities is much different than before. The intensity in which I execute them has also changed radically. (Spoiler alert for younger men: I'm much more focused, so the intensity is greater.)

I hope that from all the stories that I've shared in this and prior chapters—drawn from my friends' and my own experiences—you can see that when there is coherence, an alignment of our lives to our priorities and a set of inner and outer practices that support and animate our lives, we typically experience a sense of grace and ease that does not occur when we are stuck in Man Box culture. Our lives unfold with purpose and meaning, often with many surprises that lead us onward to yet another chapter that we have not yet imagined and is waiting to occur. With hindsight we can look back and see how even the most radically disconnected and disruptive life transitions contribute in a fundamental way to the later chapters in our lives, as if it was all part of an elaborately designed plan that we can only comprehend in a rear-view mirror.

GETTING STARTED

The best way to get started designing your life is to download the PDF of the book *Designing Your Life,* which Burnett and Evans make available online, and read the first chapter. There is so much wisdom in their introduction that your perspective on what constitutes a good, successful life will be forever changed. Read the chapter carefully and repeatedly. Internalize its insights. Think about how they might change the way that you approach the problems that you are currently trying to solve and the priorities that you are pursuing.

Then, if you feel inspired, start working your way through the exercises. I have found myself returning to the visual maps that they generate over and over again, as they guided and expanded my thinking about the multiple directions in which I might head to build meaning and purpose in my life. And I'm grateful that recently my son suggested that we work through the process again together, as my "maps" did change in small but material ways, reflecting the change in my circumstances and priorities over the past five years.

I think you will find these exercises particularly helpful:

- the health/work/play/love dashboard,
- the workview/lifeview/integration reflections,
- the wayfinding log, charting your energy and engagement as you navigate your daily tasks over the course of three weeks,
- mindmapping (rapid fire image generation related to energy, engagement and flow, to find the golden nuggets of what animates your soul),
- odyssey planning (life option generation),
- prototyping (talking to individuals and exploring concrete examples of things you might do, instead of conceptualizing and researching options that in reality you might hate).

Perhaps the most important benefit of the process is that it forces you to reframe your dysfunctional beliefs, based on heavily researched data and the decades of Burnett and Evans's experience guiding individuals on to their next chapters.

Having followed their step-by-step process twice, I can tell you that no matter what the ultimate outcome of your engagement with these practices is, you will emerge with a much deeper understanding of your purpose in life. And you'll discover that once you set your intention to make a shift, your life will indeed begin to move forward. Remaining engaged with your design team as you do, you'll have the support and reinforcement to make the changes you desire happen.

It's really that simple. So, what are you waiting for?

CHAPTER 9

MAKE A SHIFT

Up until this point, we have focused on several key beliefs that our culture of masculinity conditions into us so deeply that they prevent us from fully expressing the many wonderful ways that we are constructed as men. It is now time to pull our focus away from the changes that we might make as individuals to the larger cultural shifts that may or may not be happening. The questions that we will explore are: Where are we in our evolution as men? Has any real progress been made in making a shift to heal the deep wounds that our culture of masculinity has created? Where are we stuck? Is there hope that we will ever get to a point where 21st Century Males are perceived as the healthy, restorative presence in our society that men can and should be?

To answer these questions, I'm going to helicopter in, pick you up, and gather a group of eight other men, so that together we can all examine a topographical view of the "new male" territory that guys have been exploring over the past 50–60 years. We want to map the trails that have been blazed through the wilderness, as guys grapple with the idea of what it means to be a man in today's world. We'll use as our guides the leaders of groups of men who have been "getting naked" as collectives for decades. In taking this tour with me, you may find yourself wanting to become a member of one of these Naked Man Collectives, in order to connect and bond with a community of guys doing the work of becoming whole, fully formed men. (Think Chapter 1, "The Incomplete Man," where we started our journey.) I highly recommended that you check out their websites.

■　■　■

Our first stop will be to pick up Robert Heasley. Robert is a psychotherapist and former university professor with a PhD from Cornell. A former co-director of the Men's Center for Growth and Change in Philadelphia, he was also co-founder of the first domestic violence prevention program for men in Anchorage, Alaska, in 1980. Robert has been deeply immersed in grappling with the negative impacts of our culture of masculinity on men from a wide range of backgrounds, and has helped to address issues of violence, isolation, failed relationships, sexual anxiety, as well as sexual acting out. He has taught extensively at the university level in the area of sexuality, gender and counseling, developing the first course to be taught specifically focused on men and masculinities at two universities. His research focuses on men and relationships, issues of intimacy, raising boys, fathering, healing from sexual abuse and other sexual challenges. His wife, Betsy Crane, is a former professor and director of human sexuality studies at Widener University near Philadelphia. Robert became active in the men's movement through the feminist movement in the '70s.

Now 76, he traces his involvement in men's work back to age 23 when his oldest child, a son, was born. This is when he entertained the questions: "What does it mean to be a father, and is that something different than being a mother?" and "What is expected in raising a son that is different from raising a daughter?" As he became exposed to feminist analysis of gender and masculinity, Robert came to understand the historic pressure on parents to raise their sons to assure they were not like girls. To be masculine, the theory goes, is not a one-dimensional set of behaviors, but rather a "take-whatever-steps-necessary" approach to assure boys not be feminine. This framework was not the one Robert used in raising his son (nor for raising his daughter, who came along six years later).

Robert was born into a working-class Catholic family where he was the next-to-the-youngest of four boys and three girls. Of the four boys, he was the one who failed horribly at the masculine qualities of hunting, fixing cars, and being "tough." While his dad was a competitive boxer in his own youth, and Robert's older brothers joined the military after high school, Robert's boyhood dream was to go to college, study literature, or to become a dancer.

Robert grew up in fear of his father's bouts of intense anger when stressed by the challenges of his factory job and part-time work as a mechanic to keep the family fed. Expectations of men at that time prevented his father from "allowing" his wife to work, even though she had been an office worker before they married. Robert was also aware that work and the way masculinity was constructed at that time kept his dad out of the emotional and intimate lives of his children, so Robert sought another model for parenting. "I wanted to raise my son the way my mother had raised me—kind, nurturing, emotionally supportive and engaged, along with encouraging skills and knowledge that would help me in school and life in general."

At a deeply personal level, Robert shared that he was sexually molested by a stranger at age eight, and again by different men (strangers, again) when he was 11 and 14. At 14, he ran away from his home in Western Pennsylvania to New York City—a boy confused about "belonging" in his family and his sexual vulnerability. Living for a week on the streets of NYC, men would solicit him for sex. A priest that he turned to after Mass helped him return home.

"I never told anyone about any of the abuse but I lived with the effects in terms of fear of men and confusion about my own sexuality. Like many boys who experience sexual abuse, the effect can be confounded by the experience of physical arousal along with the sense of incredible fear, shame and guilt. At the time, no one ever spoke of male sexual abuse, and there was little in the way of language to explain or even interpret what occurred.

"I think the reason why I was attracted to feminism is that feminism back then was about rejecting men, challenging the legitimacy of the patriarchy, and understanding that masculinity itself had its own hierarchy when men dominated not only women, but other men (and boys) as well. Women were disrupting gender and gathering support not only for expanding opportunities for women but for ways to 'be' a woman. What was not articulated at the time was that we were raising boys through a highly restrictive set of expectations, limiting the nurturing they need, and not acknowledging the harm being done to boys—by restricting their emotional awareness and their voices when hurt, scared, or confused."

By 1977, Robert was living in Alaska, studying at the university, and became involved in a group establishing the first women's shelter in the state. It became clear that women who came to the shelter after experiencing what was often severe physical abuse were usually returning to relationships in which they were being abused again. This led Robert to co-found a men's domestic violence prevention program in 1980 in Anchorage, and he continued to work in this area more recently in Philadelphia.

"When I first started running groups for men who 'battered' women, I was young, I wasn't doing my best work because of my own history of abuse, I really distrusted men, and hated men who were involved in abusing others. It wasn't my best act. But once I started to listen to the men's stories, I began to feel compassion and have empathy for men, and how the male journey set men up for destructive behaviors.

"In 1986, I taught my first class on men and masculinity. There were 26 students, all women, no men. Why were the women taking a course on men? They wanted to understand how better to relate to their boyfriends, fiancés, husbands, and how to raise better sons. I understood and supported that but was struck by the idea that women were 'doing' men's work for them.

"In the mid-1980s, as a graduate student at Cornell, I also got involved with an organization called The National Organization for Changing Men. The organization grew out of an emerging feminist men's movement. The organization was pro women, feminism, gay-affirming and dedicated to making changes in men's lives and the meaning of masculinity.

"The framework back then was that men were the problem. And it is true that men are the cause of most violence, are at greater risk of suicide, less likely to seek mental health interventions, and even exert less self-care regarding health. We can see the result of this tension, and the confusion men live with, in our society today. The anxiety of guys who feel displaced has risen to a feverish pitch. Take a look at the messages that male mass shooters leave behind. They are all variations on a theme that 'women (gays, communists, etc.) are denying my right as a man to be seen as dominant.'

"Men, on one hand, are seen as broken, and the various forms of the men's movement have been an attempt to 'fix' men. By contrast, women have been viewed as being repressed, and the focus of the women's movement has been on liberation and opportunity. We now know that the way we have thought about men is incomplete. It is the system that men grow up in that is the real problem—not inherently men themselves. We raise boys telling them that they cannot do what girls do. But then, when we rightly began to raise girls to believe that they can do what boys do, it diminished what some see as uniquely belonging to boys, and guys can feel displaced. By seeing the feminist movement as expanding the possibilities for men as well as women—by re-imagining the lives of boys and men, we can engage in the process, pro-actively, of making new meanings of men's lives."

This part of our conversation made me reflect on Richard Reeves' analysis that what is needed now is a societal investment focused on improving the well-being of men.

Robert went on. "I must admit though, that my involvement in men's work has also been about finding myself, and helping other men do the same. I did not need to fit in with the traditional masculine (even if I could), but I also did not want to be on the margins. For the longest time, gay men felt like they needed to present as straight to fit in. I can relate to that. I was on the margin, too. But I didn't want to bring the margins into the Center. Instead, I wanted the Center to expand its range of possibilities out to the margins, much as many straight young men are adopting some of the behaviors of their gay brothers today.

"This is an oversimplification, of course, as we are not monoliths, and there are so many nuances and variations in gender formation, but one of the interesting outcomes of feminism is that on the whole, we raise girls to be women, not feminine. Yes, there is still a lot of pressure on young women to adhere to gender stereotypes, but at the end of the day, girls are encouraged to define who and 'how' they want to experience and express themselves—no matter their choice, adult females become 'women.' And yet, we continue to place too much focus on raising boys to be masculine, denying them 'manhood' if they do not conform. This too often leads to young males obsessing about imitating what some authors call 'manhood acts' that restrict those ways of being that are not 'manly.' Why? Because of parents' fear of the loss of power that will occur if our boys are not adequately masculine, and the fear that our boys will be hurt by other boys. It's all about power.

"The question of what is feminine and what's masculine brings us to the issue of archetypes. What is masculine about them? Why do we need them? Do we really need containers and labels to describe our experience? Sometimes I wonder. Perhaps we do. The problem is that language is both liberating and limiting. We search for words to describe the full spectrum of our experience as human beings. They don't exist. So we resort to labels that are incomplete descriptions of who we are. What we're seeing now is the breakdown in that taxonomy."

We discussed whether the current "pronoun" movement, however well-intended, is the answer, as choosing pronouns often reinforces the old stereotypes/patterns/identities even as individuals try to break them.

Robert continued. "There's also another problem. It's the inner narrative in men that does not have an outer voice, because men are forced into certain behaviors in order to fit in. As a result, men have secrets, a secret life. All men do. It's because of the way in which we are raised. We have to hide many things that we love. Boys stop singing in church in the 3rd or 4th grade to appear masculine. We stop expressing affection for each other in the 2nd grade for the same reason. But we still love music and want male friends."

Looking at the clock and realizing our conversation might go on for hours, and that Robert had a hard stop to see a patient, I switched gears. "Okay, we can agree that there are huge challenges ahead of us, but are things changing? We have not talked about that yet. You have been at this for a long time. You would know."

"I do think we're making progress, but there is a tremendous backlash right now precisely because we are making gains in dismantling our dominance-based culture of masculinity. These gains threaten the very nature of the hierarchy of men, the patriarchy, and indeed the very idea of masculinity, because traditional notions of masculinity are losing their meaning and power. There is clear evidence that men who do not buy into the traditional patriarchal stereotypes are doing just fine—are better fathers, more engaged friends and the like, and boys raised without the limitations of traditional masculinity are doing even better!"

■ ■ ■

Let's move on and gather insight from a Gen Xer who is one of the men carrying the torch for the granddaddy of men's groups: The ManKind Project. Because Boysen Hodgson is the director of communications for "MKP," and so damn articulate about all this stuff, we're going to want to spend considerable time with him. Again, I will let him tell you about his journey in his own words.

"In many ways I am both a typical and atypical Gen Xer." Boysen paused, collected his thoughts as to where to begin, then continued.

"I was raised in Upstate New York, in a very rural, homogenous area of the state. My parents divorced at age 11, so I was a latchkey kid. I lived in two worlds. Much of the time I was with my mom, a single mom trying to raise 3, then 4, then 5 boys. I was with my dad on Wednesdays and every other weekend. He was a small-town veterinarian, beloved in the community. Handsome, outgoing, charismatic. But he had a lot of secrets. That's what ended their marriage. And from there, my world felt like chaos—with moving, changing schools, a string of new step-mothers and siblings, step-fathers, moving again, and again.

"I actually have six brothers—I am either #2 or # 3 in birth order, depending upon which side of the family you are talking about—so I grew up surrounded by men. And the unspoken norms around masculinity that I absorbed growing up were very close to what we talk about as 'Man Box' stuff these days. In the area of New York where I was raised, there is still a ton of unhealthy aspects of traditional masculinity in play.

"In my case, I received two very different messages about being a man. From my mom I got, 'Don't be like your dad.' From most people around me I heard, 'You are so much like your dad.' I internalized those two messages deeply. I lived in two different worlds. What I showed to the world was very different from what was on the inside. I was successful and accomplished on the outside, but in relationships, even friendships, I felt unknown, a cipher.

"By my late 20s, I was miserable, isolated, and alone. My world was very small. I was in a dead-end job and an unhealthy relationship, both of which I was responsible for creating, and I was too scared to do anything bigger.

"Complicating things was the fact that because of my mom's taste in books, from my teens on I started to read a lot of new-agey self-help books: *The Road Less Traveled, Way of The Peaceful Warrior, The Book (on the Taboo of Knowing Who You Are), Games People Play, Jonathan Livingston Seagull, Siddhartha, Zen and the Art of Motorcycle Maintenance* and so many more. I took all this esoteric stuff, which I still love by the way, and used it as a way to spiritually bypass all the negative stuff I experienced—keeping people at a distance, overthinking everything, and not holding myself accountable for my own actions and behaviors. Inside me, in the quiet voice, I knew I had work to do. I knew there was another way, but I just kept choosing smallness.

"Then one of my younger brothers went through MKP's New Warrior Training Adventure ['NWTA'], and the other men in my family did too, from 1996 to 1999. They loved it, it blew them wide open. But I was so afraid of being seen, telling the truth about myself, and being vulnerable in front of other men, that I could not make myself go through the program. It wasn't until the pain became big enough that I was willing to take that risk.

"There came the moment about six months after the end of that long relationship when I had met the woman who is now my wife, and I realized that just weeks into the relationship, I was repeating the old patterns. I had to do something. In some ways what happened to me is a perfect example of what motivates men to make a change, which I have now observed in hundreds of men over the years. It's really two things: hearing a call deep down in our guts that there is something more for us, and pain.

"In every training program, there's always a guy who says that he's here because he heard about the program from another guy who went through it . . . and there was just something about him that he trusted, some strange attractor. That's the call. That's the Hero's Journey. The call is always some variation of 'Do you want to experience an adventure?'

"As for the pain, there is no question that men are hurting today. We feel isolated. We frequently don't have a sense of purpose in life. We are confused about what our role is supposed to be. And we have been saturated in a two-dimensional view of what it means to be masculine.

"The focus on getting ahead makes it very tough to figure out what we are experiencing, and feeling, and what we want, and who we want to be close to, what our vision is for the future.

"MKP invites men to go through a difficult initiatory process, a hero's journey in order to find the softness, grief, and joy inside of them, and discover what lies underneath our fear, guilt, grief, rage, and shame. We give men a community of practice with other men who are on this journey of figuring out who they are in the world, and what they want for themselves, their friends and families.

"There's a huge evolution going on at MKP right now as to what the hero's journey looks like, but that's really nothing new, because the program has always been evolving from the very beginning. It got started with three guys who sat around a kitchen table in Milwaukee, Wisconsin, in 1984. Myth, archetypes, and Jungian psychology were very popular back in the '70s and '80s. Very different from today. But the power of myth and stories to bring men through the hero's journey continues, even as some definitions of masculinity dissolve.

"This is very hopeful for me. This is exactly what MKP was designed to do from the beginning—bust open rigid definitions of what it means to be a man. And that's exactly what our groups are doing now, as we exist in a culture where this is very much up in the air.

"Today, we have men's groups in over 26 countries, and run trainings in fourteen regions of the world. Across the US, we will be offering 50 New Warrior Training Adventure weekends this year, plus 100 additional training programs. In the US, we also support over 700 men's groups that have been pulled together by program participants.

"The content of our programs has changed a lot over time, but the framework remains the same. (In the beginning the founders didn't even realize that they were doing an initiation ritual until they were seven years in. That's pretty funny when you think about it.) Our core insight has always been that there is this thing within men, indeed all human beings, that is waiting to be fully expressed. For men there aren't many containers where they can go to their full expression and be safe, supported.

"Recently, we have been going through another huge evolution. There is a spiritual aspect in our work. In fact, developing spiritual awareness within men is in our mission statement. For a long time, this component of our work has been informed, in part, by indigenous spirituality. We've used some symbols, language and ceremony that resemble or have roots in Native American traditions. There are men in the work with decades of connection to Native people here in the US and in other countries, as well as a number of Native men who are part of the organization and very committed. It's beautiful, and meaningful. I've loved having these processes be part of the work, but it's become increasingly clear that as an organization, we had to find a new way. As mostly nonnative men, I think it's our responsibility to self-educate and act in ways that reflect cultural awareness and respect. In the last few years, with a lot of work and a lot of pain, we've changed all the processes that resembled or were rooted in Native American spiritual practice. We can hold on to and honor the influence of Indigenous ways of seeing and thinking without using language or ritual that offends or alienates some of the men we're trying to serve.

"Our goal has always been to help men get grounded, see how we are all connected, see how we are connected to nature and to something bigger than ourselves. We will continue to do that, and to build respectful relationships with other cultural traditions. It's all about con-nection. It is my personal hope that someday MKP guys will be sitting in local circles with indigenous people from many tribes, with love and respect. Those wisdom traditions are powerful and healing."

Recognizing once again the conversation was running long, I asked, "Given what you are seeing at the weekend retreats this year, do you believe that we are making a cultural shift? Especially among younger men who are going to be taking on the role of leading the charge? Do you have any evidence from the frontlines to share?"

Boysen responded, "Yes, I'm getting lots of reports that younger men are coming to NWTA for two reasons. First, very much like their fathers, they are looking for ways to break out of the remaining con-straints of '50s–'60s corporate culture. They want to be in touch with the 'wild man' inside of them that this culture stifles. Second, they want to be connected to other men, and in a space where competition is not the number one game. A place where there is an awareness that men can come and be open and vulnerable, collaborate and support each other, and bond in community. And leave feeling good about being a man."

I interjected, "Yeah, young men are not getting many positive mes-sages about being male today." Boysen agreed.

I then asked him one final question. "Given the size of the organiza-tion and its reach, is there any conflict within MKP between men who identify as 'traditional males' and 'progressives'?" I had witnessed both groups as being present at my own weekend experience, so I knew both were active in the group.

Boysen grimaced a bit, as if to say that he should have expected me to raise that thorny issue. Then he smiled and offered this observation. "Are you familiar with Steve McIntosh's work around integral philoso-phy? He has a book called *Developmental Politics*."

I replied, "No."

"Well, I think that's the best way to describe what is going on inter-nally. Integral theory talks about tension that needs to be managed, and that's a good thing. Here's how that theory plays out at MKP. Our programs speak to both groups of men. Some of the values that we talk about—warrior energy, grit, strength, responsibility, accountability, authenticity, integrity—are really important in 'traditional' male models. Other core values are key to more 'progressive' types—lover energy, empathy, compassion, respect, intercultural understanding, interconnectivity. There's definitely a push/pull tension between the two groups—not a peacefully co-exist situation. Integral theory says that in this tension is the space where creativity occurs. It provides the richest places where we can grow."

"That seems like an insight that all men should take to heart during these times," I mused.

░ ░ ░

Our next stop will be to pick up Owen Marcus. Owen likes to introduce himself this way: "I never intended to work with men. I never intended to work on my connection skills. Only after a series of unsatisfying relationships was my dissatisfaction strong enough for me to do what I resisted doing: sitting in a men's group to learn to develop my relationship skills. I immediately realized that I was not the only one struggling. Then, to my surprise, I found myself enjoying sharing with and listening to other men."

An executive coach, as well as a former bodyworker who has helped scores of professional athletes, Owen used his decades of postgraduate training with Ron Kurtz and Peter Levine, Ph.D., and other developers of new fields of psychotherapy to create a somatic-based model that works for men. He trains men how to use their bodies and innate ability to heal to step out of our habitual stress response. (See Chapter 2 and Chapter 4 regarding the importance of somatics, using our bodies to make a shift.) In 2015, he created EVRYMAN with a couple of co-founders to provide a new space and build communities of practice where men could do this work. Owen has been involved in men's work for over forty-five years, so he also has a solid perspective on the current state of things.

Once again, I asked him whether he thinks that things are changing, and where we might be stuck.

He responded, "Yes, I think we're making progress. Men's work is evolving, but the problem is that it's not happening fast enough. We're stuck in an old paradigm of men's work that doesn't grab younger men.

"Back when I first got involved, the men's movement started as a response to the women's movement. At the time we were trying to find validity for men to be emotional. We did a lot of work with mythology, drums, getting naked in the woods, to unleash what was inside of us. There was a ton of momentum in the beginning. But all movements have to evolve, but the men's movement didn't. It got stuck for awhile.

"Today, the conversation about masculinity is going right over guys' heads. The only people who talk about masculinity are in the media or academics. Think about it. What guy wants to talk about his masculinity?!"

He paused for a second. I did not respond, stumped.

"Yeah, right. None do. So we have to change the model of men's work, so that the men's movement isn't such a new age-y old model. The future of the movement is doing the inner work that men need and want to do. That's why we started EVRYMAN. That's what it's all about.

"We believe that the power of men's work is in the collective, the interdependent, the tribal experience among men. That's consistent with Sebastian Junger's book *Tribe*. Men need a safe space in order to do the inner work that needs to get done. The biggest difference between therapy and this inner work is that therapy is one-to-one, and it's conducted between an expert and a patient. It helps but it is not the answer. Men's work is peer-to-peer, tribal. It succeeds because we're all doing it together. It takes us back to our ancestral roots.

"You know, Alice Armstrong makes an accurate and important observation in her book *Making Sense of Men*. She says, 'Women don't have a commonly understood code of honor as men do.' Men need a space where we can be seen and recognized for who we are as men."

He went on. "One of the benefits of our work is that you discover your ability to contribute to another man's life. There is no other venue where just showing up adds to another person's journey.

"Another critical aspect of our work is that we focus on the physiological aspect of men's experience. Our goal is to get guys to open up, emotionally. But ask a guy how he feels. Most men *can't respond*, even if he would like to, because we grew up in a culture that feminizes feeling. Men are criticized for both expressing their emotions ('men don't cry'), and not expressing them ('you are such a stone, cold, silent, remote, detached'). So what's the solution? We show men how to feel emotions in their bodies, both in their present experience, and where they have stored their trauma. Most men instinctively know how to do that, and the journey takes off from there . . ."

Again, I interrupted—it's something that, according to my wife, like all men, I'm really, really good at—and moved the conversation to the general state of things.

"So Owen, I get that this new model of men's work is a terrific experience, but are we as a culture or society making a shift? Beyond men getting more in touch with their emotions, and building healthier relationships at work and home, are there bigger, broader changes going on? Are we ever going to move beyond the crap that is still going on? Look at how much trauma men are still experiencing and causing . . ."

"Hell, yes, Mark. Look, I've been doing this work for a long time. I do see change happening, but it's like the Berlin Wall. When it came down, it surprised the hell out of everyone. No one saw that coming. It seemed to happen overnight at the time, but of course it didn't. In any major shift there is organic movement below the surface that evades institutional or public awareness. Then boom! It happens. Things tip. Just like that."

Seeking a fourth opinion on all this, I reached out to Charles Matheus. Charles is another Cornell University graduate (what is in the water supply up there?) who has been involved in men's work for a long time, with a particular focus on helping men and boys develop a healthy version of masculinity. Now an executive coach helping men find vitality, purpose, and success, he has been hosting *Remaking Manhood | The Healthy Masculinity Podcast*, where he and Mark Greene interview thought leaders in this space. It's a wonderful program that rewards repeat listening.

"What is it going to take to make a leap forward?" Charles mused. "Well, first you have to understand where I come from, the experience that I bring to answering this question, the number of times that I have been present and witnessed a transformative moment, the falling away of the artifice, the protective armor, the revelation of vulnerability, humility, the deep desire to be seen and loved for who they are . . . as boys and men.

"And now I have to confess that I am willfully naïve and optimistic, innocent. My optimism comes from standing across from men and boys who need very little to get to a place of belonging. Not very far underneath the mask that we put on about what it is to be a man is our humanity, as Judy Chu, Carol Gilligan, and Niobe Way point out. Judy Chu says, 'All it is going to take is culture change, and culture change happens all the time.' I've taken that to heart over and over again, and I can name the moments."

"Okay, Charles. I take your point, but if that's the case why is it that we also sense that in some ways it isn't happening, or it isn't happening fast enough? Why do we feel stuck?"

"There are a couple of reasons. Our economic system has a lot at stake in keeping us in place, making us compete for the rewards that it distributes.

"But I think that the real reason underneath it all is fear. We think that we will lose power if we switch to a form of masculinity that is heart-centered, kind, collaborative. The reality is that an interconnected way of being male is so much more powerful. We can win collectively and collaboratively. By contrast, there is no winning in the dominance-based culture of masculinity that we inhabit. All we do is age out and die. When we make the switch to this other way of being male, of being human, we don't lose power. In fact, it's the opposite. We gain power. And it's not that hard to unlearn the behavior that is holding us back.

"I talk a lot about how to overcome fear of making a change in my book, *Leadership and Masculinity: Embracing New Strength.*

"The first step is to build self-awareness. We need to look at what is happening in our body to create space between your Self and ego. Don't believe in everything you think. Separate our true humanity from our ego because the ego is deeply invested in the status quo. We need to develop a healthier relationship with our egos. Change is easier then. It's just a step to the side.

"The second step is to ask for help. The relational field develops when we ask for help. It defangs fear. When you feel anxiety, just call someone. Taking this step takes some humility as we admit our vulnerability. It's good for us as men, and it changes the other person you reach out to.

"Third step is to take concrete action to make change in your family, community, and the world. I think that this is one of the things that the men's movement has often neglected. A lot of workshops focus on healing and self-actualization. But that is not the end point. It's just the beginning of the journey."

"I'm curious," I said. "Why do you think so much of the work seems to focus on emotions?"

"Well, for one," Charles responded, "that's a core issue for men, but it's not the whole story. Some of that is just public perception. There's a whole lot more going on in men's work."

"You mean that it's perceived as self-indulgent, privileged in some way?"

"Yes, but people don't see the pain points that I do. When they do, they are blown away. Women are craving opportunities to see men be emotional and vulnerable. That's what makes the news. Men advocating for changing the system is less interesting and messy."

"Do you think that younger generations of men are going to make the shift that we need to make?" I asked. "Peggy Orenstein's book is not encouraging . . ."

"Yeah, but I still hold onto my naivete and optimism. Younger men are confused. We need to make sure that we create systems where they can continue their growth and exploration."

███   ███   ███

Now, to get a better sense of how younger generations of men see all this, we're going to check in on Kim Evensen. A former male model of uncommon charisma and good looks, he's a captivating spokesperson whose plain-spoken gifts for communication have won a worldwide following. He speaks with the energy, enthusiasm, and self-assurance of youth. In 2017, Kim founded Brothers, a non-profit dedicated to raising awareness about the importance of male friendships and the positive effects arising from strong male relationships. His organization speaks to boys *and* men, ages 12–80, but mostly men 16–30. (And yes, of course, women often comprise half the audience, for a lot of reasons not just related to Kim's strapping, Scandinavian frame.) I am inspired by his work, and utterly convinced that his age group is going to be the one that pushes us into the future. Dropping in on Kim is a pleasure.

"I was born in Norway, but I also lived in Australia for four formative years. While there, I became obsessed with how boys and young men struggle to be vulnerable. I started to ask a bunch of questions, like: 'Why don't men ask for help from other guys?' 'Why don't men or boys hug or touch each other?' 'Why don't we say "I love you" unless we are drunk?' When I ask men in their 20s and 30s that question, most guys respond, 'Guys show, don't tell.' But that's not true. We never show our emotions.

"The truth is that men are missing out on genuine connection. We have to reclaim what has been lost. And you cannot find connection in therapy, no matter how many sessions you do. Therapists and counselors can't take the spot of a friend.

"I wrote *The Real Bro Code* for boys who have no interest in reading. In the book and my talks, I use expressions that boys use, and deconstruct their language. And, when I work with that age group, I don't use academic language. I speak to them using their own vocabulary, the memes that they toss around. I ask them, 'So, tell me why you can't say, "I love you, man"? Why do you have to add "no homo," and say instead "I love you, man, no homo"?' Then I give them practical advice, show them how to take action. And I remind them that, 'A. If it was easy, everyone would have done it,' and 'B. We have so much more relational capacities than we think we do.'

"When I'm with younger guys, I often like to use an example from the military. Soldiers know that everyone needs friendships. That's why, according to Sebastian Junger, so many vets miss the war in Afghanistan. I tell boys, 'You don't think leaning on a friend is weird when you are about to be killed, do you? So let's not wait until it's all going bad to dare to express love and compassion . . .'

"I have been asked to speak to guys in the Army almost 30 times. Each time I remind guys who they are. I challenge their use of women as currency to prove that they are 'real men.' And I remind them that friendship has to be built on love and trust. Soldiers know that. And I also talk to them about respect. Where does an attitude for respect come from? It comes from our closest relationships."

He paused, thinking and catching his breath, after the fusillade of words that had just erupted out of him.

"The problem is the norms and cultural expectations that make it hard for boys to form friendships. We have to remove all the elephants in the room first, which is what I try to do in my presentations. I told the Norwegian government that they are trying to treat the symptoms instead of solving the core issue. We need to smash down paradigms that prevent boys from forming close connections. We need to focus on connection.

"You know, I think a big part of our challenge right now is that most people who are engaged in trying to help make a cultural shift come in and talk about mental health issues, suicide, depression, substance abuse. A woman came up to me after one of my talks and said that she always feels so depressed when speakers would talk about men's mental health issues. She went on to say that she felt so much joy and hope for the future now, believing that we *actually* can make a positive change. Of course, we need to talk about mental health. We need to talk about the bad stuff. But we shouldn't use that as click bait.

"I want to be known, seen, and heard as a positive force in this space. Uplifting. I am filled with so much hope. Being full of optimism and hope has such huge value in today's world.

"I have seen a lot of change over the last six years—a lot more focus on men's health. Right after I had founded Brothers, I had a Skype meeting with Mark Greene in which I told him that I wanted to focus on boys' friendships. At the time he replied, 'Oh, that's a bit weird.' The irony is that Mark had already been writing for years about the brutal mechanisms by which our dominant culture of manhood strips boys of their natural capacity to form meaningful, authentic friendships. After giving it more thought, he agreed that this is an area that needs focus. Because the taboo around male friendships has marked us all, including me.

"Role models are so important. We need good role models for younger boys of what it looks like to have strong male friendships, so it's really important for guys in their 20s to show up and demonstrate what these relationships are for their younger brothers."

"I would add that it's vitally important older generations to do the same."

Kim closed our conversation with some sage advice for a thirty-one-year-old. "I also always tell guys, 'Show me your friends, and I will show you your future. Show me your closest relationships, and I will show you who you will become. Insecure friendships are breeding grounds for stupid decision-making. Your friends shape you/each other. If you don't practice respect in your closest male relationships, then you'll never be able to show respect to the people that you report to, and to women.' "

■ ▦ ▨

Having drunk from that firehose of passion and inspiration, let's shift over to Paul Nelson. Given all the attention that the media has given gender fluidity among younger generations of men, I think it will be useful to check in with him. As I mentioned in Chapter 2, Paul is a nationally recognized male sexuality educator and advocate, and the founder of FrankTalk.org, the first non-commercial online community for men with sexual dysfunctions. He is a licensed sex therapist who sees men daily in a clinical setting with Dr. Michael Werner, a men's sexual medicine specialist in New York City. Having counseled hundreds of men of all ages regarding sexual issues, he has his finger on the pulse of what really matters to men. He is also the newly elected president of the Connecticut Men's Gathering (COMEGA).

"I have to laugh when people ask me how long I have done men's work. I taught at an all-boys boarding school for twelve years, then supervised a boys' dorm for five years, and have been a men's therapist for erectile dysfunction for thirteen years. I'm also a father, with a son, and a daughter, and 3 brothers. That's a lot of testosterone and men's work! I am absolutely swimming in it!!!"

Paul's sarcastic sense of humor is laced with so much irony and wit that I struggle to stop laughing when I am with him. But some of the issues that we talk about aren't funny. Curious to know who attends COMEGA, I ask him whether they saw a lot of younger men at their gathering this summer.

Paul replied, "Yes, but younger men are showing up for different reasons than they did before. COMEGA got started in the '90s when *Iron John, King Warrior Magician Lover, The Power of Myth,* spoke deeply to men. In recent years, younger men have told me that the whole archetype thing does not speak to them. It's just not where their heads are. So we have decided to offer a significant range of programs that appeal to all ages.

"Our mission is to create an intergenerational community of men intentionally creating a culture shift. The highly structured mountaintop experiences that other programs offer are great, but they don't sustain you. Men need to be in community. Another problem is that historically men's work has tended to skew older, because no 32-year-old man with three kids has the time or has been able to convince his wife to let him go off for the weekend. As a result, weekend programs tend to be attended by men over 45.

"What's really interesting, though, is that younger men are truly interested in doing men's work, so we started offering monthly online gatherings, microcosms of our bi-annual weekends. And as a result, somehow the younger guys are persuading their partners to let them show up for our gatherings. About one-third of attendees are now under 40.

"COMEGA is different from lots of other programs. In terms of sheer numbers present at one time, I think we're the largest men's gathering in the East Coast. Rooted in the gatherings that got started in the '80s and then fizzled out, we do not offer a structured, directed program. We convene lots of guys and offer four blocks of five programs simultaneously from which participants cherry pick their own schedule. As a result, guys return year after year, sometimes twice a year, over and over again.

"COMEGA is open to non-binary and trans men. We always have been. About 50% of participants identify as straight; 25% as gay; and 25% as in-between. So identity is not an issue in this space. Members of COMEGA who identify as traditional men have come a long way in accepting that sexual orientation is not a thing that should be of any concern. Guys feel free to speak their truth and talk about their experience without shame or censure.

"Participants are a self-selecting group. They are men who are looking for something more than what they are getting from the men in their daily lives, and they are men whose lives aren't working. Participants cut across the full socio-economic and racial spectrum, except that high-net-worth men don't attend. I always joke around that rich men feel that they don't need friends. Of course, that isn't true, because I do live in New Canaan, but I can definitely tell you that no man who lives here would ever go near COMEGA. Sadly, making the time and finding the resources to slip away for a weekend is largely a white, middle-class privilege, but we are working on that."

I was disappointed to hear Paul's comments about men in the upper echelon of society. They are in the best position to help effect change, and it is my experience that they are often some of the loneliest men on the planet. However, his observation is consistent with a conversation that I had with another therapist in NYC whose practice focuses on Wall Street elites. For them, these issues are a very small part of overall identity issues. They are much too focused on the challenges of being a super achiever and tend to be disinterested in changing a culture in which they are successfully competing as men.

I asked Paul, "Do you think that COMEGA is achieving its mission to help men intentionally make a cultural shift?"

Paul responded with brutal honesty, "I don't know. But what I do know is that we older men in COMEGA and other men's groups must respond to the changes and needs of young men, or we will die. We have to accept that their needs are very different. For example, no one under 40 gives a shit whether you are gay or straight.

"Look, here's my take on what is going on. I think what is going to happen is that there is going to be a tipping point like gay marriage. That took over sixty years, then it seemed to happen overnight. The challenge right now is that huge segments of men are still living the bro culture. It only works for a few men, but everyone still participates in it. Getting drunk, watching sports, chasing women.

"At the end of the day, things are going to change because it has to happen. We can't keep going on this way. The men's movement and women's movement both need to give permission to men and women to be who they really are. It's that simple. That's the goal here."

　　　　　　　　■　　■　　■

Seeing some overall patterns beginning to emerge in the big picture that is developing here, let's reach out again to my soul brother, Joel Serino, whose life journey we followed in Chapter 6. As we saw earlier, Joel is obsessed with finding the realities that lie beneath the surface of things. He has been involved in many men's circles, and I thought that in his quest for "the truth," he might have stumbled upon some answers. Born at the tail end of Generation X, he offers an important critique of men's work.

"The men's circles that I have been involved in have become toxic through polarization. They focus so much energy on shadow work that there is not much room for contemplation and integration. I don't want to sit in medicine journeys or circles with too much intention anymore. Our journey is to create harmony. Not separation. Safe spaces for men and women don't focus on gender issues. They focus on unity and integration.

"In my experience, a lot of men's groups tend to be self-congratulatory. They are hedonistic, self-centered. Focused on self-empowerment. The problem is that men who feel empowered then often focus on overpowering others. Aggression. They want to take positions of power, having been empowered. I prefer to get all my orders from women. Their power is derived from speaking truth."

I thanked him for his words of caution, but then pressed on to understand how the men's work that he has done might have moved him to a new place in life.

He gave me a metaphysical answer, another bit of wisdom for the men's movement. "I am finding that I have more and more interest in a more silent approach. The things that I have been asked to do are the things that I have said I would like not to, but they feel in alignment. It's clear that I'm being asked to step up for the next generation of men and women, and do so with purity of heart. I am getting to a place where I realize that life is not about stuff to fix. It's just an expression of the universal principles. It is what it is.

"Look, the current cultural change is the repercussion of the multigenerational evolution that is going on. We're just bridge workers. You can't overvalue the importance of contemplative practice in this process. But here's the real challenge. Men always want to fix everything. The question is whether men can learn not to fix, but to trust what emerges if we become still and listen for what wants to emerge.

"The way that I see it . . . Men aren't sages, clearly, but we have been doing some of the work that sages do . . . sitting back, thinking, meditating, getting our act together. The sage doesn't have any effect on culture until she or he comes back from the cave of contemplation and re-enters the marketplace. You know this. When you visit a cave where a sage has meditated for years on end, you can literally feel the energy of the place. That energy is released when the sage returns to the world. That's happening now. Men have been in the cave for a long time doing the work. It hasn't been perfect, but our culture of masculinity is still going to make a shift now."

Okay, one last point of view, this time from Mark Greene, whose excellent summary of Man Box culture served as the springboard for our journey into this book. In many ways he agrees with Joel. A cultural shift is happening, somewhat of its own accord, because of a range of fundamental shifts in the way guys show up today. It's not that there has been some big, bold policy move or program offered by the men's movement that has triggered this shift. It's that the unit of change in our evolving culture of masculinity is the individual male, an everyday man, just regular joes doing the work of changing their own lives so that they are healthier, more connected, and more meaningful. Of course, that is what all the programs we have explored in this chapter focus on: giving men the tools they need to make their lives work.

Let's give Mark the final word on this topic.

"Masculinity [as a concept and space for activism] is a bit of a dead zone. People avert their eyes. They much prefer to deal with women's issues and other problems. The struggles of men can be a turnoff. And yet, a cultural shift is happening right under our noses, in spite of that.

"It can sound simplistic, but the bottom line is that Gen Z and millennials are a different wave of men because many of *their* fathers showed up, and showed their sons that they cared for them, instead of being absent, overly disciplining them, bullying them into manhood, or ignoring them.

"There is a really interesting study by Kevin Shafer at Brigham University measuring the impact of more engaged fathers on the social views of their adult children. Shafer's study measured degrees of engagement of dads as far back as the 1960s to the present. Shafer says that in the '60s, only about 15% of dads were what he calls 'engaged.'"

I asked what he meant by engaged. "You mean, they taught their sons progressive ideas?"

"Shafter said no. They were just there. Tossing the ball in the backyard, showing up at games, school events. It's literally being present, that's all we're talking about. Today, most dads are present in these ways.

That's a huge sea change coming out of the parenting space. And it accelerates generationally.

"Another big piece of this shift to a masculinity of expression and connection is the Stay-at-Home Dads Movement. It finally got noticed culturally about ten years ago, and how men are showing up there is transformative. Caregiving dads is creating a wave of sons and daughters who see masculinity in a completely different way."

"Okay," I joked. "So basically, you're telling me that the book I am writing is a waste of time."

Mark laughed. "Hell, no. It's a record of your journey for your sons and others of this huge shift that we are making. What it's important to pay attention to and remember. And all the work that each one of us is doing is an important piece of a collective effort to move things forward."

He paused, thinking, then said, "There's another big shift that is going on. That's permission granting."

Puzzled, I asked, "What's that? Is it like consent?"

Mark responded, "Permission granting is men being open, vulnerable and expressing our emotions in front of other men, allowing other men to see that aspect of who we are at work and in our social lives. It creates a crucial tipping point for change. Open-hearted leadership grants permission to other men around us to let go of the dominance-based culture of masculinity that is so pervasive in our personal and professional lives and trade it for something more human. Millions of men are ready to make a shift. They are the moveable middle. Permission granting is men breaking the silence, the illusion that any who want it are alone in our desire for connection and expression.

"Here's an interesting statistic for you, from a study by Catalyst. 94% of men experience masculine anxiety in the workplace, anxiety about their *performance of masculinity*.[164] 94%. Think about it. That's nearly every man in the workplace. Why is that? *Why is that??* Are guys that insecure??? Well, guess what. The answer is yes. That same study indicates that the higher the combative culture at work, the less men are willing to take a risk in calling out sexist behavior by the men around them. So, basically, everyone is walking on eggshells at work in those environments. Bullying, combative cultures are deeply retrogressive. They prevent men from changing.

"But men are pushing back, doing a lot of work to make our lives more human, more connected. More and more, men are not happy with the bullying, isolating status quo. We are sick of it and it turns out that an open-hearted approach at work yields dramatically better results in innovation, employee satisfaction, retention, financial results, mental health, etc., *and* it leads to better relationships outside work.

"These are all waves of change that are moving through society. Men are saying now, 'I don't want to *live* this way' not just 'I don't want to *work* this way.' And all these waves are cresting to a tipping point. Men don't have to run around acting like assholes anymore just to prove we are 'real men.'"

■   ■   ■

It appears that each generation has its own take on the shift that is occurring. While many men are doing the inner work that enables us to bring forth the full expression of our humanity into the world for our own well-being and the benefit of others, a cultural change of this magnitude will not occur unless we all, individually and collectively, get naked and rebuild our identities from the inside out. I do think that at the end of the day millennials and their Gen Z brothers will be the generation that helps to fundamentally reframe our perceptions of what it means to be a man. With their fathers clearing the field of any resistance, they will finally carry the ball to the end zone, declaring victory over the forces that are currently holding us back.

As evidence, I am reminded of an outdoor wedding that my wife and

I attended a couple of summers ago, when COVID restrictions eased. By coincidence, both the bride and the groom's parents are friends of ours from completely different parts of our lives.

I was expecting a staid affair observing the conventions that families with deep New England roots follow. Not too flashy. A great raw bar. Lots of good wine and cocktails. A buffet dinner, followed by a lot of dancing. All on a slice of land that has miraculously remained in the family for a hundred years or so. These are not the spaces where non-conformists thrive (except for eccentric family members summoned out of exile for the occasion).

Arriving at a sprawling complex on the Cape for a rehearsal dinner, I was excited that our period of isolation was coming to an end. I was not alone. The guests who gathered were flamboyantly dressed. People were ready to loosen up, connect, and party.

I did not anticipate, however, how far that sentiment would play out among the millennial men. They didn't seem like a demonstrative lot. It was therefore a total surprise when a string of the groom's friends offered toast after toast about how much his friendship with the groom meant to him, and how grateful he was that his buddy had chosen such a wonderful wife.

I had never heard such public protestations of love from one straight man to another before. The stories that these men shared were astounding. Their reminiscences of gastronomic feasts at home or out, reciprocal couch surfing, wilderness outings, and club hopping into the wee hours sent the mind spinning. Their willingness to reveal their strong feelings for one another in front of the patriarchy assembled demonstrated a degree of openness, transparency, and intimacy that prior generations of adult men would have never displayed. One man even joked that he had "shared a bed with the groom more than any other person in his life, with the possible exception of his wife." People looked at each other askance but laughed. The wedding left me wondering whether this was an aberrant group or an indicator that younger generations were finally rewriting the rules of the Man Box.

Later that fall I had the opportunity to dive deeper into this question, when I attended an annual alumni retreat of an all-male a cappella group. Usually, it's a multi-generational booze-fest that welcomes the new undergrads, but this year with the Delta variant on the rise, boomers stayed home. I'm glad that I did not, because I was astonished by what I witnessed when 40 men under 30 show up for each other.

When I was admitted to the group 45 years earlier, it was a decidedly straight male ensemble in which bromances existed but were not openly expressed except in displays of teasing, and a couple of gay relationships that took off. Under our jocular banter, depending on the year, the group was bedeviled by bullying and microaggressions. In 2014, after a returning undergraduate was bullied out of rejoining the group, the graduate board insisted that all new members sign an anti-bullying pledge. Hiking to the top of Mt. Oceola in the pouring rain on this retreat, I was pleased to hear the guys joking that now that they had signed "the pledge," whatever they did to each other wasn't bullying. (Evidence once again that humor is the way men process their feelings.)

After our hike, we gathered in a circle to share how being a member of the group had changed our lives. Here's what the millennial and Gen Z men had to say without boomers present:

"This is the one space where you are accepted for who you are. It's okay to express your version of being male, whatever it is."

"There will be days when you hate some guy's guts but try to be kind. At the end of the year, you won't be able to imagine life without him."

"When you leave school, you will quickly find out who your real friends are. It won't be your block mates. It will be us."

"Try not to be hard on each other. Challenging each other is fine. It strengthens us as a group. But bullying is not. Don't sink into petty bullshit."

"We will take care of you. Even when you are down and out, we will put you back on your feet."

"There will be lots of firsts. Don't give a damn about what others might say. Dive in."

"Don't judge. Stay open."

Talking to the alums in their upper twenties afterwards, I heard stories of the usual heartaches. Long-term relationships that had sadly ended. The trials of going on two or three first dates a week to find a life partner. Learning to cook vegan meals for a girlfriend.

What I did not hear was the usual locker-room, derogatory speech about women. No boasts of their sexual prowess (or aggression) with women (or men). I realize these data points do not mean that such behavior does not occur, but they are promising.

Seeing these men express new forms of masculinity in each other's company made me realize that all-male spaces can be therapeutic and productive, and not necessarily breeding grounds for a culture of dominance-based masculinity, as is commonly thought. Indeed, men might *need* safe places where they can be vulnerable, loosen up, share their emotions, develop better communication skills, and try out new behaviors without fear of ridicule or judgment. (At this retreat, men danced with each other on the deck until 5:00 AM, no questions asked.)

I understand that women may object. In these settings there is always the risk that men might fall back into the destructive mindsets that are so deeply conditioned into us. I would submit, however, that the outcomes of these spaces are largely positive. Their purpose is not to exclude women or to encourage men to think of women as "other." They are a place where men can develop the capacities to be better partners to the women and men in their lives.

So, three cheers for millennial and Gen Z men. Here's to the healthy ways of being male that they are creating.

AFTERWORD

So here we are at the end of our journey. I hope that this book has given you some ideas for ways in which we can weave together new and old forms of being male that work for you, and that together we can build an expanded, healthier culture of masculinity with a broader range of norms for men.

On our extended hike across the inner landscape of men, we have explored seven different domains that you might want to investigate further in your own way, making your own discoveries, charting your own path, and traveling with guys who are making a similar journey. I hope that this distilled list of our explorations will give you pause to reflect on how to incorporate these approaches into your own life, recalling some of the stories and guides presented within each section of the book:

- Strip Down
- Seek the Sacred Feminine Within

- Engage and Express Your Heart
- Own Your Full Sexuality Identity
- Practice Stillness
- Impose Retreat
- Reframe Success

I do believe that investigations in these areas (and other terrain that you might discover) can help us reclaim the pieces of our personalities that have been conditioned out of us and will allow us to restore the navigational tools that we all possess but infrequently use.

With a more complete inner GPS, we should be able to rebuild our masculine identities from the inside out and conduct our lives in ways that unleash our unique gifts as men for the benefit of others.

Mark Grayson
March 1, 2024

ENDNOTES

1   Richard Reeves, *Of Boys and Men: Why the Modern Male Is Struggling, Why It Matters, and What to Do About It* (Washington D.C.: The Brookings Institution Press, 2022).

2   Mark Greene, *The Little #MeToo Book for Men* (New York City, New York: ThinkPlay Partners, 2018).

3   Esther Perel, "Women Teach Men," August, 2018.

4   Peggy Orenstein, *Boys and Sex: Young Men on Hookups, Love, Porn, Consent, and the New Masculinity* (New York City, New York: Harper, 2020).

5   Peggy Orenstein, "What It Means to Be a Man," *Atlantic Monthly*, December 16, 2019.

6   Susan Faludi, "Trump's Thoroughly Modern Masculinity," *The New York Times*, October 29, 2020; and Claire Cain Miller and Alisha Haridasani Gupta, "What Makes a Man Manly? Trump and Biden Offer Competing Answers," *The New York Times*, November 3, 2020.

7   Antoni Huber, "Naked, Mute and Well Hung: A Brief Ethnographic Comparison of Kengpa and Related Ritual Performers in the Eastern Himalayas and Beyond," in *The Illuminating Mirror* eds. O. Czaja and G. Hazod (2015). Tibetan Studies

in Honour of Per K. Sørensen on the Occasion of his 65th Birthday. Wiesbaden: Verlag Dr. Ludwig Reichert, pp. 219–242 (text), 592–595 (plates).

8   John-Charles Duffy, "Concealing the Body, Concealing the Sacred: The Decline of Ritual Nudity in Mormon Temples," *Journal of Ritual Studies* 21, no. 2 (2007): 1–21.

9   ". . . during our induction physicals. In a large room, we were lined up in two lines and required to strip naked. I figured it was going to be a quick look by the examining physician as he passed up and down the line, but instead, each of the two lines were led into separate hallways where we waited in the hallway until we were called, one at a time into a room, weighed, our pulse taken, an observation for any wounds or abnormalities, and returned to the hallway. Once each of us had been examined, we were taken to the other hallway where, again we were singled out and given the old "turn your head and cough" exam. The hallways were public accessed corridors and not closed off. It has stuck in my memories all these years of my spending close to an hour lingering around wearing nothing but a pair of cowboy boots," Quora, 2020. https://www.quora.com/As-part-of-basic-training-in-the-military-do-recruits-have-to-line-up-with-no-clothes-on/answers/250331449.

10   Ian Nicholson, "Baring the soul: Paul Bindrim, Abraham Maslow and 'Nude psychotherapy'," *Journal of the History of the Behavioral Sciences* 43, no. 4 (2007): 337–359.

11   Chloe Murcock, "Fr. Richard Rohr says true evil in the flesh is really rooted in the ego, but it can still be killed," *The Chautauqua Daily*, August 20, 2020. https://chqdaily.com/2020/08/fr-richard-rohr-says-true-evil-in-the-flesh-is-really-rooted-in-the-ego-but-it-can-still-be-killed.

12   "Storm of complaints forces Vienna museum to cover up male nudes," *The Associated Press*, October 19, 2012. https://www.nydailynews.com/2012/10/19/storm-of-complaints-forces-vienna-museum-to-cover-up-male-nudes/.

13   Alfred Kinsey, Wardell Pomeroy, and Clyde Martin, "Sexual Behavior and the Human Male," *American Journal of Public Health* 93, no. 6 (2003): 894–898.

14   Alan Downs, *The Velvet Rage: Overcoming the Pain of Growing Up Gay in a Straight Man's World* (Ashland, Oregon: Blackstone Publishing, 2021).

15   Matthew Todd, *The Velvet Rage: Overcoming the Pain of Growing Up Gay in a Straight Man's World* (Bantam Press, 2016).

16   Green, Jamison (Vanderbilt University Press, 2004; Second Edition 2020).

17   Carol Hooven, "Carol Hooven on Testosterone," June 18, 2021 in *The Dishcast*

with Andrew Sullivan, podcast, MP3 audio, 1:40. https://podcasts.apple.com/us/podcast/carole-hooven-on-testosterone/id1536984072?i=1000526037974.

18   Saumya Joseph, Ankur Banarjee, "Young U.S. men having a lot less sex in the 21st century, study shows," *Reuters*, June 12, 2020; Risa Gelles-Watnick, "For Valentine's Day, 5 facts about single Americans," *Pew Research Center*, February 8, 2023.

19   Thomas Hughes, *Tom Brown at Oxford* (New York: Macmillan, 1861): 122–123.

20   Nathaniel Beck, "Christian Theology of the Body and the Body Positivity Movement," *Honors Thesis, Baylor University*, August, 2018.

21   "A Look Back at Burt Reynolds' Iconic Nude Photoshoot in Cosmopolitan," *Cosmopolitan*, September 7, 2018.

22   Matthew Rettenmund, "A Penis on Every Page: The Rise and Fall of Playgirl," *Esquire*, June 24, 2017.

23   *American Photographer*, "10 Pictures That Changed America" (January 1989).

24   Shane Duquette, *Bony to Beastly*, "The Ideal Male Body Type According to Women (Survey Results)," April 4, 2023.

25   See Shane O'Mara, *In Praise of Walking* (New York City, New York: W. W. Norton & Company, 2021), 18–21 for a discussion of the immediate impacts that occurred in the infamous "Ötzi the Iceman" experiment in 2011.

26   Jacqueline Ho, Alex Chan, Ching Luk, and Patrick Tang, "Book Review: The Body Keeps the Score: Brain, Mind, and Body in the Healing of Trauma," *Frontiers in Psychology* 12, no. 1 (2015): 704974.

27   These statistics were reported by Way during her presentation *The Crisis of Connection among Youth* at Trinity Spiritual Center on November 20, 2022. Specific citations for the data from that presentation are available.

28   National Institute of Health: National Center for Biotechnology Information, Discoveries (Craiova). 2021 Oct–Dec; 9(4): e141.

29   Center for Disease Control, *SUDORS Data Brief*, Number 2, August 2022.

30   Robin Gelburd, "A Comparison of Substance Use Disorders before and during the COVID-19 Pandemic: A Study of Private Healthcare Claims," *FAIR Health White Paper*, September 27, 2022. https://www.ajmc.com/view/substance-use-disorders-before-and-during-covid-19-pandemic-compared-in-new-study.

31   Carol Gilligan, *In a Different Voice: In a Human Voice: Psychological Theory and Women's Development* (Cambridge, Massachusetts: Harvard University Press, 1982); Carol Gilligan, *In a Human Voice: In Conversation with Psychologist Carol Gilligan* (New York City, New York: Jewish Theological Seminary, November 3, 2022).

32   Judy Chu, *When Boys Become Boys: Development, Relationships, and Masculinity* (New York City, New York: New York University Press, 2014).

33   Niobe Way, *Deep Secrets: Boys' Friendships and the Crisis of Connection* (Cambridge, Massachusetts: Harvard University Press, 2011).

34   Niobe Way, *Rebels with a Cause: Reimagining Boys, Ourselves, and Our Culture* (Boston, Massachusetts: Dutton, 2023), Prologue: Thin and Thick Stories. Thin stories are the easy explanations that society expects us to believe. Thick stories are the deeper answers to our questions gained from listening with curiosity and connecting the dots beneath the surface.

35   Niobe Way, *The Crisis of Connection among Youth* (Southport, Connecticut: Trinity Spiritual Center, November 20, 2022).

36   Orenstein, *Boys and Sex.*

37   Niobe Way, The Crisis of Connection among Youth, with additional stereotypes excerpted from her book, *Rebels with a Cause*, Prologue, 16.

38   From 1998–2007, I served as the founding CEO of All Kinds of Minds, a non-profit chaired by Charles R. Schwab whose Board and core donor base included many highly successful executives within the financial sector.

39   Mirabai Starr, *Wild Mercy: Living the Fierce and Tender Wisdom of the Women Mystics* (Sounds True, 2019).

40   Teresa of Avila, *The Interior Castle*, translated by Mirabai Starr (Riverhead Books, 2004).

41   Mirabai Starr, *Wild Mercy: Living the Fierce and Tender Wisdom of the Women Mystics* (Sounds True, 2019): 117–118.

42   Starr, *Wild Mercy*, 62–63.

43   Starr, *Wild Mercy*, 161.

44   O'Mara, *In Praise of Walking*, 145–164.

45   Susan Faludi, "Trump's Thoroughly Modern Masculinity," *The New York Times*, October 29, 2020.

46   Gloria Borger, "Josh Hawley and the 'left-wing attack on manhood'," *CNN*, November 8, 2021.

47   In English, Khaos: the betrayed promise of modernity. (Les Liens Qui Libèrent, 2023). A summary of the book can be found here in Mark Grayson, "How Do We Save Democracy," *Medium*, March 15, 2022. https://medium.com/equality-includes-you/how-do-we-save-democracy-39221916d7c3.

48   Starr, *Wild Mercy*, 145.

49   Starr, *Wild Mercy*, 149–150.

50   Starr, *Wild Mercy*, 150–151.

51   Matthew Fox, *The Hidden Spirituality of Men: Ten Metaphors to Awaken the Sacred Masculine* (Novato, California: New World Library, 2008).

52   Ann Graham Brock, *Mary Magdalene, The First Apostle: The Struggle for Authority* (Cambridge, Massachusetts: Harvard University Press, 2003); Cynthia Bourgeault, *The Meaning of Mary Magdalene: Discovering the Woman at the Heart of Christianity* (Shambala Publications, 2010).

53   Starr, *Wild Mercy*, 103–105.

54   *Playboy* 15, no. 7 (July, 1968).

55   See: Bessel van der Kolk, *The Body Keeps the Score: Brain, Mind, and Body in the Healing of Trauma* (London, United Kingdom: Penguin Press, 2015).

56   Richard Rohr, Joseph Martos, *Wild Man to Wise Man: Reflections on Male Spirituality* (Cincinnatti, Ohio: Franciscan Media, 2005): 9.

57   It is interesting to note that she was the only Titan to retain her authority under the rule of Zeus. Even the Greek gods accepted the importance of intuition.

58   Frans de Waal, *Wild Man to Wise Man: Reflections on Male Spirituality* (New York City, New York: Crown, 2010).

59   Matthew Lieberman, *Social: Why Our Brains Are Wired to Connect* (New York City, New York: Crown, 2013).

60   Niobe Way, interview by Mark Grayson, November 20, 1972, *The Crisis of Connection among Youth.*

61   Malcolm Gladwell, *Outliers: The Story of Success* (Boston, Massachusetts: Little, Brown, and Company, 2008): 91–115.

62   Starr, *Wild Mercy*, 148.

63   Starr, *Wild Mercy*, 149.

64   Kate Rademacher, *Reclaiming Rest: The Promise of Sabbath, Solitude, and Stillness in a Restless World* (Broadleaf Books, 2021).

65   Jennifer S. Lerner, Ye Li, Piercarlo Valdesolo, and Karim S. Kassam, "Emotion and Decision Making," *Annual Review of Psychology* 66, no. 1 (2015): 821. "Indeed, many psychological scientists now assume that emotions are, for better or worse, the dominant driver of most meaningful decisions in life."

66   For a summary analysis, see: Niobe Way, *Deep Secrets: Boys' Friendships and the Crisis of Connection* (Cambridge, Massachusetts: Harvard University Press, 2011), 43–67 or the following authors and their work: Dan Kinlon and Michael Thompson (*Raising Cain: Protecting the Emotional Life of Boys*, 1992), Daniel Goleman (*Emotional Intelligence*, 1995), William Pollack (*Real Boys*, 1998), Michael Gurian (*The Wonder of Boys*, 2000), Leonard Sax (*Boys Adrift*, 2007), Michael Kimmel (*Guyland*, 2008).

67   Itziar Uriquijo, Natalio Extremera, and Garazi Azanga, "The Contribution of Emotional Intelligence to Career Success: Beyond Personality Traits," *International Journal of Environmental Research and Public Health* 16, no. 23 (2019): 4809.

68   Reeves, *Of Boys and Men.*

69   The fact that Title IX has had an enormous impact on women's sports begs the question as to whether a coordinated national effort is required to effect change, as Richard Reeves suggests in his book.

70   Compare US attitudes to mental health treatment with those in uber macho Argentina where 1 in 6 individuals are in therapy. Albert Brok, "On Argentina's psychology industry, culture," YouTube, 2017, 5:32. https://www.youtube.com/watch?v=G8_U-mBBc9k.

71   The legendary Olga Silverstein, who coincidentally published the now dated *The Courage to Raise Good Men* (London, United Kingdom: Penguin Press, 1994) just before we started working with her.

72   J. Abraham Vélez de Cea, "Ramon Panikkar (1918–2010): Life and Legacy," *Buddhist-Christian Studies* 31, no. 1 (2011): 215–219.

73   Paul Ekman, Richard J. Davidson, Matthieu Riccard, and B. Alan Wallace, "Buddhist and Psychological Perspectives on Emotions and Well-Being," *Current Directions in Psychological Science* 14, no. 2 (2005): 59–63.

74   Catherine Shainberg, *Kabballah of Light: Ancient Practices to Ignite the Imagination and Illuminate the Sou* (Rochester, Vermont: Inner Traditions, 2022), 149–150, 150–151, 289–290.

75   "Science of the Heart: Exploring the Role of the Heart in Human Performance," *HeartMath Institute*, 2016. (For an excellent introduction to heart-centered practice, watch Matthew Wright's lectures at Trinity Spiritual Center on Prayers of the Heart); See Matthew Wright, "Opening the Eye of the Heart; How Ancient Wisdom Can Alter Your Life," Trinity Spiritual Center, Sept 29, 2021. https://www.youtube.com/watch?v=5NleN5f_PZk&list=PLLwV20GZMs1fLhvFvqljr_uWcmhb49T5d&index=1.

76   Way, *Rebels with a Cause*, Chapter 4 of manuscript, 12.

77   Way, *Rebels with a Cause*, Chapter 4 of manuscript, 15.

78   Way, *Rebels with a Cause*, Chapter 4 of manuscript, 31.

79   Saliha Bava, PhD, and Mark Greene, *The Relational Workplace: How Relational Intelligence Grows Diverse, Equitable, and Inclusive Cultures of Connection* (New York City, New York: ThinkPlay Partners, 2023).

80   Saliha Bava, PhD, and Mark Greene, *The Relational Book for Parenting: Raising*

Children to Connect, Collaborate, and Innovate by Growing our Families' Relationship Superpowers (New York City, New York: ThinkPlay Partners, 2018).

81   Oren Jay Sofer, *Say What You Mean* (Shambala Publications, 2018), 249.

82   An excellent summary of the research base regarding gender differences in the experience of touch is contained in the introduction of Ana Aznar and Harriet R. Tenenbaum, "Parent-Child Positive Touch: Gender, Age, and Task Differences," *Journal of Nonverbal Behavior* 40, no. 4 (2016): 317–333.

83   Allan Schore, "All Our Sons: The Developmental Neurobiology and Neuroendocrinology of Boys at Risk," *Journal of Infant Mental Health* 38, no. 1 (2017): 15–52.

84   Carol Gilligan and Judy Chu, *When Boys Become Boys: Development, Relationships, and Masculinity* (New York Cit, New York: New York University Press, 2014).

85   Valerian J. Derlega, Robin J. Lewis, Scott Harrison, Barbara A. Winstead and Robert Costanza, "Gender differences in the initiation and attribution of tactile intimacy," *Journal of Nonverbal Behavior* 13, no. 1 (1989): 83–96.

86   Valerian J. Derlega, Robin J. Lewis, Scott Harrison, Barbara A. Winstead and Robert Costanza, "Gender differences in the initiation and attribution of tactile intimacy," *Journal of Nonverbal Behavior* 13, no. 1 (1989): 83–96.

87   Orenstein, *Boys & Sex*.

88   Other words that stem from this root are: "consensus," "consensual," "sensual," "sensory," "sense" (cognition).

89   Richard Kearney, *Touch: Recovering Our Most Vital Sense* (New York City, New York: Columbia University Press, 2021); Bessel van der Kolk, *The Body Keeps the Score: Brain, Mind, and Body in the Healing of Trauma* (London, United Kingdom: Penguin Press, 2015), 217.

90   Mark Grayson, "Lost at Sea: The challenges of reinventing a dominance-based culture of masculinity," *The Good Men Project*, April 16, 2021. https://goodmen project.com/featured-content/lost-at-sea/.

91   "Victims of Sexual Violence: Statistics," *Rape, Abuse & Incest National Network* compilation of research from multiple studies, whose bibliography can be found at https://www.rainn.org/statistics/victims-sexual-violence.

92   Kearney, *Touch*, 106–107.

93   Kearney, *Touch*, 108.

94   Kearney, *Touch*, 180–181.

95   Way, *Deep Secrets*.

96   *Webster's Dictionary* (1923).

97   Hanne Blank, *Straight: The Surprisingly Short History of Heterosexuality* (Boston, Massachusetts: Beacon Press, 2012), 1–21; Jonathan Ned Katz, "The Invention of Heterosexuality," in Routledge International Handbook of Heterosexualities Studies (United Kingdom, Routledge, 2020).

98   Laura Chen, Hassan Murad, Molly Paras, Kristina Colbenson, Amelia Sattler, Erin Goranson, Mohamed Elamin et al., "Sexual Abuse and Lifetime Diagnosis of Psychiatric Disorders: Systematic Review and Meta-Analysis," *Mayo Clinical Proceedings* 85, no. 7 (2010): 618–629.

99   Bennett McIntosh, "The Science of Sex: Historian and philosopher Sarah Richardson interrogates the science of sex and gender," *Harvard Magazine*, November-December, 2019. https://www.harvardmagazine.com/2019/10/sarah-richardson-science-sex.

100 National Health Statistics Reports in 2011 and 2016 pre COVID, indicate that approximately 3% of heterosexual males 18–44 reported that they have engaged in anal or oral sex with another man. This number is believed to be grossly under reported.

101 Tony Silva, *Still Straight: Sexual Flexibility Among White Men in America* (New York City, New York: NYU Press, March 2021).

102 Alfred Kinsey, Wardell Pomeroy, Clyde Martin, "Sexual Behavior in the Human Male," *American Journal of Public Health* 93, no. 6 (2003): 894–898.

103 Ritch C. Savin-Williams, *Mostly Straight: sexual fluidity among men* (Cambridge, Massachusetts: Harvard University Press, 2017).

104 Savin-Williams, *Mostly Straight*, 2.

105 Savin-Williams, *Mostly Straight*, 11–21, 166–68, 170–176.

106 Savin-Williams, *Mostly Straight*, 34.

107 Savin-Williams, *Mostly Straight*, 35.

108 Jane Ward, Not Gay: *Sex Between Straight White Men* (New York City, New York: New York University Press, 2015).

109 Ocean Vuong, "Reimagining Masculinity," *Paris Review*, June 10, 2019.

110 Orenstein, *Boys & Sex*.

111 Orenstein, *Boys & Sex*, 11.

112 Nils Hammarén and Thomas Johansson, "Homosociality: In Between Power and Intimacy," *SAGE Open* 4, no. 1 (2014), 2158244013518057.

113 Wil S. Hylton, "My Cousin Was a Hero. Until He Tried to Kill Me," *New York Times*, May 18, 2019.

114 Publius Terentius Afer (Terence), *Heauton Timorumenos (The Self Tormentor)*, "homo sum: humani nil a me alienum puto," line 77 (163 BCE).

115 "When Americans Say They Believe in God, What Do They Mean?," *Pew Research Center*, April 25, 2018. https://www.pewresearch.org/religion/2018/04/25/when-americans-say-they-believe-in-god-what-do-they-mean/.

116 Malcolm Gladwell, *Outliers: The Story of Success* (Boston. Massachusetts: Little, Brown and Company, 2008).

117 Mihaly Csikszentmihalyi, "Toward a psychology of optimal experience," in *Flow and the foundations of positive psychology: The Collected Works of Mihaly Csikszentmihalyi* (Dordrecht, Netherlands: Springer, Dordrecht, 2014).

118 "Education Pays," *U.S. Bureau of Labor Statistics*, Last modified date: Sept 6, 2023.

119 Sr. S. Satchindananda Saraswati, *The Yoga Sutras of Pantanjali*, "There is no value in digging shallow wells in a hundred places. Decide on one place and dig deep."

120 Shane O'Mara, *In Praise of Walking: A New Scientific Exploration* (New York City, New York: W. W. Norton, 2019), 145–164.

121 Sally Bowles, first President of Emily Hall Tremaine Foundation (1993–2001), former Deputy Commissioner of Welfare, State of Connecticut; staff person coordinating the Rockefeller Foundation's initiative supporting the struggle to end apartheid; education advisor to Mayor John Lindsey; one of the founders of the Peace Corps.

122 Catherine Shainberg, *Kabballah of Light: Ancient Practices to Ignite the Imagination and Illuminate the Soul* (Rochester, Vermont: Inner Traditions, 2022), 128–281.

123 Courtney Cowart, *An American Awakening: From Ground Zero to Katrina | The People We Are Free to Be* (New York City, New York: Seabury Books, 2008), 56.

124 Courtney Cowart, "What is Corona Trying to Teach Us?: Plug in and bring your gift," interview by Mark Grayson, *The Good Men Project*, April 10, 2020.

125 Cowart, "What is Corona Trying to Teach Us?"

126 Cowart, "What is Corona Trying to Teach Us?"

127 Courtney Cowart, *An American Awakening: From Ground Zero to Katrina | The People We Are Free to Be* (New York City, New York: Seabury Books, 2008), 38–58.

128 Nate Bennett and G. James Lemoine, "What VUCA Really Means for You," *Harvard Business Review*, January–February 2014.

129 Elizabeth Gilbert, "Your elusive creative genius," TED2009, February, 2009, 19:15. https://www.ted.com/talks/elizabeth_gilbert_your_elusive_creative_genius.

130 Ephrat Livni, "Albert Einstein's best ideas came when he was aimless. Yours can too," *Quartz*, June 8, 2018.

131 Grayson, "The Lessons of Corona for Men," *The Good Men Project*, April 12, 2020.

132 Mark Greene, "The Man Box: The Link Between Emotional Suppression and Male Violence," *The Good Men Project*, October 2, 2018.

133 Mantak Chia and Douglas Abrams, *The Multi-Orgasmic Man: Sexual Secrets Every Man Should Know* (San Francisco, California: Harper Collins San Francisco, 1996).

134 Chia and Abrams, *The Multi-Orgasmic Man.*

135 Perel, "Women Teach Men."

136 Perel, "Women Teach Men," 14–17.

137 Frank Pega, Bálint Náfrádi, Natalie C. Momen, Yuka Ujita, Kai N. Streicher, Annette M. Prüss-Üstün, Technical Advisory Group, Alexis Descatha, Tim Driscoll, Frida M. Fischer, Lode Godderis, Hannah M. Kiiver, Jian Li, Linda L. Magnusson Hanson, Reiner Rugulies, Kathrine Sørensen, and Tracey J. Woodruff, "Global, regional, and national burdens of ischemic heart disease and stroke attributable to exposure to long working hours for 194 countries, 2000–2016: A systematic analysis from the WHO/ILO Joint Estimates of the Work-related Burden of Disease and Injury," *Environment International* 154, no. 1 (2021), 106595.

138 Raphaël Liogier, *KHAOS: Théorie de la modernité réelle* [*KAHOS: Theory of Real Modernity*], (Paris, France: Editions Les Liens qui Libèrent, 2023).

139 As reported by the United Nations, the World Bank, the International Monetary Fund, and many other research organizations, women in the developing world are the de facto head of household and often the primary economic engine for growth as farmers, caregivers, educators, entrepreneurs, and volunteers. In the US, half of all households are headed by women. Laurie Goodman, Jung Hyun Choi, Jun Zhu, "More Women Have Become Homeowners and Heads of Household: Could the Pandemic Undo that Progress?," *Urban Institute*, March 16, 2021.

140 Richard V. Reeves, "The underreported rise in male suicide: Boys and men are four times more likely to take their own lives, but you could be forgiven for not knowing that," *Substack*, March 13, 2023.

141 St. Paul, Galatians 2:15–16 (NSRV).

142 Fairfield Country Day School, Fairfield, Connecticut.

143 See Chapter 2.

144 For an excellent discussion of the impact that flickering back and forth from executive mode to default mode has on creativity, see Shane O'Mara, *In Praise of Walking: A New Scientific Exploration* (New York City, New York: W. W. Norton, 2019), 148–153.

145 See Chapter 6.

146 Dacher Keltner, *Awe: The New Science of Everyday Wonder and How It Can Transform Your Life* (London, United Kingdom: Penguin Press, 2023).

147 Keltner, *Awe*, 128.

148 Keltner, *Awe*, 133–135.

149 Keltner, *Awe*, 138–141.

150 O'Mara, *In Praise of Walking*, 18–21.

151 Will Duncan, "Everyone Can Meditate" (hosted event, Trinity Spiritual Center, Southport, CT, October 13–14).

152 Way, *Rebels with a Cause*, 1–22.

153 Alan Downs, *The Velvet Rage: Overcoming the Pain of Growing Up Gay in a Straight Man's World* (Ashland, Oregon: Blackstone Publishing, 2021).

154 R. Ramchand, M.S. Schuler, M. Schoenbaum, L.Colpe, L. Ayer, "Suicidality among sexual minority adults: Gender, age, and race/ethnicity differences," *American Journal of Preventative Medicine* 62, no. 2 (2022), 193–202; "Gay and Bisexual Men's Health," Centers for Disease Control and Prevention, December 12, 2022. https://www.cdc.gov/msmhealth/index.htm.

155 Richard Reeves, *Of Boys and Men*.

156 Erica Sweeney, "14 Signs You're Stuck in a Scarcity Mindset," *Men's Health*, December 16, 2022.

157 Isabel Behncke, PhD Oxford University, MPhil Cambridge University, MSc University College London. Dr. Behncke's PhD dissertation was the first comprehensive study of play behavior in wild bonobos known to science.

158 Matthew A. Killingsworth, Daniel Kahneman, and Barbara Mellers, "Income and emotional well-being: A conflict resolved," *Proceedings of the National Academy of Sciences (PNAS)* 120, no. 10 (2023), e2208661120.

159 Howard Thurman, "Baccalaureate Address" (commencement speech, Spelman College, Atlanta, Georgia, 1980).

160 Bill Burnett & Dave Evans, *Designing Your Life: How to Build a Well-Lived Joyful Life* (New York City, New York: Knopf Doubleday, 2016), xxii–xxiii.

161 Brendan Gill, *Late Bloomers* (New York City, New York: Artisan/Workman Publishing Company, Inc., 1996).

162 Hindu stages of life. The four asramas are: *Brahmacharya* (student life), *Gṛhastha* (householder life), *Vanaprastha* (forest walker/forest dweller or retired), and *Sannyasa* (renunciate or renounced life).

163 Sara Lawrence-Lightfoot, *The Third Chapter: Passion, Risk, and Adventure in the 25 Years after 50* (Cambridge, Massachusetts: Sarah Chrichton Books, 2009).

164 S. DiMuccio, N. Sattari, E. Shaffer, J. Cline. "Masculine anxiety and interrupting sexism at work." Catalyst 2021. https://www.catalyst.org/reports/masculine-anxiety-workplace/.

INDEX

ACKNOWLEDGMENTS

A long life with many unexpected twists and turns has put me in the position of having an unusual number of people to thank. Collectively, it is their wisdom, experience and insight that informs the content of the book. I am greatly indebted to each and every one of you, named and unnamed in the following acknowledgments, who have been fellow sojourners on this wonderful adventure with me.

At the top of the list of travelers that I want to thank are my wife, Sarah, and our two sons, Parker and Philip, for their love and patience when recording my "lab notes on life" invaded our time together for many years. Your willingness to let me share our stories and those of our friends, along with your input and support, has made this a better book. It stands as a testament to what can happen when we allow ourselves to be open, accessible, and vulnerable.

There is an endless list of individuals that I need to thank for helping me pull this manuscript together. First and foremost, I want to express my gratitude to my agent, Tim Brandhorst, for successfully shepherding me through the process of publishing a book. His advice and assistance has been invaluable. I also need to thank Beth Beaudin for preparing the manuscript for publication, Stephen Foster for his painstaking copy editing, Kostis Pavlou for creating such a captivating cover design, and Susan Gerber for designing the interior pages, effectively pulling all our efforts together. Cecily Stranahan and Evi Coghlan carefully read and commented on my first draft, and Christine LePorte meticulously proofread the final typeset manuscript. Thank you for all your efforts.

The framework for this book came together because of the intelligent, gentle probing of Jane Kosstrin at Doublespace who worked with me to develop Naked Man Collective, a website for men exploring the new masculinity terrain. Jane helped me to distill my ideas into seven key points that became the springboard for this book.

I would also like to give a special shout-out to Parker and Philip, who helped me formulate the basic ideas contained in this book on the many long hikes that we have taken. They have both read multiple drafts of my essays and these chapters. Both are excellent writers and unafraid to give me the direct feedback that I need to hear from their respective generations. (One is even doing his Ph.D. in rhetoric.) I am most grateful that they suited up to be a part of my team. I also want to thank Brett D'Elia for his many insightful contributions to my own thinking, as I rambled on and on while we were working out.

I want to thank all the experts and men whose research and experience have fleshed out the book's key themes. Any list I offer is bound to be incomplete, but I need to name several here. First, I must thank Mark Greene and Niobe Way for the many ways that they each contributed to and expanded my own thinking. I must also thank the litany of men who opened up and allowed me to share their experience in the book: Boysen Hodgson, Charles Mattheus, Owen Marcus, Joel Serino, Morris Holbrook, Robert Green, Bob Vuyosevich, Robert Heasley, Paul Nelson, Lynn Weigel, Steve Smock, Kim Evensen, Chris Gaglione, Biddle Duke,

Lynn Weigel, Br. Carl Sword, Cullen Cowan, James Houghton, Joschi Schwarz, Jamie Curtis, Seth Aidinoff, Peter Hasapis, Mark Kutolowski, Thomas Benton, Michael Banten, Weller Hlinomaz, Harry Schmitz, Dylan Mello, Alex Langshur, and many more.

I have a group of muses to thank for encouraging me to write this book. They include: Ellie Duke, who was working at Los Angeles Review of Books and edited the very first essay that unlocked a torrent of ideas; Lisa Hickey, Publisher, The Good Men Project, along with Lisa Blacker and Kara Post-Kennedy, Executive Editors. Supporting me as I tackled one thorny topic after another were Catherine Ventura, Andrew Frothingham, and Nicholas Latimer, each urging me to soldier on. I have Leslie Meredith to thank for convincing me that I could actually write this book, and Mirabai Starr for believing in me as well.

Of course, writing a book like this isn't possible without holding up the lives of the *real men* that I am proud to call my family and friends: my dad, step-dad, brothers, step-brothers, brothers-in-law, nephews, and my wife's and my many cousins are all amazing men They, along with the close male friends Stockton, Mark, Fred, Stu, Bobby, Ian, Nicholas, Stephen, Andrew, Peter, Biddle, Brett, Jamie, Lynn, Alex, Robert, Murph, Adam, Sandy, Rich, Neal, Kirk, Cullen, and Ricky, who have been a such a big part of my life for so many years, have made this book what it is.

As I progressed through my twenties, thirties, forties, and early fifties, I was extremely blessed to have some of the best male mentors a guy could want: Lee Rosenberg, Chuck Schwab, Bob Eubanks, Amo Houghton, and Peter Grauer. Thank you for your patience and guidance.

Although it's a cliché to say that behind every successful man is a strong woman, in my case, it's an understatement. I would say that there is a whole platoon, thirty or so, of women who have made me who I am as a man today.

Starting with my wife, my mom, and my sister—three forces of nature that you best not cross. They embody a love so fierce, deep, and undying that you know you'll be okay, whatever may befall you.

Then there's a litany of women mentors and colleagues, from whom I have learned how to be an effective leader. (Indeed, in many ways I have learned as much or more from them as I have from their male counterparts.) Evi Coghlan, Eileen Horowitz, Sally Bowles, Alexa Culwell, Mary Dean Barringer, Diane Morris, Jocelyn Hong, Jodell Seagrave, Virginia Cargill, Cecily Stranahan, Alane Kelly, and Chris Whyte (without whom I could have never endured ten years of commuting).

I should also pay tribute to the two women who read the coming-of-age novel that I wrote after college and confirmed that I was a writer, and I should never forget it: Elizabeth Aldrich and Elizabeth Becker. Your words have proven to be prophetic.

These are the men and women who have inspired this book, and for that I will be eternally grateful.

ABOUT THE AUTHOR

Mark Grayson grew up in a small town in Ohio and in remote parts of Central Texas. He worked his way through Harvard College and Columbia Business School, then began his career in the entertainment industry in Los Angeles. Mark helped launch and scale the educational television production company Rabbit Ears; the education non-profit All Kinds of Minds; and most recently Rocket21, a safe online platform that encourages children to begin to explore their dreams for the future.

Currently the Founding Director of the Trinity Spiritual Center, Mark's series of conversations with high-profile thought leaders has drawn comparisons to Krista Tippett's On Being. In its first three years of operations, the Center was awarded two prestigious Constable Grants and has garnered the attention of national media.

As a private citizen concerned about the declining state of our democracy, Mark has successfully advocated that Members of Congress appropriate $2.3 million in funding in FYE 2023 for the creation of the

Lewis-Houghton Civics and Democracy Initiative at the Library of Congress. The program will offer music-driven curricular resources that will help secondary school educators teach American history and civics in anticipation of our 250th anniversary in 2026.

As a Featured Columnist for The Good Men Project Mark has reached thousands. In over 50 essays published over the past five years, Mark has explored a broad range of themes, eliciting strong positive feedback from readers.

Mark is married to the former actress Sarah Houghton and has two sons, Parker and Philip. Together, they manage to care for their rambunctious Havanese, Phoebe.

www.ingramcontent.com/pod-product-compliance
Lightning Source LLC
Chambersburg PA
CBHW060909120626
46553CB00001B/261